"The perspectives and exercises offered here are right on target; they arise from a clear understanding of the bonds of love and how these bonds work in adult relationships . . . We hope that this book will help you do just that—shape your precious relationship into a more satisfying and lasting bond."

From the Foreword—**Susan Johnson**, *EdD, Emeritus Professor of Clinical Psychology at University of Ottawa, Ontario, Canada and Developer of Emotionally Focused Therapy*

"The second edition of this workbook for couples is a fantastic resource made even better! It faithfully mirrors the process of Emotionally Focused Couple Therapy (EFT). In-depth explanations and reflective exercises will help you to explore your emotions, articulate them better for yourself, and express them to your partner. It's like having two master EFT therapists come home with you, envelop you in warmth, and guide you to improve your relationship or reinforce and build on your sessions if you are working with a therapist. The authors have broadened the scope of the workbook by integrating complexity around culture and the trauma of oppression, and by including examples of diverse couples. I will recommend this guide to every one of the couples in my practice!"

Marlene Best, *PhD, Clinical Professor of Clinical Psychology, University of Ottawa, Canada, and Certified EFT Therapist, Supervisor and Trainer*

"This workbook, based on Emotionally Focused Therapy, includes excellent exercises that focus on helping couples create positive communication patterns in place of the destructive ones that negatively affect their relationships. Drawing on extensive research and clinical experience, this book will help couples strengthen their trust in one another as well as heal past hurts. I recommend it for use in marriage enrichment groups, as well as by individual couples."

From the First Edition—**Patricia Noller**, *PhD, Emeritus Professor, School of Psychology, University of Queensland, Australia*

"This book offers 'power tools' for couples who want to look deeply at themselves and their relationship. The authors go a lot deeper than routine techniques of marital communication—they get to the heart of the matter, and in this edition, they add insights on sexuality and culture. I urge anyone who wants to grow their relationship to read, digest, and practise what this book offers."

William J. Doherty, *PhD, Professor of Family Social Science, University of Minnesota, USA, and author of Take Back your Marriage*

AN EMOTIONALLY FOCUSED WORKBOOK FOR COUPLES

The second edition of this essential and newly updated workbook is intended for use with couples who want to enhance their emotional connection or overcome their relationship distress. It closely follows the course of EFT treatment and allows clinicians to easily integrate guided reading, reflection and discussion into the therapeutic process.

Incorporating new developments in EFT and decades of research in the field of attachment, Veronica Kallos-Lilly and Jennifer Fitzgerald include chapters that explore concepts such as attachment bonds, the three cycles of relationship distress, how to make sense of emotions, relationship hurts and more. The workbook follows the familiar and accessible format of the first edition, *Read, Reflect, and Discuss*, and weaves fresh, illustrative examples throughout, with updated content considering the impact of gender, culture and sexual orientation on relationship dynamics. Added reflections on these topics and an expanded section on sexuality dispels constraining popular myths and frees partners up to express themselves more openly.

This book is essential reading for partners looking for helpful steps to improve the quality of their romantic relationships as well as marriage and family therapists, couple therapists and clinicians training in EFT to use with their clients.

Veronica Kallos-Lilly, PhD, is a Registered Psychologist and Founding Co-Director of the Vancouver Couple & Family Institute and Vancouver Centre for EFT Training in British Columbia, Canada. As a certified EFT therapist, supervisor and trainer, Veronica provides consultation in all modalities of EFT and presents trainings internationally.

Jennifer Fitzgerald, PhD, Clinical Psychologist, is Co-Director of the Australian Centre for EFT, and has worked at the University of Queensland for the past 20 years teaching medical communication, health psychology and couples' therapy. She is a certified EFT therapist, supervisor and trainer, and teaches EFT in all states of Australia.

AN EMOTIONALLY FOCUSED WORKBOOK FOR COUPLES

The Two of Us

2nd edition

Veronica Kallos-Lilly
Jennifer Fitzgerald

Routledge
Taylor & Francis Group
NEW YORK AND LONDON

Cover images: © Getty Images

Second edition published 2022
by Routledge
605 Third Avenue, New York, NY 10158

and by Routledge
4 Park Square, Milton Park, Abingdon, Oxon, OX14 4RN

Routledge is an imprint of the Taylor & Francis Group, an informa business

[First edition published by Routledge 2015]

Library of Congress Cataloging-in-Publication Data
A catalog record for this book has been requested

ISBN: 978-0-367-44402-0 (hbk)
ISBN: 978-0-367-44403-7 (pbk)
ISBN: 978-1-003-00948-1 (ebk)

DOI: 10.4324/9781003009481

Typeset in Stone Serif
by Apex CoVantage, LLC

CONTENTS

TABLES

REFLECTIONS

FIGURES

FOREWORD

Dear Reader,

I would like to welcome you to *An Emotionally Focused Workbook for Couples: The Two of Us*. I hope reading it will encourage you to work on your relationship in a way that complements your sessions with your emotionally focused couple therapist, or with any couple therapist who is consulting with you on your relationship. Perhaps you are just wanting to learn about or enhance the bond with your mate and want to use this book to give you direction. Whatever the reason you reached out and picked up this volume, I think you will not be disappointed.

The authors of this volume are expert couple therapists who have helped hundreds of couples change their relationship for the better. They have taken the wisdom of the emotionally focused model (EFT), garnered from nearly four decades of working with couples, and numerous research projects finding that this approach shapes positive outcomes, and made it available to you in a format you can use in your own home.

The approach to relationships that forms the basis for EFT and for this volume is based on four decades of research on the bonds of attachment between adult lovers. The perspectives and exercises offered here are right on target; they arise from a clear understanding of the bonds of love and how these bonds work in adult relationships. We believe that love is no longer a mystery but something we can understand and shape. We hope that this book will help you do just that—shape your precious relationship into a more satisfying and lasting bond.

Dr Sue Johnson
(Drsuejohnson.com)

ACKNOWLEDGMENTS

Many people have directly or indirectly contributed to this book. We want to acknowledge with gratitude the assistance of our colleagues who have reviewed earlier drafts of this manuscript and/or offered helpful feedback along the way; namely, Dr. Sue Johnson, Ms. Yolanda von Hockhauf, Dr. Marlene Best, Dr. Richard Harrison, Dr. Alana Tappin and Dr. Robert Allan. Special thanks to Dr. Scott Woolley for giving us permission to use and adapt the infinity loop diagram he developed as a training tool. We would also like to express deep our gratitude to the many couples who have shared with us their journey in creating secure loving connections.

Jennifer would like to personally thank and acknowledge her academic mentor in close relationships and attachment research, Associate Professor Judith Feeney; my clinical teacher and mentor, Professor Sue Johnson; my friend and colleague, Dr. Veronica Kallos-Lilly, for traveling so often to Australia to teach EFT; my late parents, Florence and Ned Churchward, for giving me a secure start in life; and my husband, William Fitzgerald, and our children, Dominic, Michael and Madeleine, for their unwavering love and encouragement over so many years.

Veronica would like to thank Dr. Sue Johnson, for being an inspiration, mentor and secure base over the past 30 years; Dr. Jenny Fitzgerald for being a safe haven friend and colleague; and my parents, Agi and Pista Kallos, for their enormous love and belief in me. I would like to dedicate this work to my precious ones: Bob, for living out the words on these pages with me day in and day out and for holding my hand as we walk through life together; Drew and Maddie, for all the sunshine you bring into my world; and Buddy and Luna, for reminding me to go outside and take walks.

CHAPTER 1

INTRODUCTION

Who is This Book For?

If you are content in your couple relationship, needing help with your relationship or recovering from a relationship breakup, then this book could well be beneficial to you. This book is for people who want to understand and experience how to build a secure bond with a relationship partner. We have written this book for couples, because love relationships are the central focus of our professional lives. As therapists we have been invited inside the lives of many, many couples; in so doing, we've witnessed the anguish of broken relationships, the hard work involved in repairing relationships and the joy of healed relationships. We want to help you make your relationship as happy and secure as possible.

We are reaching out to people of all ages and identities relating to gender, sexual orientation, culture, ethnicity, race and social position in romantic relationships of all stages. While it has been suggested by others that men and women are inherently different, maybe even coming from different planets,[1] we honor the ways that our shared humanity transcends our various identities. We believe people from all over planet Earth need each other to live well and typically seek romantic partnership for love, belonging, sexuality, closeness, security, companionship and/or comfort. These core needs for love, safety and acceptance cut across all of our identities. Although how we express our basic emotions and needs is unique and influenced by many factors, including our temperament, family rearing, social position and experiences, religion, culture, coping patterns, and our previous love relationships. Have you been invited to show vulnerability and ask for comfort in your life? Have you been socialized to shut down your emotions or to be ashamed, forever feeling vulnerable or helpless? In couple relationships that are working well, partners are able to tune into, respect and respond to their own and each other's emotions and needs. So, whether you are newly committed or in a relationship of long standing, whether you are straight, lesbian, gay, bisexual, two-spirit, transgender, queer, intersex, asexual, pansexual or other nonconforming identities (LGBTTQIAP+), and whether you feel quite satisfied or very dissatisfied within your love relationship, we expect you will find something in this book that will be useful for you.

Whether your problems are about money, in-laws, children, sex or pretty much anything else, this book will help you, not by giving you advice about managing money, dealing with in-laws, raising children or fulfilling sexual desires, but by helping you to go deeper into understanding yourself and your partner and what happens *between you* when problems in these or other areas occur. This book aims to assist you to understand and influence the dynamics of your relationship so you can find lasting solutions; solutions that will keep your relationship strong no matter what challenges you face now or in the future.

If you are content in your relationship, but it's lost some of its spark, you and your partner may be able to use this workbook on your own to enhance your relationship. However, you may already be working with a therapist who has recommended this book. If your relationship feels troubled, it may be best to work with a therapist trained in Emotionally Focused Therapy (EFT) for couples and use this workbook to complement your therapeutic process. If you picked up this workbook on your

DOI: 10.4324/9781003009481-1

own and are finding it difficult to use independently, you can locate EFT therapists around the world by visiting **www.iceeft.com**.

What is Emotionally Focused Therapy for Couples?

The principles we will recommend in this book are drawn from an approach to couple therapy called Emotionally Focused Therapy, or EFT for short. The approach was developed in the 1980s by Dr. Susan Johnson (Emeritus Professor at University of Ottawa; Founder of the Ottawa Couples and Family Institute and the International Centre for Excellence in EFT) and Dr. Leslie Greenberg (Emeritus Professor at York University, Toronto).[2,3] These researchers developed the first EFT manual following many, many hours of watching and analyzing recordings of couples therapy sessions, all the while asking questions and delving into the whys and wherefores of the change process. Much research and training continue all over the world, to expand knowledge and awareness of the principles of using EFT to help couples change their distressed relationships into relationships of security and safety.

Earlier approaches to couples therapy had focused on helping partners change their own behaviors or thoughts; other approaches focused exclusively on the interactions between partners.[4] Individual approaches to therapy had often targeted individual emotions and needs without paying attention to the impact of interactions between partners. It took these two gifted and dedicated clinician researchers to open the way to a unique approach that neatly integrates a focus on who we are as individual emotional beings and how we interact in relationships that matter the most. In other words, EFT helps partners tune into their important feelings and needs and then put those feelings and needs across in ways that draws the other closer and invites a positive response.

EFT is an approach to couples therapy that works. Not only do couples usually like the approach, they usually experience substantial change, even in relationships that have been characterized by significant distress and heartache. Research has established that 86 to 90 percent of couples undertaking a course of EFT report significant improvement and 70 to 75 percent of couples recover from their distress.[5,6] These changes have been found to last over time, even in conditions of high stress such as having a seriously ill child,[7] as well as betrayals like affairs.[8] The approach and its related educational programs have been tested in a range of different populations, including with couples where one partner is depressed,[9] experiencing sexual difficulties[10] or health problems such as heart attack[11] or cancer.[12]

The initial model of EFT therapy was later strengthened by Dr Johnson's integration of knowledge about attachment and bonding in close relationships. This influential theory of close relationships will be described in more detail throughout the book. No longer do emotions need to be swept away under the carpet; instead, and none too soon, in this model of therapy, each partner's emotional experience is respectfully acknowledged, understood and worked through. Together, partners learn how to live in their relationship so as to create the closeness and security they desire. They learn to recognize their emotional needs for safety and connection and learn to ask in soft and non-blaming ways for their partners to help meet their needs. Emotions, as EFT founder Sue Johnson says, are "the music of the attachment dance."[13] As emotions are understood and responded to, the dance changes; couples are then able to move from turmoil and struggle on the "dance floor," to movements of grace, harmony and closeness.

How Will This Book Help You?

We draw on extensive research with happy and unhappy couples, as well as our clinical experience and wisdom gained from treating hundreds of distressed couples over the years. Our aim is to support you to achieve relationship success through three important steps: First, we want to help you discover how you and your partner react to each other when your important relationship needs are not being met; second, we want to help you gain a deeper understanding of your own, and your partner's emotions; and third, we would like to help you talk to each other about your emotions, needs, hopes and longings in ways that strengthen your relationship.

Hence, this book will offer you a framework for *personal reflection* and *meaningful conversations with your partner*. These reflections and conversations will help you to heal past hurts, strengthen trust and develop a relationship that could look and feel very different from the relationship that has been troubling you in the past.

In this edition we have attempted to build in more content and reflections on the impact of one's culture and experiences of discrimination on relationships. Our hope is to speak more directly to the range of lived experiences among our readers. Throughout this edition we have consciously adjusted our language and pronouns to be more inclusive. For instance, you will see "they" or "their" at times to replace he/she and his/her. As two cisgender, heterosexual, white women, we do not see ourselves as experts on the experience of racial trauma or know what it is like to be a target of discrimination or to feel a lack of belonging because of not being a part of the dominant culture. We only wish to make space and acknowledge the tremendous impact of these experiences and help open up deeper conversation between partners, especially partners who may come from different backgrounds. Others may have similar life experiences but have coped with them in different ways. As attachment therapists we know that these conversations can be powerfully connecting. When we feel a topic is outside the scope of this book or our own expertise, we will provide ideas for additional reading.

How to Use This Book? What Can You Do to Help Yourselves and Your Relationship?

We have presented our material using a simple, recurring format: Read, Reflect, and Talk. There are extra copies of the worksheets at the back of this book, so there is a copy for you and your partner. We would like to suggest that you take the book in small bites, digesting each piece before moving on to the next. We encourage you to read and reflect on each piece (perhaps with some written notes) before you share with your partner. Alternatively, you may prefer to read the chapters aloud to each other, reflect on the exercises quietly, and then ask each other the questions with genuine curiosity, even if you have discussed some of the same subjects in the past. The reflection time will help you to slow down and give space for ideas to take shape and for feelings to become clearer or for new feelings to emerge, before you discuss together. Don't forget to pay attention to the love tips along the way—keep your eye out for the heart symbol.

Talking about feelings, disappointments, needs, hopes, longings, and other important aspects of your relationship is likely to stir up a range of emotions for you. These stirred-up emotions will need to be handled with care. Recognize that if you have decided to work through this book together, there is a part of each of you that is invested in connecting with each other in a new way. Building on that assumption, we offer conversation guidelines that provide a framework for sharing your personal reflections with one another.

L-O-V-E Conversations

To have a loving relationship, you will each need to communicate in a sensitive, loving way. You may feel very far from being able to do that right now, but we have come up with a way of approaching your conversations, called L-O-V-E conversations, that will give you a platform for creating some safety in your discussions. You may like to make a flash card of the following simple words to help you stay focused on keeping your conversations "L-O-V-E conversations" throughout the discussion activities of this book.

When we communicate with each other, remember to

Listen with an
Open heart and mind
Validate and acknowledge each other
Express our thoughts and feelings softly, simply, and slowly.

Let's look at the L-O-V-E conversation guide more closely.

L-O-V-E: *Listen*: It is not by chance that L-O-V-E conversations start with listening. So often we want to do the talking, fixing, pleading or controlling. Necessary as it is to express our feelings and points of view, effective communication starts in the heart with a willingness to listen to the other (be it partner, child, colleague or stranger). Listeners tune into words, but they also tune in to feelings; for what is said in words, but also for what is said by facial expression and body "language." So, while opening your ears and heart to listen to your partner, keep a careful eye on their face as well. Some readers may be inwardly groaning by now, because you have received many messages from your frustrated partners about your lack of ability to tune into feelings. To you, we say, "Don't give up. We would like to help you with simple steps to discover that you probably are better at understanding your own and your partner's feelings than you realize. Please read on." Tempting as it may be to interrupt your partner while they are talking, we encourage you to resist that urge. Listening without interruptions conveys respect and a willingness to understand your partner's perspective.

L-**O**-V-E: *Open*: An open mind is really just another way of saying, "I'm trying to listen to you as though we have just met, and I haven't had time to develop any negative assumptions as yet." It means attempting to put aside, as much as possible, the judgments and presumptions that creep in with relationship difficulties. It means being humble enough to realize that maybe there is something to learn if I listen to you with new ears. An open heart means taking in your words and allowing them to impact me. Allowing your words and experiences to move me.

L-O-**V**-E: *Validate*: Before thinking about a quick reply to your partner's message, we would like to suggest that you slow down for long enough to validate and acknowledge what you have just heard your partner say. Press the pause button (or even better, the delete button) on self-defending comments and knee-jerk reactions. Make an effort to acknowledge that what your partner has just said is a legitimate experience for them. When you validate your partner, you are demonstrating respect for their view of reality even though it may be different from yours. It helps your partner feel heard and cared for too.

If you just don't get what your partner is saying, be honest, but in a supportive way. For example, instead of exclaiming, "That's ridiculous!" or "I reject what you say" which invalidates your partner's position, you could try, "I'd like to get what you are saying there, but it is pretty confusing for me right now." If you think you understand what your partner has said, but you really don't agree with it, you can be honest in a validating way. For example, "I am finding it hard to agree with you there. I see it quite differently, but I do get that you are trying to help me understand your experience." If you feel bad about what your partner says, you can share how you are impacted by their disclosure. For example, "When you tell me how you feel, I feel bad, embarrassed; but thank you for telling me honestly what is going on for you right now."

L-O-V-E: *Express*: Satisfying relationships typically involve conversations about feelings, hopes, dreams and disappointments. When one partner is willing to disclose something of his or her "inner" life, and the other partner is willing to listen and validate what is shared, it is emotionally meaningful and the bond between these two people is strengthened. So, disclosure is important and signals to the other person, "I trust you enough to tell you something personal about myself; you matter enough for me to want to let you in." Sometimes, it can be scary to disclose; indeed, in violent or disrespectful relationships, it is often not wise to do so. Disclosure works best when the disclosing partner has received some strong signals that the other is interested, open and responsive. Sometimes, before disclosing, you may decide that you need to "test the waters" first; for example, with a question like, "Would you be willing to listen to what I've been thinking about since that last fight we had?" Or "I've wanted to talk to you for a while now about my concerns about . . . would it be an okay time now for me to talk to you?"

Just as listeners don't always have to agree with what their partners say, disclosers can't always demand that their partners are ready to listen immediately. Especially if you have multiple responsibilities (e.g., small children crying, business phones ringing) it is definitely helpful to agree on a time to talk that is mutually suitable for deeper conversation. Some years ago, when over a hundred happy couples in Brisbane, Australia, were asked to report on how they repaired hurtful events in their relationship, more than 60 percent spontaneously indicated that choosing the right time to talk to each other about the event was an important part of the repair process. For some couples, this meant waiting ("Our relationship is too important to rush this"); for others, it meant making a priority of talking immediately ("Don't let the sun go down on our wrath").[14]

You and your partner will need to talk about when you feel it will be most comfortable and helpful to talk over the reflections in this book. Some couples may find it works well to make a regular time each week to work on the reflections and discussions that this book will guide you through. Honoring the "appointment" could be a good way to signal to your partner that your relationship matters and you want to help improve the quality of your day-to-day lives.

When disclosing to your partner, it will help if you speak in a way that does not totally demoralize or destroy your partner's sense of worth and importance to you. Hence, we suggest you aim, wherever possible, to use a *soft* tone, rather than a harsh voice. Avoid swearing, name-calling or trading insults. These negative exchanges usually end up building barriers rather than breaking them down. The aim of this book is to help you discover new and better ways of interacting.

Choose *simple* words; stay close to the essence of what you are feeling and wanting to convey. Try not to bamboozle your partner with too many abstract ideas or an analysis of their character. *Slow down* the pace so that you can express yourself more clearly and help your partner to grasp the important ideas you want to convey. Speaking softly, simply, slowly[15] gives your partner a chance to listen non-defensively. If you have trouble speaking softly, simply, slowly, it may mean that you are feeling stirred up with strong emotion. Pause. Take a few deep breaths. Picture the stress flowing out of your body as you breathe out. Remind yourself: "Slow down, don't rush, take a deep breath. Talk about my feelings not my partner's faults."

Reflection 1.1 Ready to have a L-O-V-E conversation?

Let's begin your first L-O-V-E conversation on a positive note. Identify the last time you had a good moment or interaction with your partner, felt close, relaxed, enjoyed an activity together, or noticed something you appreciate about your partner. Describe the situation or quality you appreciate and the good feelings it evokes. Take turns sharing your good moments.

Description of Good Moment: ______________________________

____

____

____

Good Feelings Evoked: ______________________________

____

Debrief Together: How do you feel inside about sharing your good moments and feelings with each other? In this moment how do you feel toward each other (e.g., closer, warmer, embarrassed, cautious, happy, calm, relaxed)? ______________________________

____

If you get stuck and begin going off track in this exercise, simply stop the conversation, congratulate yourselves and each other for trying and recognize that this is a unique way of talking that will take time to hone. Remember the old saying, "Rome wasn't built in a day." You will likely need to give time and effort to talking through topics with your partner, especially as they become more challenging. Help each other feel encouraged by agreeing to meet in the near future to try again and by sharing with your EFT therapist what happened so that they can help you make sense of it. Small steps, often, will get you a long way along the path. More about how to share your feelings and concerns in a way that strengthens your relationship bond will be developed as we go along.

Limitations of This Book

If there is physical or sexual violence in your relationship, we absolutely encourage you to seek professional help, if you are not already doing so, to manage these harmful aspects of your relationship. The same is true if there is excessive verbal abuse, hostility, ridicule or contempt. If you or your partner has serious problems with addictions, gambling or health problems such as severe depression, traumatic stress or psychosis, we encourage you also to seek professional help to enable you to have the health and stability to be able to work on your relationship. These and other problems can strain a couples relationship, just as continuing to live in a distressing relationship can lead to deterioration in any of the problems as listed. Help is available and change is possible. For help in your local area, see your local doctor for a referral to an appropriate professional or consult websites such as the Find a psychologist or counselor page detailing the psychological associations in your area.

Importantly, if you find that attempting the exercises in this book consistently leads to problems (such as escalation of conflict, raised voices, endless discussion that does not reach a satisfying resolution or conversations that leave you feeling more distant from each other), we encourage you to seek professional help. Consult the list of EFT couples therapists around the world at **www.iceeft.com**.

This book is a workbook and offers you and your partner step-by-step opportunities to reflect on your relationship and discuss together your concerns and fears, your hopes and longings. It is written as a resource for couples who are interested in relationship enhancement or for couples who are attending therapy with an EFT trained therapist to strengthen or rebuild their relationship bond, as manualized by Sue Johnson in her recent books, including *Hold me tight* (*HMT*).[16] You can use this book as a companion throughout the therapy process, to bridge the progress you are making in therapy to the outside world and to document your journey along the way as a reference for the future.

If You Are a Therapist Using This Book with Your Clients

Over the years several of our therapist friends have asked us for advice on using this workbook with their clients. The feedback we have received is that reading the chapters, doing the exercises and sharing their responses offers clients helpful structure and support to work on their relationship between sessions. Much like therapy, the chapters and reflections build on each other incrementally and deepen gradually. In order to get the most out of the workbook we suggest that couples go through it slowly in small bite-sized chunks and not get ahead of where their therapy is at in terms of the EFT tasks and stages.

Every couple and therapist system will work at a different pace, so the suggestions here rely heavily on the therapist's attunement to their clients' needs throughout the therapeutic process. Chapters 1 and 2 introduce readers to the notion that security in love relationships involves building a strong emotional bond. Chapter 2 provides concrete and practical examples of what it looks like to provide a safe haven and secure base as a partner. Inviting the couple to look for positive examples helps them notice existing strengths in their relationship. Chapter 3, which invites partners to explore the quality of their early family relationships and cultural influences, helps partners make connections about how their histories can impact their current relationship patterns. Couples tell us that it supports their understanding of themselves and their partner while helping them develop compassion as they come to know each other's history. These chapters fit nicely with the first few therapy sessions (conjoint and individual) as they can create hope and help partners see the "bigger picture" of each other and their relationship.

Chapter 4 corresponds to stage one of EFT in which partners begin to see how distress in their relationship bond shows itself in patterns and reactive cycles of interaction. This chapter describes the three main cycles, and couples identify their main problematic interaction pattern. Exercises enable partners to notice their own behaviors in the pattern and how they trigger and "pull" each other into their reactive cycles, reinforcing what they are realizing in early sessions of EFT. Chapters 5 and 6 help couples make sense of their emotional world, stirred up in these cycle interactions. The workbook gradually shifts from more reactive to core emotions in Chapter 5, as you will likely be doing in your sessions as you move deeper into stage one with your couples. Chapter 6 goes into some depth about the main core emotions. Here the workbook can support your couples in understanding and expanding their emotional language to describe what they are experiencing. The EFT model teaches us that the upsetting emotions couples feel in their negative cycles are grounded in their attachment needs not being met. Chapter 7 will support your in-session work by reinforcing the attachment frame that cycle behaviors are a couples best attempts at getting their needs met. In this chapter, partners are encouraged to tune into and share the positive intentions behind their typical actions in the cycle. Chapter 8 then further elaborates on socially useful but potentially sensitive emotions such as shame, guilt, hurt and jealousy.

Chapters 9 through 11 correspond to stage two of EFT. This section of the workbook starts with a checklist to assess a couples readiness for stage two, a tool that we are told is useful for clients and therapists alike. As you help first the withdrawn partner to engage and then the protesting partner become more vulnerable, Chapter 9 can support partners to reflect on the work they are doing in session about their deeper attachment fears and needs and give them a structure to continue their conversation through the week. It is recommended that this chapter be taken slowly and broken up between these two change processes as we do in therapy. Chapter 10 deals with healing relationship injuries. The EFT model informs us that it is difficult to fully complete stage two when there are relationship injuries that have not been healed. Similarly, it is difficult to heal relationship injuries without doing some stage two work. Thus, your guidance in the timing and movement between Chapter 9 and 10 will be important in supporting your couples. In other words, couples may come back and revisit parts of Chapter 9 after working through a hurt or relationship injury in therapy and the reflections of Chapter 10. Filled with stories of change, Chapter 11 can provide both inspiration and a roadmap of the change process, illustrating how a variety of couples with different initial concerns successfully traversed the ground they traveled.

Finally, Chapters 12 and 13 correspond to stage three of EFT. Chapter 12 focuses on consolidating new secure cycles of relating, revisiting initial content issues and problem-solving as a team. The reflections and stories of couples revitalizing their sexual relationship can help facilitate these potentially sensitive conversations both in and out of the therapy office. As therapy is coming to an end it is time to look back together at the ground traveled and create the couples own story of change. We know that transitions in a couples life cycle create stress and therefore a good part of Chapter 13 is devoted to looking ahead, anticipating needs at various stages of life and providing resources for additional reading.

As a final note, we would like to suggest that this resource works best as a companion when the therapy leads, and the workbook follows. The workbook helps partners make sense of what comes alive and is discovered in their sessions, expanding their understanding of what happened. Just like good EFT, clients have an experience and then process the meaning of their experience. In-session experiential exploration will also deepen your couples engagement with their personal reflections and sharing on their own, which can spark new material for the next session. It's important not to lose the experiential nature of EFT which could happen if the sessions become an intellectual review of their workbook reflections. Rather, use the workbook as a jumping off point to ask your couples if anything they worked on between sessions particularly moved them, surprised them or triggered them.

Our Sincere Hope to All Our Readers

We hope this book will give you a chance to change the music of your relationship dance. If you have felt lonely, angry, sad or scared on the dance floor of your relationship up until now, we would like to help you gain a new perspective by taking a few steps back, slowing down and discovering what is happening. From there, you can, if you are both willing to risk something new, learn to play different music and create a new dance.

References

1. Gray, J. (1993). *Men are from mars, women are from venus*. London: Thorsons.
2. Greenberg, L., & Johnson, S. (1988). *Emotionally focused therapy for couples*. New York, NY: The Guilford Press.

3. Johnson, S. (2004). *The practice of emotionally focused couple therapy: Creating connection* (2nd ed.). New York, NY: Routledge.
4. Christensen, A., Atkins, D. C., Baucom, B., & Yi, J. (2010). Marital status and satisfaction five years following randomised clinical trial comparing traditional versus integrative behavioural couple therapy. *Journal of Consulting and Clinical Psychology, 78*, 225–235.
5. Johnson, S. M., Hunsley, J., Greenberg, L., & Schindler, D. (1999). Emotionally focused therapy: Status and challenges. *Clinical Psychology: Science and Practice, 6*, 67–79.
6. Beasley, C., & Ager, R. (2019). Emotionally focused couples therapy: A systematic review of its effectiveness over the past 19 years. *Journal of Evidence-Based Social Work, 16*, 144–159.
7. Gordon-Walker, J., Johnson, S., Manion, I., & Cloutier, P. (1996). An emotionally focused marital intervention for couples with chronically ill children. *Journal of Marital and Family Therapy, 28*, 391–399.
8. Halchuk, R. E., Makinen, J. A., & Johnson, S. M. (2010). Resolving attachment injuries in couples using emotionally focused therapy: A three-year follow-up. *Journal of Couple and Relationship Therapy, 9*, 31–47.
9. Denton, W., & Coffey, A. (2011). Depression: Enemy of attachment bond. In J. Furrow, S. Johnson, & B. Bradley (Eds.), *The emotionally focused casebook: New direction in treating couples* (pp. 87–112). New York, NY and London: Routledge.
10. Johnson, S., & Zuccarini, D. (2011). An integrated model of couple and sex therapy. In J. Furrow, S. Johnson, & B. Bradley (Eds.), *The emotionally focused casebook: New direction in treating couples* (pp. 219–246). New York, NY and London: Routledge.
11. Tulloch, H., Johnson, S., Demidenko, N., Clyde, M., Bouchard, K., & Greenman, P. (2020). An attachment-based intervention for patients with cardiovascular disease and their partners: A proof-of-concept study. *Health Psychology*. Advance online publication. https://doi.org/10.1037/hea0001034
12. McLean, L., Walton, T., Rodin, G., Esplen, M. J., & Jones, J. (2013). A couple-based intervention for patients and caregivers facing end-stage cancer: Outcomes of a randomized controlled trial. *Psycho-Oncology, 22*, 28–38.
13. Johnson, S. (1998). Listening to the music: Emotion as a natural part of systems theory. Special edition of *The Journal of Systemic Therapies, 17*, 1–17.
14. Feeney, J., & Fitzgerald, J. (2012). Relationship education. In P. Noller & G. Karantzas (Eds.), *The Wiley-Blackwell handbook of couples and family relationships* (pp. 289–304). Malden, MA: Wiley-Blackwell.
15. Furrow, J., Johnson, S., Bradley, B., Brubacher, L., Campbell, L., Kallos-Lilly, V., Palmer, G., Rheem, K., Woolley, S. (in press). *Becoming an emotionally focused therapist: The workbook* (2nd ed.). London: Routledge.
16. Johnson, S. (2008). *Hold me tight*. New York, NY, Boston and London: Little Brown and Company.

CHAPTER 2

ATTACHMENT BONDS

The Best Chance of Survival

You might expect that a book for couples would start with descriptions of "falling in love," "making love" or "how to communicate." However, we are starting with the heart of what unites all people! Eighty years ago, child psychiatrist John Bowlby at the Tavistock Clinic in London said,

> Finding oneself alone in a strange place, perhaps in darkness, and met by a sudden movement or mysterious sound, few of us would be unafraid. Were we to have with us even one stout companion, however, we should probably feel much braver, and given many, our courage would quickly return. Being alone, like conscience, "doth make cowards of us all".[1]

Bowlby declared what many practitioners and researchers of his time had been reluctant to admit; that is, *humans need other humans*. Our natural state is to need each other for companionship, intimacy and support to negotiate life's twists and turns and to share life's joys and sorrows. This fact applies whether you are male or female and no matter what strata of society or country of the world you come from. For some of you, it may be a relief to have this basic need for closeness acknowledged. For others, it may be a foreign idea that it is normal and healthy to depend on other people. For others yet, it might be a threatening idea to depend on other people or have others depend on you. You may be used to being completely self-sufficient.

So bear with us please. Before we talk more about communication, emotions, interactions, sex and other topics important to couple relationships, let us establish the basics: as humans we need other humans, and not just any human, but humans who are special to us. Whereas earlier generations of mental health practitioners had proposed that it was *infantile* for adults to need other people for support, Bowlby understood the crucial importance of the special and irreplaceable bond that develops between young children and their caregivers *and* between adults and their relationship partner, close relatives and friends. In fact, knowing that we exist in the minds of at least a few important others is a crucial part of feeling secure in the world, no matter what age you are. He said the need for relationship bonds follows us "from the cradle to the grave."[2] This refreshing notion transformed the world of medicine, education and psychology.

Nowadays, most patients facing painful procedures, worrying tests or major surgery are routinely accompanied by loved ones; sick children can have a parent sleep on a couch near their hospital bed; women giving birth in hospital can be held and encouraged by the partner or support person who loves them. Typically, infants and young children placed in nursery schools and childcare centers are supported while they adjust to separation from their parents; and clinical psychologists and psychiatrists attend carefully to the interpersonal world of their patients to foster their wellbeing. Fortunately, now, these practices, which honor the vital importance of close relationships for our bio-psycho-social wellbeing, are taken for granted, but it was not always so.

DOI: 10.4324/9781003009481-2

A Brief History of Attachment

Following World War II, John Bowlby was asked by the World Health Organization to report on the impact of maternal deprivation on young children. He studied children who had been orphaned, left in hospitals for weeks or months with little or no contact with parents or who had experienced prolonged separation from their mothers who themselves had been ill or hospitalized for long periods. What Bowlby discovered has helped us appreciate the special nature of the emotional bond that develops between young children and their caregivers. Bowlby called this *emotional* tie *attachment*. Other people can provide food or attend to the basic physical needs of the child, but it is the emotional connection between children and their primary caregiver/s that is so essential for the child's development and survival.

Following discussion with a range of scientists studying behaviors of animals in groups, information processing in the human brain and normal child development, Bowlby proposed that the child's urge to seek proximity to a caregiver is "hard wired" into the human brain and enhances survival. When this bond is ruptured through prolonged or permanent separation, protest and despair typically ensue. Furthermore, this predisposition to turn to others for help when in need is a survival mechanism that follows us throughout the lifespan.[3]

Other researchers expanded Bowlby's work, carefully examining many aspects of the relationship between caregiver and infant. Interestingly, they discovered that caregivers' *sensitivity* and *responsiveness* to the baby's needs throughout the first year of life were crucial in developing the baby's sense of security in the world and confidence that future needs would be met.[4] Some of the important aspects of this sensitivity are: 1) how quickly caregivers respond to their infant's distress; 2) if the attempts to relieve the distress actually provide comfort; and 3) if the physical contact is tender and soothing.

Safe Haven and Secure Base

Attachment theory suggests that young children use their attachment figures (mothers, fathers, grandparents, typically the people who care for them) in two very important ways. First, an attachment figure is seen as a *safe haven* to whom they turn when frightened, ill, tired or bored. The safe haven is a place to access attention, love and care. Second, an attachment figure is a *secure base* from which children explore the world when everything is safe. Safety promotes curiosity, and so a secure base encourages exploration and bolsters one's confidence to try new ventures. Bowlby noticed that when the relationship is working well, these attachment behaviors (e.g., turning to the caregiver when frightened, protesting if separated, exploring off into new territory when safe) keep the *distance* between the mother and child flexible and comfortable. As such, a secure attachment promotes both closeness and autonomy and there is fluidity in the movement between closeness and autonomy.

Next time you go to a park or children's playground, notice these attachment behaviors on display: Little children run, climb, laugh and play with just an occasional glance to a watchful caregiver who sits on a park bench nearby; come the arrival into the play area of a large and barking dog, many young children will instantly move in the direction of the parent on the bench, and typically will find the caregiver already on the move toward them. Child and adult meet and a comforting cuddle provides reassurance to the little one that protection is at hand, the danger is not as bad as first thought, or has now passed; the child at some point then disengages from the caregiver's embrace to run back and play, the adult resumes his or her place on the park bench: Over time, the ability to *access* the known and *responsive* caregiver facilitates secure attachment. This bond helps to preserve the safety and survival of not only the young; people of all ages feel more secure if there are at least a few trustworthy others *to whom* they can turn for support, help or encouragement, and *from whom* they can venture forth into the world.[5]

Romantic Love as Attachment

More recently, researchers have proposed that romantic love can also be thought of as an attachment bond: Romantic partners can offer a safe haven to each other in times of need, and a secure base from which each can explore and develop his or her potential.[6] When any of us, young or old, has emotional needs, it is a natural survival strategy for us to want to turn to one special person, or a few close others, for support and comfort. Seeking and maintaining contact with a few *irreplaceable* others is a primary motivating force in us all.

When individuals know, without a shadow of doubt, that their partners will be their "stout companion," as Bowlby quaintly expressed it, in any time of need, and further, when there is lived experience of this responsiveness consistently over time, a *secure bond* between the partners is established and maintained. In other words, when we feel secure in our love relationships, such security is a profound psychological resource that has been found to be associated with reports of higher relationship quality, more positive emotions, more emotional expressiveness, more constructive ways of dealing with negative emotions, more curiosity and tolerance for ambiguity and more constructive coping with stress.[7,8] Scientists are even discovering that a strong, supportive relationship carries with it physical health benefits such as reduced risk of heart disease,[9] improved immune functioning[10] and ability to cope with pain.[11]

Infants who are allowed to be dependent on their caregivers in their early development are observed to grow up to function more confidently and independently in the world. So, too, the dependence on a partner that develops in a secure couple relationship actually fosters autonomy and self-confidence, leading to *interdependence* between the partners. From the safe haven and the secure base of the couple's relationship, two individuals go out into the world feeling stronger, more confident and better equipped to face the ups and downs of daily life; this security spills over to benefit their children, coworkers and community.

Reflection 2.1 Look at your relationship through the "lens" of attachment security

Safe haven

Partners give each other support and comfort in a number of ways. Some examples might include:

- Listening when the other is worried;
- Being attentive when the other is sick;
- Helping practically when the other is tired;
- Inquiring about your partner's feelings;
- Staying engaged patiently when your partner is confused;
- Discussing and debriefing events of the day together;
- Expressing concern and/or providing physical comfort when your partner is sad or hurt.

How does my partner give me support, comfort and encouragement? *(Take your time. Try to find at least* one *positive answer to this question.)*

____

____

____

If you can't find a positive answer to this question, acknowledge that you feel blocked on it instead of shifting the focus to your partner's flaws. Sometimes past hurts and current anger can make it difficult for us to see the positive ways in which our partners are attempting to respond to us.

How could I offer my partner a safe haven in hard times? Think of specific things you do/could do (no matter how small).

____

____

____

Secure base

Partners encourage each other to grow and develop, for example, by:

- Supporting each other's work and activities
- Asking questions that reflect curiosity in each other's opinions
- Listening to each other's hopes and dreams
- Taking an interest in each other's studies, community activities, hobbies
- Acknowledging each other's capabilities and possibilities for growth
- Bolstering each other's confidence with encouragement ("You can do this").

How has my partner encouraged me to grow and develop? *(Try to find at least* one *positive answer to this question.)*

____

____

____

How could I support my partner's dreams and aspirations to grow and develop?

____

____

____

What Partners Really Need from One Another

In romantic relationships, partners typically need or long for acceptance, closeness and understanding, and also to feel loved, appreciated and important. These needs are normal, and having these needs met in a healthy and mutually satisfying way enhances the physical and mental health and overall quality of life of both partners.

> Some people may get caught up in unhealthy ways of asking to have their attachment needs met, but the basic need to feel safe and loved is healthy.

Attachment is essentially about safety and survival. When your attachment needs are not met in your primary relationship, it is normal to feel some combination of fear, uncertainty or anxiousness. When you turn to your partner with these feelings and are greeted with understanding, compassion and reassurance, essentially *emotional responsiveness*, you will likely be comforted and feel secure again. Emotional presence is the "solution" to insecurity. In *Hold me tight*[12] Sue Johnson captures the essence of emotional presence in the acronym: A.R.E.

*A*ccessibility: Accessibility means that I can access your attention, presence and support when I need it. Consider your answers to the following questions: Can I reach you physically and emotionally? Can I get your attention? If I reach for you, will you be there? Will you be open and receptive to my feelings? Can I depend on you to make me a priority?
*R*esponsiveness: Responsiveness means that I can count on you to respond to my cues and needs. Consider your answers to the following questions: Will you tune into my feelings? Will you empathize with me? Will you express sensitivity and compassion? Will you comfort me when I need it?
*E*ngagement: Engagement means that you will keep me close and cherish me as someone who holds a unique place in your life. Consider your answers to the following questions: Will you confide in me? Will you let me close and share your vulnerabilities, doubts and worries? Will you listen to my feelings and allow yourself to be affected by them? Are you interested, curious, drawn to me? Will you tune into my (and your) relationship needs and cues? Will you express your affection to me in your words, gestures, the way you look at me and/or touch me? Will you accept my affection expressed in these same ways?

Reflection 2.2 How is our emotional presence?

Describe a recent example of when you were accessible to your partner.

____

____

____

In this scenario, how did you respond to your partner?

____

____

____

How would you describe your level of engagement?

____
____
____

What would a casual onlooker say about the quality of your engagement as a couple?

____
____
____

Now, describe a recent example of when your partner was accessible to you.

____
____
____

In this scenario, how did your partner respond to you?

____
____
____

How would you describe your partner's level of engagement?

____
____
____

What would a casual onlooker say about the quality of your engagement as a couple?

____
____
____

Developing the Emotional Bond

As you can see, emotional security between you and your partner needs to be developed very consciously. It is not automatically assured; neither does it happen by chance. If you turn to your partner in times of need, seeking comfort, support and care, and find them *not* available and *not* responsive, it is not surprising that you could end up feeling lonely, afraid, hurt or angry. When momentary doubts are repeatedly ignored, dismissed or otherwise not tended to, they can expand and eventually evolve into deeper fears and insecurities.

Some typical fears include being rejected, abandoned or considered a failure; fear of not being accepted or valued; and fear of being controlled. These fears are legitimate for the person concerned and become easier to understand when they are considered in the light of his or her experiences in current or previous close relationships (which we will consider in Chapter 3).

Some common fears in relationships are expressed as:

"I don't know for sure if my partner is there for me"
"I am invisible in this relationship"
"No matter how hard I try, I can't seem to please my partner"
"My opinions don't carry much weight"
"I don't feel wanted"
"I don't think my partner finds me attractive"
"I can't get my feelings heard"
"I am powerless to make an impact"
"There's not much space for my needs in this relationship"

Feelings of insecurity in your relationship can evolve when you feel like you can't openly acknowledge your fears and get a comforting response. Or when you feel like your partner isn't there at a time when you need them the most (such as when dealing with serious illness, the birth of your baby or the death of your parent), you may come to believe that your relationship bond is insecure. That is, you may believe that you can't turn to your relationship when you need support. Similarly, if you are unresponsive or reactive to your partner's needs over time, they will understandably feel negatively impacted. An insecure relationship bond results in distress for you, your partner and your relationship.

Reflection 2.3 Insecurity creates fear and distress

Perhaps you or your partner has said some of these statements. As you read the statements again out loud, *SLOWLY*, notice which ones strike a chord with you. Notice (and note down) the impact of saying and feeling those words. Do you sense the distress in the listed statements earlier? How would you describe it in your own words (feelings or sensations in your body)?

____

____

____

Share with your partner how you are impacted. Remember to: Listen with an Open heart and mind, Validate and Express yourself softly, simply, slowly.

We consider this level of distress to be an *understandable reaction* to relationships that feel insecure. When feeling insecure, a range of negative emotions can emerge. For example, you may feel hurt, angry, fearful, sad or ashamed. These feelings may be familiar to you from many interactions that have followed the pattern you identified in Chapter 2. You may like to think of these reactions as a *protest* that your core needs for security are threatened. Further, you may have expressed your protest in ways that triggered negative emotions in your partner; they may also have recently experienced feelings of fear, hurt, anger, sadness or shame. One way to think of it is that the intensity of the protest may reflect how important this relationship is to you.

Professor John Gottman, from the University of Washington and researcher of couple relationships for many decades, sums up the essence of relationship distress in his comment that distressed couples become *overwhelmed* by negative emotions and *trapped* in constricting cycles of interaction.[13] If you do relate to some of the fears and uncertainties expressed in the outlined statements, you may be feeling quite discouraged. However, it can be reassuring to know that these types of distressing relationship experiences are evidence of an insecure relationship bond that *can be repaired.*

Our aim is to help you walk through the process of how to deal with negative emotions and distressing interactions so as to restore or build a secure attachment bond with your partner. You may do this on your own with your partner, or in conjunction with an emotionally focused couples therapist. In the following chapter we will help you to better understand your and your partner's attachment needs.

References

1,2. Bowlby, J. (1969/1982). *Attachment and loss: Vol. 1. Attachment* (p. 119). New York, NY: Basic Books.

3. Bowlby, J. (1979). *The making and breaking of affectional bonds*. London: Tavistock.

4. Ainsworth, M., Blehar, M., Waters, E., & Wall, S. (1978). *Patterns of attachment: A psychological study of the strange situation*. Hillsdale, NJ: Lawrence Erlbaum.

5. Bowlby, J. (1988). *A secure base*. New York, NY: Basic Books.

6. Hazan, C., & Shaver, P. (1987). Romantic love conceptualized as an attachment process. *Journal of Personality and Social Psychology, 52*, 511–524.

7. Feeney, J. (2008). Adult romantic attachment. In J. Cassidy & P. Shaver (Eds.), *Handbook of attachment* (pp. 456–481). New York, NY and London: Guilford Press.

8. Mikulincer, M., & Shaver, P. (2007). *Attachment in adulthood: Structure, dynamics and change*. New York, NY: The Guilford Press.

9. Coyne, J., Rohraugh, M., Shoham, V., Sonnega, J., Nicklas, J., & Cranford, J. (2001). Prognostic importance of marital quality for survival of congestive heart failure. *The American Journal of Cardiology, 88*, 526–529.

10. Robles, T., & Kiecolt-Glaser, J. (2003). The physiology of marriage: Pathways to health. *Physiology and Behaviour, 79*, 409–416.

11. Coan, J., Schaefer, H., & Davidson, R. (2006). Lending a hand. *Psychological Science, 17*, 1–8.

12. Johnson, S. (2008). *Hold me tight*. New York, NY, Boston and London: Little, Brown and Company.

13. Gottman, J. (1994). *What predicts divorce?* Hillsdale, NJ: Lawrence Erlbaum.

CHAPTER 3

MY PARTNER AND ME

What Influenced Who We Are and How We Are in Close Relationships?

The person that you are today is the result of a unique combination of many factors in which you were raised, including your genetic inheritance, socio-political climate, social position, culture, upbringing, schooling, life experiences in general and your experiences in close relationships. All those influences interact to shape the person you are. The same applies to your partner. As a couple, those unique influences have met and, to some extent, joined to create your identity as a couple. Sometimes "the meeting and joining" goes smoothly, other times it can be confusing, painful and difficult. In this chapter we will focus on your history of attachment relationships. Aspects of your earlier relationships and life experiences are likely to have influenced your beliefs about yourself and close others, and your needs in a close relationship. We understand that for some of you the thought of looking into such a topic is interesting and fun, for others it may feel uncomfortable, even threatening. Let's take it a step at a time. To begin, take some time to reflect on how you typically feel in close relationships.

Our Beliefs and Expectations in Attachment Relationships

Although we may not be consciously aware of it, we all gain a sense of ourselves, our value and our lovability through our life experiences. So, if your caregivers and early love partners have been warm and attentive, you will likely see or "define" yourself as a person who is lovable and worthy of receiving care and attention. Through experiences of significant people tuning into you and valuing you, you will come to value your own thoughts, feelings and needs as an important part of yourself. It follows that you will most likely be motivated to listen to these parts of yourself and express them to significant others. If you struggle to see and appreciate who you are because you have not had such experiences to draw upon, it will be more challenging to accept your opinions, feelings and needs as valid, and therefore it will also be difficult to communicate them well to others.

Beliefs about others focus on trusting that we can express our wants, fears and needs to our partners and that they will be there for us. Over the years our clients have expressed it best as: "a soft place to land," "having someone to lean into," "knowing my back is covered," "a safe place to rest my weary head." When we are confident that others will be there for us, there is an anticipation that we can reach for our partners and that reaching will "pull" for a caring response, such as acknowledgement, compassion and/or practical help. We are talking about healthy, realistic expectations here (such as, asking for help when sick or reassurance when afraid); we are *not* talking about an elevated sense of entitlement in which one partner might make unreasonably high demands of the other (such as demands to be adored to the exclusion of all other family or friend relationships). If your beliefs about others are that they are not dependable or responsive, it would make sense that you would keep your feelings and needs inside. Being anything but self-sufficient could seem unnecessary or even risky.

DOI: 10.4324/9781003009481-3

Reflection 3.1 Attachment beliefs and expectations

The following questions look at how confident you feel that others will be there for you and how comfortable you feel about getting close to others and letting others get close to you. See Appendix A for more worksheets.

MARK AN ESTIMATE ON THE LINE FROM 1 (NOT AT ALL) TO 10 (VERY MUCH).

To what extent do I feel confident that my partner or close others will accept me?
1 (not at all) 10 (very much)

____

How confident do I feel that my partner or important others will be there for me if I need them?
1 (not at all) 10 (very much)

____

To what extent do I see myself as a person who is worthy of care and support if I need it?
1 (not at all) 10 (very much)

____

To what extent do I feel comfortable letting my partner or important others close to me?
1 (not at all) 10 (very much)

____

How confident do I feel about asking others for help or closeness?
1 (not at all) 10 (very much)

____

To what extent do I feel comfortable giving support to my partner or important others?
1 (not at all) 10 (very much)

____

At which end of the continuum do most of your responses lie? These reflective questions draw on the two basic human concerns described here that establish the ground work for how the "meeting and joining" plays out in an intimate relationship:

1. you believe you are lovable and worthy of attention and care, and
2. you trust others to be there for you.[1,2]

If you have generally positive, nurturing experiences with others, you will likely feel deserving of love and anticipate loving responses to requests. You will also likely feel comfortable asking for what you need in your close relationships. You will likely make those requests in a loving way that sends a clear signal about what you need. You will also respond to similar expressions from your partner with an open heart.

Requests may sound like:

- "Will you come with me to the colonoscopy tomorrow? I'm really nervous about the procedure."
- "I'm feeling anxious about my presentation at work, can you sit with me and let's go over it together."
- "Something unsettling happened today that I'd like to talk over with you."
- "We've been so busy these last few weeks, I've missed you. Let's make sure we spend some time together on the weekend to reconnect."
- "I need a bit of time to 'de-stress', and then I can join with you and be present."

What Determines Our Answers to the Two Fundamental Questions?

The two fundamental questions in the mind of any person establishing a close partnership are: "Am I lovable and worthy of care?" and "Can I depend on my partner to be there when needed?" It is disturbing and painful to have doubts about one's own lovability and worthiness, just as it can also be deeply disturbing to feel unsure of the dependability and responsiveness of a partner. Our ability to answer confidently, "Yes, I am worthy of care!" and "Yes, my partner will be there for me!" was initially conceptualized as being influenced by at least three factors related to our attachment experiences.

These include:

1. the quality of our parent's relationship,
2. the quality of the care we received from our attachment figures when growing up, and, of course,
3. the quality of our own romantic relationships.[3]

However, we wish to acknowledge that these three factors are themselves strongly affected by many *intersecting* and *intergenerational* influences such as mental health and/or substance use difficulties in the family, poverty and the trauma of marginalization and oppression within the social structure. These influences, being voiced throughout North America and other parts of the world, highlighting racism against black, Indigenous and other people of color (BIPOC) and discrimination against people who identify as LGBTTQIAP+ all impact attachment security profoundly. Altogether, these experiences will have left an indelible imprint, which influence or shape the beliefs we hold about ourselves, and our close relationships.

If, overall, we grew up experiencing safety in our community, received consistent and supportive care in our family, were fortunate to live in a home where our parents or caregivers had a good relationship and if our partner is supportive and reliable, there is a very good chance that we will have positive beliefs about our own worth and also about being in close relationships. These are the typical background stories of individuals with secure attachments in adulthood.

If, however, the care we received was inconsistent, unreliable or in some way not supportive of our welfare (for example, the family or social environment may have felt/been conflictual, frightening, unpredictable, rejecting, abusive or neglectful), or if we have felt let down or "injured" by previous romantic partners, then it is likely that we will feel somewhat unsure about our own worth and to some extent unsafe in close relationships. Similarly, if we have witnessed ongoing conflict between our parents/caregivers that was not effectively repaired, it is likely to affect our expectations of relationships. Such are the typical background stories of individuals who report feeling insecure in their close relationships in adulthood.

Reflection 3.2 My own attachment history

Take some time now to reflect on your own history of attachment relationships.[4]

Childhood

When you were upset by something as a child, did you have a "lap"[5] to climb up onto to be held and comforted? Who, if anyone, did you go to for comfort when you were young?

How did this person or people generally respond to you?

How consistently did you get these responses?

What did you learn about asking for comfort and security from these experiences?

If your first answer was "no," how did you comfort yourself?

How did you learn *not* to turn to others for comfort?

Observations of your parents' or caregivers' relationship

Choose three adjectives to describe your caregivers' relationship:

What did you learn about relationship bonds from observing your own parents' or caregivers' relationship, or being reared by a single parent or being reared by multiple caregivers?

____

____

____

Adulthood

Have there been times when you have been able to confide and find comfort with your partner? Describe a time when this went well.

____

____

____

How do you typically approach your partner for attention and contact?

____

____

____

Have you ever turned to alcohol, drugs, sex or material things for comfort?
Please describe what was going on and what you did to cope.

____

____

____

Have there been any particularly traumatic incidences in your previous romantic relationships that make it difficult to approach your current partner?

____

____

____

If you have had positive childhood experiences of attachment, it is natural to want to extend them into your love relationships. If you have grown up in an environment with challenging attachment experiences, it is natural to feel a sense of emptiness and yearning for what was missed. We think of coupling as providing a *second chance* to do it over and experience the safe haven a close relationship is meant to be. This can be accomplished, *even with partners who have never experienced a secure relationship before*. Even if your relationship does not feel like a safe haven today, it can be transformed. We have seen this happen time and time again.

These personal reflections may stir up some difficult feelings. However, they can also help you become aware of important life experiences that have formed the basis of your current beliefs about relationships and the giving and receiving of support. The same is true of your partner and so if you can share and receive your responses in the spirit of an open mind and heart, you may discover some new understanding and share a new experience of confiding and support.

It can also be helpful to realize that your and your partner's responses in difficult interactions may relate, *in part*, to experiences, hurts and disappointments that predate your relationship. In tense moments responses such as reactive anger, rejection, dismissal or an all-out shut down, can feel deeply personal. However, it can be helpful to see beyond what is right in front of you; that what is happening between you now is reminiscent of past hurts and traumas for you or your partner, and ways you each learned to cope. Sharing your stories and linking them to your reactions in your relationship can help you draw on that broader perspective and not take things as personally.

Coping with the "Less than Ideal"

The human psyche has remarkable resiliency to cope with differences and unfavorable attachment circumstances. Researchers have identified that there are essentially two ways to cope with attachment—impoverished environments. Our built-in drive to survive seems to prompt some individuals *to turn up their watchfulness* for signs of availability or rejection from others, and other individuals *to turn down their needs* for closeness and support.[6]

> Whether you turn up your watchfulness for signs of availability or turn down your needs for support, these approaches reflect your best attempts to manage distress.

Typically, individuals whose attachment "antennae" are kept on high alert tend to feel uneasy or anxious that others might let them down and not want to be as close as they themselves desire in close relationships. These individuals often report feeling preoccupied with their ability to access their partners. They tend to appear clingy or attempt to monitor and control their partners.[7]

By contrast, individuals whose attachment antennae are kept turned down low report being uncomfortable with too much closeness and prefer to see themselves as self-sufficient and avoid depending on others very much. Both these responses make sense in the context of a challenging upbringing, lack of safety in the world or troubled romantic relationships in the past. However, what was helpful for survival then, in previous significant relationships, may not be so helpful now, in your current romantic relationship.

Reflection 3.3 How my past influences me

How have your own child and adulthood attachment relationships shaped your beliefs about being able to expect others to be attentive to your needs?

____

____

____

How have societal influences or norms shaped your expectations of others being attentive to your needs? (For example, concerning your culture, race, birthplace, religion, social class, abilities, etc.)

____

____

____

Complete the sentence(s) that apply to you:
When my antenna is turned up, I notice myself engaging in these behaviors:

____

____

____

When my antenna is turned down, I notice myself engaging in the following behaviors:

____

____

____

Cultural Influences on Who We Are and How We Are in Close Relationships

Before moving on to understand more about your patterns and emotions, we wish to draw attention to the powerful impact of culture, race, religion, gender and sexual orientation on relationships. Many couples in the world have made a great success of establishing a romantic partnership that includes cultural differences. Sometimes, however, cultural differences can be misinterpreted and become polarizing and upsetting. Partners might be of different ethnicities or may come from the same background but of a different "status" or social position. Or in the case of immigration, one partner may be a first generation arrival and the other partner's family goes back several generations and is thus more assimilated to the dominant culture. Alternatively, partners may have religious differences, or one partner was raised in economic adversity and the other in more affluent circumstances. These differences have the potential to create a gulf between partners, resulting in conflict or tension around significant matters in family life, such as communication, parenting, religious observances, lifestyle, substance use, moral viewpoints, how manners and respect are conveyed and values around money, to name just a few possibilities.

Other couples may bring differences in their backgrounds in terms of gender roles, with one partner holding conservative and fixed ideas about gender expectations in home and family life, and the other holding more liberal or flexible views and ways of sharing household tasks, child care and financial responsibilities. The trap for couples in all these scenarios is when attitudes, comments or behaviors that have been shaped through different cultural backgrounds are not well understood, or interpreted as meaning "You don't love me! I don't matter to you!" or "I'm not valued or respected by you!" Similarly, difficulties can easily arise if differences of view or behavior are labeled as a fault or peculiarity in the other. Security, on the other hand, can be built through having L-O-V-E conversations about your differences and what they mean to you. As a couple, it is possible to navigate them by sharing your basic needs and weaving them together to form a relationship tapestry that is uniquely your own.

Individualism Versus Collectivism

In addition to differences in life experiences and world views, couples with mixed ethnicities can bring different beliefs and ideas about communication, closeness, and how emotion and love are expressed. One example is when a traditionally reared Asian person and a Westerner of European heritage form a committed relationship. Recent research conducted in Australia and Hong Kong asked Westerners of European descent/Chinese couples to comment on what they thought was necessary for a long-term successful relationship. One Western woman wrote: "I think it's through verbal affirmation. I think you need to tell your partner you love them and tell them that they're beautiful and give them verbal affirmations." By contrast, a Chinese woman wrote: "There is a Chinese saying that 'Love is to be held in your heart rather than put it in your mouth.' If a guy says I love you every day, he is considered to be just saying it, not doing it, because there would be no need to say it if doing it."[8]

If a couple has not arrived at an understanding about such contrasting beliefs, can you imagine how it might lead to doubts or mistrust? Encountering these cultural differences, a woman of European heritage might actively seek what she is needing by probing and questioning her mate about their lack of expressiveness: "What do you like about me?" or "How come you never complement me before we go out together?" She may push for more affirmation or affection in the relationship. By acting on these individualistic needs her Chinese partner may feel overpowered. Thus, a person of Chinese heritage may be more likely to keep quiet about this difference and adapt their expectations to their partner's behavior in order to maintain harmony.

These contrasting views and expectations can be understood as a collectivism-individualism continuum. Broadly speaking, in individualist cultures, people are defined by their individual characteristics and validation of these forms self-esteem. Young people are encouraged to grow up independent and express their unique feelings and preferences. In contrast, in collectivist cultures, people are defined by their relationship with others and self-esteem is derived from fitting harmoniously into the group. Suppression of individuality for the benefit of group harmony is considered a sign of maturity.[9] People of Asian, Middle Eastern, African and Latin-American countries tend to be high in collectivism whereas European and former European colonies tend to be high in individualism.[10] Thus, both of the responses listed are equally valid based on cultural expectations but may need to be explored for partners to better understand where each is coming from and avoid negative power dynamics. Intercultural couples who make a success of dealing with their differences of cultural background typically talk openly about the defining characteristics of their respective backgrounds, and over time many create a "third reality,"[11] which integrates what the couple consider the best aspects of both cultures and does not privilege one culture over the other.

Religious and Racial Discrimination

Another important lens through which to explore culture in your relationship involves the life experiences of marginalized groups, such as people of color or people who have suffered religious persecution. Couples can also struggle when one partner comes from a group that has suffered racial or religious discrimination and the other partner comes from the privileged, dominant group. People who have been exposed to chronic racism or religious persecution throughout their lives understandably carry an extra load of stress and trauma and very likely intergenerational trauma that may be out of their conscious awareness.

One woman told us about attending functions with her family at the Jewish community center. While participating in activities there, she experienced a confusing combination of feelings, including a deep sense of belonging, as well as an inexplicable restlessness which came out as impatience with her children. Her partner would then rush to the kids' defence, leaving her feeling guilty and abandoned. When the couple explored this issue together, she revealed that both of her parents were Holocaust survivors and she had been the victim of anti-Semitism herself on a few occasions, growing up in a largely Anglo-Saxon neighborhood. She generally felt safe in everyday life. However, going to Synagogue or attending the Jewish identified community center left her feeling "exposed, like a sitting duck" and engulfed in fear. Her suffocating fear was replaced with immediate relief upon leaving the premises. Whether living with low-grade fear or an acute sense of threat, these feelings can seep into one's relationships in unhelpful ways. Especially if in the form of heightened emotional reactivity, edginess or in some cases restricted emotional expression. However, with some self-reflection, this woman was able to find ways to let her partner know when the fear came and be receptive to comfort and reassurance.

Another story we wish to share is of a couple with an African American husband, Jamar, and wife, Holly, whose parents were third and fourth generation Polish and French. They poignantly illustrate how racial stress, culture and class differences can strain a relationship. Jamar was raised in relative poverty and was determined to be a good provider to his wife and family when he grew up. In contrast, Holly was raised in an affluent home in which she had much freedom, but not much support from her parents. She had always dreamed of having a warm, close-knit family. With Jamar's focus on being a reliable breadwinner, however, Holly once again felt on her own much of the time. She experienced Jamar as emotionally absent and criticized him for working too much. For Jamar her criticisms felt like attacks that cut to the core of his identity as a "good" man and dependable partner. When they argued, Jamar would feel diminished inside. Unbeknownst to Holly, her sharp words brushed against a deep sense of inferiority that he had internalized as a young boy of little means who was teased for being "too black." Jamar avoided sharing these painful feelings with Holly, believing that as a white person, she would never be able to truly understand him. Instead he would close down and turn to work to manage his frustration. At other times Jamar would become hostile and question how she could be so needy when she had everything she could possibly want. Jamar never felt like he belonged in the social circles they frequented and even in Holly's family who were slow to accept him at the beginning.

As a young person he had internalized a concept of himself as inferior which was reinforced in their relationship through a pattern of Holly criticizing and demanding when she felt lonely and Jamar distancing angrily when he felt judged. Jamar's racial identity and world view, shaped by chronic discrimination, made it difficult for him to trust his wife's ability to understand and respond to him. Also, coming from a more collectivist culture, Jamar tried hard to just "carry on" instead of letting Holly know how her words affected him. Holly's relentless pursuit of her needs was congruent with the individualistic culture and privilege in which she was raised. However, it only served to reinforce Jamar's mistrust. It would have been better instead to open up and share how she missed him at times when he worked so hard. Fortunately, Jamar and Holly were able to heal their relationship through therapy (which you can read about in Chapter 11) and L-O-V-E conversations aimed at understanding how differences in culture and social position, communication patterns and negative racial experiences were impacting them both.[12]

We turn now to inviting your own reflection on the religious, cultural or racial influences in your own life and relationship. Before doing so, we wish to acknowledge that in these few paragraphs our examples cannot be exhaustive and thus touch briefly on some groups and not on others. We hope you can catch the spirit of our message that you and your life experiences matter, even if we do not speak directly to your own cultural heritage. Also, we hope our examples inspire some avenues of discussion, rather than create assumptions about any particular group. We aspire to acknowledge the significance of culture and discrimination, invite you to be curious about your own and your partner's background and to create a space for some rich conversations.

Reflection 3.4 Reflection on our cultural influences

How have culture, race, ethnicity, religion, gender roles, social position/power or other contextual influences shaped my identity? What positive or negative messages have I internalized about myself? Who has helped me in exploring my identities in these various areas?

How might the pain of racial, cultural, social class or religious oppression play a role in my life? How do I cope?

Upon reflection, what assumptions do I bring into our relationship based on my background that affect us?

What disagreements do we have that can be better understood if we look at them through the lens of racial, cultural, social position/power or religious impacts and or stressors?

How have we handled these differences? What have been some positive or negative aspects of the way we have dealt with our different backgrounds?

What are still sensitive issues from our backgrounds that can trap us into negative interactions?

These conversations can be sensitive, and misunderstandings based on differences in background can contribute to hurt and distress. Meeting in L-O-V-E will help you care for each other and perhaps also discover something new.

Unique Experiences of People Who Identify as Lesbian, Gay, Bisexual, Transgender, Two-Spirit, Questioning, Intersex, Asexual, Pansexual or other Identities (LGBTTQIAP+)

How freely humans have experienced and expressed their gender and their sexuality has varied across time and through many different cultures. Importantly, how you, the readers of this book, think and feel about your gender identity, sexuality and sexual orientation is valid and vital to attend to in your relationship. Your gender identity may align with the sex you were assigned at birth, but it may not. Your sexual orientation may align with the expectations of your family of origin, significant caregivers or local community, but it may not. While it is beyond the scope of this book to adequately address the full range of experiences of people who identify as **LGBTTQIAP+**, we want to nonetheless take some time to respectfully acknowledge and honor wherever you are at in this journey. Complexity and variation from the considered norm of your place or time regarding gender, sexual attraction, behaviors and fantasies, as well as social and emotional preferences and lifestyle, have likely posed significantly negative and painful experiences for you.[13] We want to welcome you in the fullness of your humanity into this space and hope that the exercises and suggestions in this book will be of support to you and your relationships.

The research literature on same-sex relationships validates what our shared humanity already knows deep inside, that attachment process functions similarly across all love relationships.[14,15] Despite this, we know that living in a world that marginalizes and punishes nonconformity, many individuals have experienced pain and harm along their developmental pathways to adulthood and continue to experience discrimination throughout their adult lives.[16,17] You may very well have had negative experiences, rejection or trauma in coming out to yourself, your family or friends, and possibly developed internalized negativity toward yourself as a result. Also, **LGBTTQIAP+** couples typically carry an additional load of the stress navigating everyday life in a cisgender, hetero-dominant world.

LGBTTQIAP+ partners may also have had very different experiences in their developmental pathways to adulthood, with coming out, for example, being relatively safe for one partner but negative, anxiety-provoking or traumatic for the other. Some communities are more accepting of diversity than others, such that differences in how "out" a partner is can understandably create sources of tension within the relationship. In the next chapter you will meet Angela and Denise, a couple who struggled with exactly this issue and you can read about their story of change in Chapter 11. Similarly, couples where one partner experiences gender dysphoria or is in the process of transitioning is likely to experience a complex soup of emotions including fear, shame, sadness, uncertainty, anger, despair, excitement . . . all of which are valid and normal given the circumstances.

We therefore want to create space and safety here for readers who identify as **LGBTTQIAP+** to reflect with some depth on the unique experiences that have shaped how you see yourself and helped or hindered you on your journey to be your authentic self. We are mindful that some readers may be in an early phase of exploring their identities. If this is the case, we offer some additional resources which we hope will be helpful in supporting you in this process.

Additional resources . . .
safezone.uncc.edu/allies/theories
www.nbcnews.com/feature/nbc-out/best-black-queer-books-according-black-lgbtq-leaders-n1231309
the519.org/education-training/training-resources/our-resources
myhusbandbetty.com Helen Boyd's Trans 101 lecture

Reflection 3.5 Reflections on the pathways to developing LGBTTQIAP+ identities

What do I remember as important experiences in my pathway to developing my gender identity, identities or sexual orientation?

____

____

____

Who helped me on that journey? Who didn't help me, and instead made it hard and painful? What messages have I internalized about myself, positive or negative, as a result of these interactions?

____

____

____

Did I have peers who provided a sense of safety and belonging? Who else has helped me develop my identity?

____

____

____

Do we have differences in how open and "out" we are with family, friends or co-workers? How do we navigate these differences as a couple?

____

____

____

How is our relationship impacted by the ongoing stress of marginalization and discrimination? Do I tend to turn my "antennae" up or down? How do I cope?

____

____

____

How could we help or better support each other as a couple?

____

____

____

Take some time to share the reflections in this chapter with your partner. Carve out time to create space for this sharing to be the priority, without rushing or multitasking. Take turns sharing your stories in small chunks. When you are listening to your partner's story, just provide your full attention, even if you have heard some parts of it before. Allow yourself to be touched by what your partner is saying, but do not feel responsible for making it better or for providing solutions to problems. Close your L-O-V-E conversations by expressing how it felt to participate in the sharing and listening. Notice and comment on what helps you feel heard and closer to each other. If there has been particularly sensitive content to your reflections and disclosures, help each other to slow down, breathe and center for a few minutes before moving onto something else in your day. New and deeper understanding for you both may be reached through several conversations, not just this one. Handle each other with care in honoring the journey you have taken to explore your childhood experiences, earlier romantic relationships and the impact of culture and discrimination.

If you have identified that you are somewhat anxious about rejection or avoidant of closeness, or that you have had a turbulent journey in close relationships so far, this does not mean that you are doomed to have unhappy or unsuccessful romantic relationships or that you are in anyway a defective human being. Understanding how each of you predominantly feels in close relationships can be helpful because it provides you and your partner with an opportunity to get a better understanding of each other and the impact you may be having on each other. Understanding can also lead to healing and change; relationships can change for the better and as they do, perceptions of yourself and your partner can change as well. Anxious partners can discover that they are in fact lovable and that their partners can be reliable and responsive. Avoidant partners can discover that their partners can be accepting of their need for space and individuality. Importantly, couples can work together to understand and respect each other's sensitivities and help each other to feel more secure.

In the following chapter we will take a closer look at the ways that couples can get caught up and stuck in negative interactions, typically as a result of feeling insecure in the relationship. Identifying the negative patterns opens the way to changing them and building greater security.

References

1. Bowlby, J. (1973). *Attachment and loss: Vol. 2. Separation, separation and anger*. New York, NY: Basic Books.

2,3. Hazan, C., & Shaver, P. (1987). Romantic love conceptualized as an attachment process. *Journal of Personality and Social Psychology*, *52*, 511–524.

4. Furrow, J., Johnson, S., Bradley, B., Brubacher, L., Campbell, L., Kallos-Lilly, V., Palmer, G., Rheem, K., Woolley, S. (in press). *Becoming an emotionally focused therapist: The workbook* (2nd ed.). London: Routledge.

5. Johnson, S. (1992). Personal communication.

6. Brennan, K., Clark, C., & Shaver, P. (1998). Self-report measurement of adult attachment. In J. Simpson & S. Rholes (Eds.), *Attachment theory and close relationships* (pp. 46–75). New York, NY and London: The Guilford Press.

7. Feeney, J. (2016). Adult romantic attachment: Developments in the study of couple relationships. In J. Cassidy & P. Shaver (Eds.), *The handbook of attachment: Theory, research and clinical applications* (3rd ed., pp. 435–463). New York, NY and London: The Guilford Press.

8. Hiew, D., & Leung, P. (2017). Cultural diversity in couple relationships. In J. Fitzgerald (Ed.), *Foundations for couples therapy: Research for the real world* (pp. 82–91). New York, NY: Routledge.

9. Hofsteder, G., Hofsteder, G. V., & Minkov, M. (2010). *Cultures and organisations: Software of the mind* (3rd ed.). New York, NY: McGraw-Hill.

10. Dawlish, A. F. E., & Huber, G. L. (2003). Individualism versus collectivism in different cultures: A cross-cultural study. *Intercultural Education*, *14*(1), 47–56. Retrieved July 2, 2010, https://doi.org/10.1080/1467598032000044647

11. Perel, E. (2000). A tourist's view of marriage: Cross-cultural couples-challenges, choices and implications for therapy. In P. Papp (Ed.), *Couples on the fault line: New directions for therapists* (pp. 178–204). New York, NY: The Guildford Press.

12. Nightingale, M., Awosan, C. I., & Stavrianopoulos, K. (2019). Emotionally focused therapy: A culturally sensitive approach for African American heterosexual couples. *Journal of Family Psychotherapy*, *30*(3), 221–244.

13. Malpas, J. (2020, March). *Can couples change gender and sexuality?* Online presentation, Second Australian Assembly on Affect and Attachment, Brisbane, Australia.
14. Fingerhut, A., & Peplau, L. (2013). Same-sex romantic relationships. In C. J. Patterson & A. R. D'Augelli (Eds.), *Handbook of psychology and sexual orientation* (pp. 165–178). New York, NY: Oxford University Press.
15. Ridge, S. R., & Feeney, J. A. (1998). Relationship history and relationship attitudes in gay males and lesbians: Attachment style and gender differences. *Australian and New Zealand Journal of Psychiatry, 32*, 848–859.
16. Allan, R., & Johnson, S. (2017). Conceptual and application issues: Emotionally focused therapy with gay male couples. *Journal of Couple and Relationship Therapy, 16*(4), 286–305. https://doi.org/10.1080/15332691.2016.1238800
17. Mohr, J., & Jackson, S. (2016). Same-sex romantic attachment. In J. Cassidy & P. Shaver (Eds.), *The handbook of attachment: Theory, research and clinical applications* (3rd ed., pp. 484–506). New York, NY and London: The Guilford Press.

CHAPTER 4

WHAT HAPPENED TO US? THREE CYCLES OF RELATIONSHIP DISTRESS

Most couples experience mutual attraction, understanding and closeness early in their relationship. As you reflect back on the early stages of your relationship, what attracted you to one another, how your relationship developed, it may be difficult to make sense of how your relationship has evolved over time to the point of wanting to pick this book up for help. All couples experience a range of emotions, good and bad, and times together, both happy and difficult. Some couples are able to weather difficult moments or misunderstandings and "bounce back," resolving them relatively easily. Whereas other couples can become "caught" in misunderstandings that evolve into big disputes affecting how fundamentally close, secure, and respected they feel. It is only when these negative interactions become a regular pattern and your positions in them become rigid that it can be problematic. Over the years, getting stuck again and again in similar misunderstandings and arguments, not being able to resolve your differences can affect your relationship bond, leaving you feeling confused, disappointed, and disheartened. For some couples it may not be the case that you've been close and now feel you have drifted apart, but rather that you are searching to create a closer bond than you've ever felt before. Regardless of how you came to this point, this chapter will help you look at your relationship in a new light. We will describe common relationship dynamics[1,2] that we see in our clinics and ask you to reflect on patterns in your own relationship.

When you experience conflict or difficult interactions with your partner, do you notice that your conversations follow a typical course? If so, you are like many couples who recognize that their arguments or tense conversations tend to follow a familiar, repetitive pattern, regardless of the topic (e.g., household tasks, finances, decisions). Although you may not know what sets it off, you likely recognize that these conversations are emotionally charged. How the conversation goes and the emotional chain reactions that occur are more important than the topic of the conversation. We will help you tune into how your difficult conversations evolve and what makes them feel so charged. The way you react to each other in these moments is likely your best attempt at handling the situation but may in fact drive you further apart. You know how unsatisfying it can be when your interactions take a negative turn, spiral down, and leave you feeling unresolved and distant. If you begin to pay attention to the steps you each take in your conversations over and over in different situations, you will probably notice a pattern.

If you and your partner have troublesome conflict or interactions that you would like to change, becoming acquainted with the pattern that spirals your relationship down will be the first step in changing it. Relationship experts have long described three different patterns or "dances" reflective of distressed relationships.[3] We characterize these as: Protest-Withdraw, Be Loud to be Heard, and Avoid Conflict at any Cost. As you are likely well aware, these negative interactions can be set off by a variety of triggers as minor as someone feeling cranky or preoccupied or as major as one of you having serious doubts about the relationship. The most common dance, illustrated next by Patricia and William, is the Protest-Withdraw pattern, which typically occurs when both partners are desperately trying to get

DOI: 10.4324/9781003009481-4

their needs met and stay together. As you read the descriptions of these three different patterns, notice if your relationship fits one more than the others. Notice which partner you identify with most in the stories. *(Please note the three couples described are drawn from our clinical experience, to illustrate common patterns of conflict and interaction we see in distressed couples. As with all the clinical stories told in this book, the partners are a composite of several people and details described have been changed to protect their privacy.)*

Protest-Withdraw: Patricia and William

Patricia and William are a British, cisgender, heterosexual couple in their mid-thirties who had recently migrated to Canada. Patricia, a clothing designer, and William, a high school History teacher, had purchased their first home and were embarking on a task that surely promised to be exciting and bonding: Decorating together!!! Today, they were looking for a living-room sofa. By the third furniture store, however, it was quickly becoming apparent that their ideas were very different. They couldn't even agree on a color choice. William gravitated toward an overstuffed, patterned sofa and Patricia liked a brown leather sofa with clean lines. Finding no compromise, the couple were getting worn out and discouraged. Patricia began insistently trying to convince William her preference was more in keeping with current design trends. Feeling put down, William dug his heels in and defended his taste with logical, practical arguments. Patricia then stated curtly that since design was her area of expertise, he should trust her. Hearing the frustration escalate in her voice, William backed down and gave in to avoid an argument.

Although they apparently reached agreement on a sofa, neither felt good inside. Patricia had an unsettled, jittery feeling in her stomach. William felt down and deflated. When Patricia noticed William's mood, that jittery feeling in her stomach grew. Several times she approached William to ask him if he was "really ok" with their decision. Each time he reassured her quietly, but he remained remote.

If you take a close look at this couple's interaction, you will notice how Patricia and William each take certain steps that interplay to produce a disconnection between them. When Patricia experiences an apparently irreconcilable difference with William, she tries to convince him to agree with her. When that doesn't work, she escalates her attempt to resolve the issue by becoming demanding. (She doesn't tell him how anxious and insecure these differences make her feel.) Instead Patricia becomes "bigger," more convincing and confrontational. We can view her steps in the interaction as attempts to "get them on the same page" because their differences feel threatening to her. Her goal is *to close the gap between them* the only way she knows how, by insisting.

William defends his position initially, in reaction to what he hears as Patricia putting down his design sense. He shuts down his hurt feelings and becomes distant and logical in his counter arguments. Eventually Patricia's arguments wear him down; William puts his own preferences aside and capitulates to her in order to prevent further conflict. However, the whole interaction leaves William with a sour feeling and he retreats into himself. We can view William's steps in their interaction as withdrawing with the goal being *to protect him from hurt and protect their relationship from conflict.* The trouble is that their resolution feels "hollow" and seems to have been arrived at in a way that has affected their connection. Patricia tries to reconnect with William by seeking reassurance and he responds half-heartedly.

Later that day at the soccer field, William was to coach their son's game. William always arrived early to set up the field and Patricia followed later with their son. Today, the team was playing at a different field and it had slipped William's mind to tell Patricia. He tried to reach her on her mobile phone but got no answer. Meanwhile, Patricia had shown up at the regular field and was alarmed not to find William or the rest of the players. She couldn't reach anyone because she had left her mobile charging at home. By chance, one of the other parents happened to be driving past and stopped to tell her where the game was relocated. When they arrived, the game had already begun, and Patricia was flustered.

She tried to talk to William, but he brushed her off with an irritated tone and focused on coaching the game. Patricia felt snubbed when she had "done nothing wrong." Throughout the game it seemed as if William ignored Patricia and although outwardly she maintained her composure, inside she fumed.

They maintained a tense politeness for the next several hours, through dinner and their night-time ritual with their son. However, after he fell asleep Patricia approached William to talk about the day and let him know she was hurt by his behavior earlier in the day. William denied he had a "tone" and said she was making mountains out of molehills. Trying to be understood, Patricia became more insistent and accused him of being insensitive. William steadily explained that he could not attend to her while he was coaching and left the room with an air of exasperation. They spent the rest of the evening in separate parts of the house.

Do you notice a similar pattern in the steps of Patricia and William's two interactions? Patricia tends to press harder when she does not feel like she is getting through to William. She tries to push him to respond in order to manage her feelings of insecurity. William, on the other hand, also feels uncomfortable when he and Patricia disagree. William worries about not pleasing her and feels like a failure when this happens. However, William handles his difficult feelings by trying to defend himself logically, minimizing the problem, and staying calm by closing off emotionally. The more closed off William appears, the more intensely Patricia tries to make contact. The more Patricia pokes and pushes to get through, the more distant William becomes. The cycle of interaction feeds on itself. Both partners will feel unsettled until their connection is restored. What follows is an infinity loop that illustrates how partners influence each other.

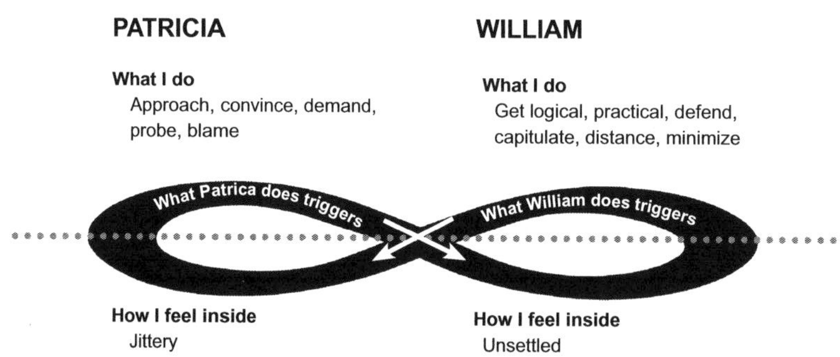

Figure 4.1 Patricia and William's relationship dance with behaviors and feelings
Infinity diagram adapted from Scott R. Woolley, Ph.D.©[4] and labeling adapted from Lucy Pascal, M.S.W.[5]

We have illustrated Patricia and William's negative cycle as an example to follow. The complete version with all of the layers filled in is reproduced by permission in Appendix B. Here we focus on the first layer that portrays how their pattern of relating looks on the surface in terms of how Patricia and William act toward each other.

As you progress in this book, we will be completing all the layers of the cycle in Appendix B, which will give you a sense of the dynamics involved in your negative interactions. As in the example outlined, you can leave the feelings or emotions layer vague if you are unsure. We will be helping you to discover and crystallize your emotional experience in later chapters. For now, it is important to notice that if you follow the arrows, you will see the following: What Patricia does with her feelings of distress (jangled, anxious, hurt) in the relationship triggers William's distress (unsettled, anxious) and in turn how he behaves on the basis of his unsettled feelings will further add to Patricia's jitters.

NEGATIVE CYCLES FEED ON THEMSELVES: How I deal with my difficult emotions are *both* a REACTION to a threat and become a fresh TRIGGER for my partner.

The cycle illustrated on the previous page is made up of a series of steps that have repeated again and again in different contexts over years of being together, evolving into a pattern. EFT couple therapists think of this cycle as a dance that partners create together in their ways of being and coping in the relationship, especially when one or both are feeling threatened, stressed, tired or hurt. When we feel insecure or threatened in our relationships, there are basic responses that we are wired to have. The stress response prepares us for fight, flight or freeze and these responses translate into interpersonal behaviors of pursuit (fight) or avoidance (flight and freeze). In times of distress or upset in a relationship, often there is one partner who pursues the other in some way with the goal being to make contact, to keep the connection alive or get a response from the other. This partner may criticize, complain, blame, poke or try to manage and control things. The other way to respond is to protect the relationship and the interaction from getting worse by withdrawing, shutting down, being super logical, placating or avoiding difficult topics. Let's take a closer look at both of these ways of coping within relationships.

Although it may not be apparent, when one partner is pursuing the other in a negative way, often what they are "protesting" is the loss of the connection in the present moment or more generally in the relationship. If **protesting partners** could say what their gut is calling out, it might sound something like:

> "Oh no, please don't shut down. That feels too lonely for me. Stay with me, respond to me, I need you to be there right now! I wish you could see how much I need you."

This would send a very clear signal to their partners; however, for many couples that feels too risky to say for a variety of reasons, including messages from family, society and culture, like "Don't wear your heart on your sleeve," "Adults should be self-sufficient" or "It is weak to feel sad, afraid, unsure of yourself, or insecure." Also, once negative cycles show up repeatedly in a relationship, it can feel risky or threatening to open up and be vulnerable. Instead, protesting partners may complain, accuse or demand and then their distress signals do not come across clearly. Instead of sounding like "I need to connect with you," it comes across as "How come you never listen to me!" or "You don't care about anyone else but yourself!" or "I expect an apology from you!"

If these phrases have a hint of familiarity to you, do not get down on yourself. Protesting is a natural thing to do when it has not felt safe or worked to be more open and vulnerable. However, it is possible to change these patterns of behavior between you and your partner and create a place where you can take the risk to express your feelings and needs. Here is a list of behaviors that people engage in when they are desperate to get their partner's attention or response.

Protesting Behaviors

Probing, poking
Questioning
Accusing
Demanding
Clinging
Nagging
Blaming
Criticizing
Complaining
Confronting
Attacking
Putting the other down
Interrogating
Yelling to make my point
Following around the house
Phoning or texting repeatedly
Picking arguments
Controlling
Judging
Disapproving.

In *Protest-Withdraw*, partners who tend to withdraw or avoid difficult interactions are quietly protesting conflict and disharmony, which can feel very jarring for some people. Again, although not apparent, partners who tend to placate, defend, distance or close off emotionally during tense conversations are typically trying to minimize conflict in the relationship and avoid disappointing their partners. They may also be protecting themselves from the distress they feel when they do disappoint their partners. They may appear paralyzed, distant or even unaffected during difficult conversations. However, research has shown that their bodies are quite keyed up (heart pounding, palms sweating) suggesting that they are experiencing considerable physical discomfort and physiological distress during potentially conflictual interactions.[6] If *withdrawing partners* could clearly express their own dilemma in tense moments, it might sound something like:

> "Let's keep the peace. I'm nervous when you're unhappy or when our relationship does not feel harmonious. I wish you could see that I am trying to fix the problem between us because I care."

Maybe you identify with the withdrawing position just described? Life may have taught you to be guarded with your feelings; that it's safest to shut down your feelings because they can make things worse. Or perhaps you have never had anyone really help you tune into your feelings. It's difficult to express your emotions when you don't know how to tune into that part of yourself. Instead you may feel blocked and try to minimize the problem or fix it logically. See this list of withdrawing behaviors that people typically use when they are trying to make things better. Note that similar lists of feelings, thoughts and behaviors are available on Douglas Tilley's website.[7]

Withdrawing Behaviors

Reasoning
Defending
Clamming up
Appeasing
Placating
Accommodating
Smoothing things over
Minimizing the problem
Giving advice or problem-solving
Using humor
Dismissing
Deflecting
Counter blaming
Criticizing
Withdrawing, leaving the room
Numbing out
Avoiding
Not responding
Shutting down
Yelling to shut things down

If Protest-Withdraw does not sound familiar, there are two other patterns to consider. These patterns also draw on protesting and withdrawing behaviors, but they express themselves in different combinations, as you will soon discover.

Be Loud to be Heard: Angela and Denise

The second pattern, Be Loud to be Heard, typically consists of two partners who tend to protest or seek contact with each other in ways that are confrontational and difficult to respond to: demanding, complaining or criticizing. When threatened in the relationship both partners approach each other harshly, instead of sharing the vulnerable feelings that are evoked by the threat. Partners stuck in this pattern tend to escalate quickly, express anger readily, and argue frequently. Angela and Denise, a lesbian cisgender couple who are middle-aged, call their negative cycle "the blame game." Their main triggers center on interactions with Denise's family, a large, expressive Polish Catholic family who, although aware of their daughter's sexual orientation, tend to dance around it with denial. Although Denise has been "out" for over two decades, Angela feels that Denise minimizes their relationship when around her family and this has undermined Angela's sense of importance and value to Denise. Coming from a smaller Scottish Canadian family, Angela initially went along to Denise's family functions but would stay in the shadows during the event. Later she would pick a fight with Denise to see if she was still capable of getting Denise's attention. Somehow, it was comforting for Angela to reaffirm that she was important enough to get a reaction from Denise. However, as the years have passed, Angela has begun to refuse to participate in family functions, because she does not feel accepted by the family or supported by Denise in confronting them. Denise feels threatened and deserted by Angela's refusal to participate. Denise handles her feelings of abandonment by begging Angela to come along, badgering her and eventually demanding that she come: "If you don't come with me to family functions, then we have no relationship!" Angela hears a threat in the air and responds angrily, blaming Denise for not sticking up for her . . . their escalating cycle is off and running again.

If this pattern sounds familiar to you, perhaps you can take reassurance in the knowledge that the energy inherent in the *Be Loud to be Heard* pattern is a lot about the intensity of feelings you and your partner have toward one another. You can learn to channel those feelings into a strength by finding ways to reach out and respond back to each other more lovingly.

Avoid Conflict at Any Cost: Wendy and Winston

In the third pattern, Avoid Conflict at any Cost, two partners tend to handle difficult or threatening situations with avoidance, withdrawing from each other physically and/or emotionally. Wendy and Winston, a heterosexual cisgender couple of Chinese heritage who were born and raised in North America, are in their sixties. Wendy is a research librarian and Winston is a university professor. When their therapist met with them, there was an empty, awkward silence between them. As Wendy talked, she was tentative about her concerns in the relationship, often checking with Winston as if to monitor his reactions to her comments. She indicated that she typically tried to avoid conflict at home, by shutting down her feelings and needs when they were not in sync with Winston's. She tended to "go with the flow" for fear of "making waves." Wendy also noted that she tended to feel depressed when she shut herself down, but it was a price she was willing to pay for the comfort of feeling like she was pleasing Winston.

Winston reported that it was actually frustrating for him that he didn't know what Wendy wanted. He said that he did not feel like a good partner to Wendy when she constantly placated him and that was painful for him. He also worried about her depression. Winston used to express his concerns more readily to Wendy, sometimes with a tone of frustration, but these conversations never seemed to "go anywhere," to use his language. In fact, they seemed to drive Wendy further into her shell.

Nowadays, Winston indicated that he keeps these feelings to himself and distracts himself by keeping busy with sports and social activities. He recognizes that his busyness helps him avoid feeling the emptiness of their connection and the pain of feeling that Wendy does not trust him enough to confide in him. He also believes that it is hurtful to Wendy when he shares his feelings with her, that she feels blamed and retreats further from him. He reports being both protective of her and fatigued by the effort of cajoling her out of her shell. However, the more activities Winston organizes, the more Wendy feels lost and unseen in the relationship. The more Wendy shuts down and retreats, the more deprived and disconnected Winston feels, and continues to try to fill the emptiness outside his relationship.

If the **Avoid Conflict at any Cost** pattern has some resonance for you, you and your partner are likely feeling some fear and cautiousness about entering into conversations about difficult feelings. We suggest that you take the activities of this book at a slow pace and give yourselves permission to take small, manageable steps with one another. There is no need to rush the process.

Reflection 4.1 What's our relationship pattern?

Identify for yourself and/or discuss with your partner which relationship pattern fits most of your difficult interactions. *It will help to remember a recent problematic interaction or conversation*. You are looking for *patterns*, not every interaction needs to fit the pattern. Read through the behaviors on the protesting and withdrawing lists. Take turns circling any behaviors that seem familiar to you in your part of the relationship dance. Recall how your partner has described your behavior in difficult or conflictual interactions. Resist the temptation to discount their description, get triggered or defend yourself. You can also try recounting and writing down a recent disagreement to track the steps in the dance you each made.

Complete the sentence: I feel threatened when ____________________

____

and then I do ____________________________ to manage.

As long as you are not currently in conflict, share your observations with your partner. You can find additional worksheets in Appendix A.

If your situation does not fit tidily into one of the three patterns just described, that is okay. Look to see if there are more steps to your dance. For instance, sometimes people who tend to withdraw might sometimes throw a "pre-emptive strike" before running behind their wall. People who typically protest can also give the cold shoulder when their partners attempt to rectify the problem. They may also tire of the pursuing position after years, lose energy and begin to withdraw their efforts. Just track the steps in your dance to identify your cycle, being as open and honest as you can, until you can achieve some agreement on how it goes between you.

You might also pay attention to the possibility that your cycle changes depending on the content area. For example, sometimes a different person pursues in the sexual arena than in the emotional arena or other areas, such as decision-making or running the household. In cisgender heterosexual couples, we typically see the sex role stereotypes played out here, with men often pursuing sexual intimacy and women emotional closeness and support in other domains, *but certainly not always*. If this is your case, your relationship may feel like there is a dominant and a secondary cycle. We encourage you to pick the dominant cycle first for the purposes of working through the exercises in this book, beginning with filling out Figure 4.2 with the actions and basic feelings you are aware of in your relationship dance. The secondary cycle that emerges in limited contexts is also important and you will have the opportunity to address those specific areas in Chapter 12.

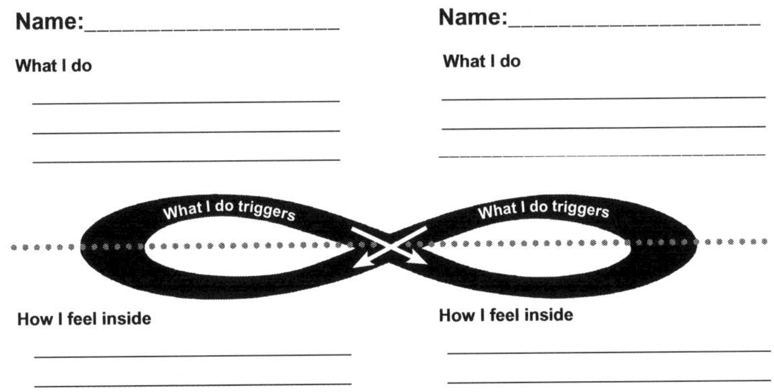

Figure 4.2 Our relationship dance with behaviors and feelings
Infinity diagram adapted from Scott R. Woolley Ph.D.© and labeling adapted from Lucy Pascal, M.S.W.

Reflection 4.2 How our cycle feeds on itself

Complete the following sentences together. They are similar to and fit with exercises from Conversation 1 from *HMT*.[8] Example: The more I go after you by *criticizing and complaining* (What I do; How I cope), the more you avoid me by *retreating and going quiet* (What you do; How you cope).

Name: ____________________
The more I go after you by ____, the more you avoid me by ________________________________.
Name: ____________________
The more I avoid you by ____, the more you go after me by ____________________.

When I (Name) ______________ don't feel on solid footing (secure, connected) with you, I react by ____________________, and then you ______________________________________ in ____________________ response.
When I (Name) ____________________ don't feel on solid footing (secure, connected) with you, I react by ____, and then you respond by ________________________________.

No matter what your relationship cycle is, you are probably already recognizing the irony of the dance of distress:

> The very thing one of you does to cope with feeling hurt, lonely, inadequate and/or insecure triggers fear in your partner. The way each of you handles that fear brushes on tender places in the other, perpetuating the distress cycle.

Can you see how your behaviors fit together and feed on each other? If you can, you have just identified your relationship dance; this is a very important step in starting to change your relationship. As a playful exercise, Sue Johnson suggests that you might like to decide on a nickname for your relationship dance.[9] Having a shared name to reference it and an understanding of what it looks like and sounds like will help you start to work together on a common goal: noticing your negative cycle when it is happening in real time. Some examples of nicknames our clients have used for their negative cycles are The Elephant, OP (Old Pattern), The Sensitivity Cyclone, The Trap and The Void. Our cycle nickname is:

____

Now when you start to trip into your cycle, just try to notice it. Noticing yourselves carrying out the behaviors you and your partner identified in the list will cue you. At this early stage, you will likely not be able to change it to a new, positive dance, but perhaps you can start to interrupt and unlatch from the negative cycle just by acknowledging it ("We've just got caught in The Trap!"), and expressing a desire to avoid it ("Don't let's go there!"). For some couples a little humor or playfulness can defuse conflict, for others humor can inflame it. Perhaps ask each other what would help to defuse the tense moment; recognizing that protesting and withdrawing do not work.

> Although the lists of behaviors do not conjure up a pleasant picture, remember that the reason for them is to keep contact in some way, and establish safety for yourself and the relationship.

Both are legitimate and important goals. For the people who do more active protesting, there is typically a desire to access your partner, and get a response from them. For people who do more avoiding or withdrawing, the motivation to shut down the interaction is typically to prevent things from getting worse. Partners also protest or withdraw in order to protect themselves from getting hurt or feeling too vulnerable. Regardless of the position you take when you feel threatened in your relationship, the world can feel lonely and insecure when you don't feel like you have your partner to lean on. However, recognizing how you impact each other, how your behaviors fit together to create this cycle, is the first step in working together. Being able to recognize and name your dance when it begins to happen can give you the tools to interrupt the cycle. Try not to get discouraged if you cannot stop the cycle every time. Notice that you *can* gain some control over the cycle sometimes, and that may create some hope that you can learn to do it differently if you work together. The following chapters will help you understand the emotions that make these negative cycles so charged, so you can begin to understand them and find different ways to express yourselves.

References

1. Watzlawick, P., Beavin, J., & Jackson, D. (1967). *Pragmatics of human communication: A study of interactional patterns, pathologies and paradoxes*. New York, NY: Norton.
2. Fogarty, T. (1976). Marital crisis. In P. J. Guerin (Ed.), *Family therapy: Theory and practice* (pp. 325–334). New York, NY: Gardner Press.
3. Gottman, J. M., & Levenson, R. W. (2002). A two-factor model for predicting when a couple will divorce: Exploratory analyses using 14-year longitudinal data. *Family Process, 41*, 83–96.
4. Woolley, S., & Kallos-Lilly, V. (2011). How to avoid cycle impasses. *The EFT Community News, 11*, 2–5.
5. Pascal, L. (2013). Personal Communication.

6. Gottman, J. M., & Levenson, R. W. (1988). The social physiology of marriage. In P. Noller & M. A. Fitzpatrick (Eds.), *Perspectives on marital interaction* (pp. 183–200). Clevedon: Multilingual Matters Ltd.
7. Tilley, D. (2003). *When we are not getting along: My feelings, thoughts and behaviors checklist.* Douglas Tilley LCSW-C. Retrieved February 18, 2013, from www.douglastilley.com/Forms/Your Relationship ThoughtsFeelingsand Behaviors.pdf
8, 9. Johnson, S. (2008). *Hold me tight.* New York, NY, Boston and London: Little, Brown and Company.

CHAPTER 5

EMOTIONS

How to Make Sense of Them

Falling in love, getting to know a romantic partner, maintaining a couple relationship, raising a family, caring for a partner in older age—all these stages of couple and family life—involve a range of vivid emotional experiences.[1] When our emotional experiences are positive, such as when we feel happy, comforted, excited or interested, we are typically feeling good. However, when our emotional experiences are negative, such as when we feel lonely, hurt, angry, afraid or jealous, we are typically feeling distressed or bad. Emotions, both positive and negative, push us to behave in certain ways which impact our partners. How we feel influences how we behave; how our partners feel in response to our behaviors shape their behaviors back to us. In successful relationships, these interactions flow in positive cycles of listening, responding and disclosing; in distressed relationships, these interactions can get very unpleasant and sometimes predictable, as in the negative cycles described in Chapter 4.

We invite you now to look more closely with us at emotions, because emotional experience is such an important part of any close relationship. Chapter 5 will introduce you to the sea of emotions swirling around in your negative cycle. Depending on whether you are "snorkeling" or "scuba diving," you will encounter different sea life, and so it is with the world of emotions. If you keep snorkeling and dipping just underneath the surface of your difficult interactions, you will encounter the emotions that are most apparent in your negative cycle (e.g., frustration, resentment, helplessness, resignation). If you scuba dive, deeper underneath the surface, you will encounter deeper feelings, including your fears, vulnerabilities and insecurities. Chapter 5 will focus on distinguishing between snorkeling and scuba diving in the world of emotions and help you see what shows up when you and your partner are in your cycle. Chapter 6 will expand on and differentiate some important core emotions and help you dive deeper so that you can discover each other's fears, vulnerabilities and insecurities that are set off in the negative dance. Building a secure bond with your partner involves taking the plunge into your own and your partner's deeper emotions and needs. Exploring your emotional needs, sharing them and reaching out to each other will help you better navigate difficulties in your relationship. Chapter 8 will help you make sense of some emotions that can really rock the boat, such as contempt, shame, guilt and jealousy. It will all depend on what you can learn from those emotions and how you handle them. Let's open up our discussion about emotions by looking at how they provide us with important information.

How Emotions Help Us Survive

Emotions help us to survive, because *emotions give us vital information about changes in our environment* and prompt us to take action at far greater speed than conscious thought.[2] For example, the glimpse

DOI: 10.4324/9781003009481-5

of a snake-like object on a forest track prompts a hiker to halt and pull back from the spot with "knee-jerk" speed. Before the hiker has time to think, "Is that a snake?" the hiker's feet have moved away from possible danger. The hiker reacts to it emotionally with fear and responds with self-protection before consciously thinking, "It is a snake." As the moments pass, additional processes in the hiker's brain will carefully evaluate the object and decide that while it looks like a snake in color and shape, it is actually just a stick or a thick vine. Phew! The hiker's emotional reaction prompted immediate action that increased chance of survival.

Emotions also provide useful information to others through distinctive facial and vocal expressions. People across cultures have been found to recognize common emotional expressions in posed or natural photographs,[3] which supports Charles Darwin's view that facial expressions of emotions are universal.[4] In our close relationships, the constant sending and reading of signals about emotional states, especially through facial expressions, informs and guides our interactions.[5] Being perceptive and responsive to our partner's emotions can help them feel cared for and prevent difficulties from arising. Conversely, being oblivious to our partner's needs can engender feelings of neglect.[6]

Not only do emotions give information to others and ourselves, they *prompt us for action*. When an emotion is triggered by a change in the environment, for example, you hear your partner cry out loudly and suddenly in pain, you will typically have a physiological response to the initial perception that something bad has happened. In this case, the sound of a partner's cry might trigger a flood of fear in your body (such as increased heart rate, pale skin, dilated pupils), leading to a thought, "Has my partner fallen?" Finally, after only microseconds of sensing, feeling, thinking, you will get into action: Fear will push you, in this case, to move quickly to their aid.[7]

Here are some examples of basic **core emotions** and how they can prompt us for different actions:

- **Fear** prompts us to protect ourselves and others
- **Surprise** prompts us to pause with widened eyes to take in the novel moment
- **Anger** prompts us to stand up to a perceived threat
- **Sadness** prompts us to seek comfort
- **Shame** prompts us to hide and not want to be seen
- **Joy** and happiness in a relationship typically move us toward others with positive energy (e.g., relaxed, playful, affectionate).

> Emotions are distinct from behaviors. For example, feeling annoyed does not mean we automatically go on to act aggressively. Emotions prepare us for action, but wisdom and being able to regulate ourselves helps us to act in socially appropriate ways.

Neuroscientist Jaak Panksepp sums up the importance of emotions when he says, "Emotions are our inherited ancestral tools for living."[8] He reports that our core emotions, which are found across species, urge us to survive, because they urge us to play, explore, reproduce, care for others, protect ourselves from danger, grieve and relate to others.

Gender Differences in Emotional Experience and Expression

Perhaps you have heard your partner mutter in frustration: "Why do some women have to get so emotional!" or "How come some men are so hopeless about talking about feelings!" In either of these situations, achieving a safe emotional connection with your partner may feel very difficult. Perhaps you may fear that your partner will express either too much or too little emotion when you want to discuss important issues or solve relationship difficulties. The question of gender differences in emotional experience and expression has intrigued scientists, clinicians and the public alike. Research based on cisgender populations certainly has found that women see themselves as being more expressive of emotions than men[9, 10] and having more confidence in the expression of most emotions.[11]

Whereas some gender differences are observed in the expression of emotion in favor of women expressing emotions more freely than men, we have certainly encountered men who are emotionally expressive and women who are less so. However, we believe that, fundamentally, all people experience the same basic emotions in response to loss, threat or violation and to love and care. Where the differences emerge is in the *expression* of these core basic emotions. We argue that much of the observed gender differences in emotional experiencing and expression are the direct result of socialization. Parents, educators and society have done boys and men a disservice by creating child-rearing environments that encouraged male children to disconnect from their vulnerable feelings and their capacity to experience and express love in close relationships. Similarly, many girls and women have been socialized to feel ashamed of feeling angry, outspoken or confident.

Fortunately, parents and educators in the Western world today are less inclined to take such a gender-stereotyped approach to child rearing. Allowing young boys and men to acknowledge and express their vulnerable emotions and girls and women to express assertion, confidence and appropriate anger is now more accepted and is likely to be helpful for the mental and social health of future generations. In particular, in close relationships, the ability for people of all gender identities (whether binary or fluid) to access, understand and talk about a range of emotions is typically valued and appreciated by their partners. Let's turn now to helping you make sense of your own emotions in the context of your relationship.

Emotions Are at the Heart of Your Relationship Dance

In close relationships, partners are experiencing emotions and acting on them day in and day out. At any moment, one partner's action is likely to trigger an emotional response in the other partner. Let's consider William and Patricia, who you met in Chapter 4. When William *sees* a dark frown come over Patricia's face, he might *feel* an uneasy stirring that something is wrong, followed by a *thought*, "Oh no, what have I said to upset her?" followed by a quiet *departure* into another room. *Seeing* William's departure triggers a new emotional sequence for Patricia. She *feels* hurt and frustrated and *thinks*, "Why does he always have to disappear when we have important things to discuss!" which may prompt a *shout* of protest, "There you go again, always running away when the going gets rough." The *sound* of her angry voice triggers a fresh response in William, and so the sequences of triggers, feelings, thoughts and actions go back and forth between them, like links in a very long chain.

Think now about some of the emotional experiences that occur for you in your relationship. Think of your partner and what they do (facial expressions, vocal tones, behaviors) that stimulate emotional responses in you. Slow down, take your time and picture the moments. Allow yourself to tune in to how you recall feeling in your body at that moment, or imagine how you might feel if any of the following were to happen:

Reflection 5.1 Emotion tracking exercise[12]

If my partner . . .	Immediately in my body I sense . . . (Is this safe or is it threatening for me?)	Other feelings in my body may emerge . . .	Typically, I feel . . .	Typically, I think . . .	Typically, I do . . .
Example: Arrives home early from work looking serious	Uh-oh	My eyes widen and my mouth might open. My attention focuses on the unexpected arrival	I feel surprised and curious to find out more	What is going on? Something must have happened!	Stop what I am doing and walk toward my partner, to find out more
Example: Frowns sternly at me	Uh-oh	My stomach clenches	I feel afraid or "on edge"	What have I done to upset you?	I find an excuse to distract myself
Arrives home from work announcing they have good news					
Calls my name in a panicky voice					
Cries in response to something insensitive I said					
Calls my name in an angry voice					
Calls my name in a playful voice					
Criticizes someone I love					
Walks away when I raise something important to me					

These scenarios are likely to have prompted memories of a range of different core emotional experiences for you such as joy, surprise, interest, sadness, fear, anger and hurt. The intensity of responses that you recall, or imagine you would feel in hypothetical scenarios, is also likely to vary somewhat from person to person.

Our responses are shaped by many factors within us as individuals and the atmosphere of our relationships. For example, in a loving relationship with high levels of trust the sight of a partner's frown may trigger caring concern and an enquiry: "What's the matter, honey?" Alternatively, in a relationship fraught with conflict, the sight of a partner's frown might trigger alarm, with vigilant thoughts such as "What will happen next?" Our emotional responses are shaped by memory of interactions with this partner, but also with memories of interactions with others in close relationships or in our community, as described in Chapter 3.

What Happens When We Ignore Our Core Emotions?

Although it is evident that our basic core emotions help us to survive, it is interesting to explore what happens if we ignore or gloss over those basic feelings. In some contexts, they can intensify, in ways that are not helpful. For example, fear can escalate into panic, anger into rage or resentment, and sadness into depression, making constructive action unlikely. The intensity of emotion in these instances has become *un*helpful. We might even feel *flooded* or *overwhelmed* by their intensity.

These sorts of reactions that seem "out of the blue" or "over" reactions triggered by your current disagreement may be linked to prior negative experiences in your current relationship. For example, an accumulation of feelings that have evolved over many unresolved arguments and negative interactions building over time, or it may be linked to previous experiences, including trauma or abandonment. For example, one man who became depressed whenever he and his wife got into conflict identified that he came from a large family in which he felt overshadowed. Experience taught him that there was no point in telling others about his needs or hurts; he would just squash them down inside and feel helpless, further leading to depression and hopelessness. Whenever his wife expressed strong opinions, he felt overshadowed (again) by her forcefulness and he closed off, spiraling down into the old, familiar, hopeless place. How this man learned to deal with his early experience of close relationships resulted in behaviors that were legitimate for him then, even though they were not helpful now because they reinforced his feelings of powerlessness. Understanding and exploring his life experiences helped this couple find better ways to deal with their interactions now.[13]

If we don't attend to our core emotions, they not only intensify, they can also shift to other emotions that overshadow and obscure the core ones. Vulnerable feelings of hurt can shift into reactive anger or cold detachment. For some people, anxious placating or passivity can veil their fear of asserting themselves and getting rejected. Similarly, if our own feelings of pain or insecurity morph into feeling joy at the suffering of another person or extreme jealousy at another's success, these emotions would not be considered helpful.[14] These *reactive emotions* that tend to protect us from feeling the vulnerability of our core hurts, fears and insecurities are further discussed later. We will focus on reactive emotions in the rest of this chapter, as you may be more aware of them at this point than the core emotions. In Chapter 6 we will return to core emotions and focus on deepening your awareness of the core emotions in your negative dance.

We understand that for some readers, it may be difficult to answer the questions about emotions in this and the following chapter. For some of you, life experiences may have given you a message that emotions are a problem, not to be listened to, trusted or expressed. If earlier experiences in your social context, family or previous romantic relationships were emotionally difficult or otherwise not conducive to opening up, you may have learned to minimize or shut down your emotions; this may have helped you to cope back then. In some extremely difficult circumstances, shutting down your feelings may have even been crucial to help you to survive. Alternatively, your early experiences may have taught you that to be heard you needed to be loud, persistent and maybe even confrontational. Now, however, in your present relationship, shutting off your emotions and withdrawing from your partner or ramping up your emotions and expressing them forcefully may not be helpful and may make it hard for your partner to feel close to you. If this is how you feel, we encourage you to try something new and attempt the reflections that follow. Take the reflections slowly, maybe in small chunks, and see what you find out about yourself and your partner.

Reflection 5.2 My emotions

What messages did I get about experiencing and expressing emotions from my culture or social context? Were there conflicting messages (e.g., between my family of origin and the culture where I lived, or between my parents and grandparents living in the home)?

____

____

____

Were some emotions OK but others not acceptable?

____

____

____

How did my family of origin respond to my emotions?

____

____

____

What messages did I get about my emotions in previous romantic relationships?

____

____

____

How did previous significant relationship partners respond to my emotions?

____

____

____

Reflection 5.3 Unhelpful intensity of negative emotion

Do I sometimes experience extremes of emotion such that I find it hard to manage the intensity of negative emotion I am feeling OR experience lack of emotion, such that I find it hard to know what I feel? If so, this is what typically happens for me:

____

____

____

How do I try to manage it?

____

____

____

Have there been times when I have experienced emotional responses about which I am now not proud? (For example, jealousy about my partner's success; pleased to see someone hurt or humiliated.) If I sit and reflect on that memory, am I able to identify an insecurity in myself that explains my reaction?

____

____

____

Reactive Emotions

In arguments and tense conversations do you ever feel . . .

- *Frustrated* or *angry* (reactive emotion) after a moment of sadness (core emotion)?
- *Anxious* (reactive emotion) about the possibility and fear (core emotion) of being rejected or seen as a failure?
- *Helpless* (reactive emotion) about letting someone know you're angry (core emotion) because your boundaries have been crossed?

Sometimes, the emotion you are experiencing is in *reaction* to a more core, primary emotion or experience. The examples of secondary or reactive emotions listed (frustration, anxiety, helplessness) are so called because they are emotions about emotions. The core emotion that is brushed against first can feel intense and scary, so the reactive emotion shows up to rescue you from being too vulnerable or exposed. You will typically bump into reactive emotions readily in your arguments and tense conversations and you will discover them by snorkeling at the surface. They may protect you by helping you to avoid uncomfortable feelings such as the hurt, sadness, fear or insecurity underneath. It can be tricky to decipher which emotions are core and which are reactive, but tuning into yourself, slowing things *way* down, and noticing which emotion comes first and then second can help you. Also, it is useful to know that core emotions are usually softer, more vulnerable and evoke responsiveness from others more readily than reactive emotions. That is even true for anger, which looks frenzied in its reactive or defensive form and grounded and assertive when it is a core emotion. Here is a table comparing and contrasting the difference between reactive and core emotions.

Table 5.1 Distinguishing between reactive and core emotions

Reactive Emotions . . .	*Core Emotions . . .*
are a reaction to: 1) vulnerable or uncomfortable core emotions in you or 2) reactive emotions in your partner	are deeply felt inside the very core of your being Are usually felt in primal parts of your body such as your heart or gut
feel like your default, your shield, the MO (Modus Operandi), the well-worn groove	feel raw, fresh, vulnerable, tender, soft, often newly discovered
Examples: "I get angry and blaming when I'm hurt"	Examples: "I feel panicked inside that I'll be abandoned"
"I throw up my hands in helplessness because there's no point in trying to talk"	"I am so sad that I failed and disappointed you"
are swimming around in your negative dance, creating waves	are discovered by slowing down and tuning deeply into yourself and your partner
Discover them by "snorkeling" and noticing the emotions at the surface of your arguments and tense conversations	Put on your scuba gear and "deep dive" Ask: what's *really* got me so distressed? Be curious: What's this *really* about for you?
trigger *even more* reactive emotions: anger, frustration, hopelessness, irritation, withdrawal	engender responsiveness: loving feelings, care, compassion, empathy, comforting, protection
escalate your negative dance to the next level	lower defenses, relax and soften your dance

It is worthy to note that child-rearing environments and culture influence our reactions to inner core emotions; for example, many men express defensive anger (reactive emotion) as a reaction to feeling afraid (core emotion), and many women cry (reactive emotion) when their primary experience is anger (core emotion).[15] For example, a husband reported that over the years several members of his family had been injured or killed in car accidents, which left him vulnerable to feeling afraid if his wife was unexpectedly late home from work. He admitted ruefully to having shouted angrily at his wife one evening when she eventually arrived home safely. She experienced his anger but did not know about his deeper fears; not surprisingly, she felt surprised and hurt by his behavior.

This couple were later able to talk about what had happened; the husband apologized for his angry outburst and also disclosed his fear of losing her through an accident. This helped the wife see her husband's anger in a different light and evoked her concern, instead of hurt. They then agreed that she would pay more attention in future to notifying him of anticipated delays to her return home. For this couple, moving away from angry and unproductive reactions at the surface to communicating about the more vulnerable emotional experience underneath the surface helped them to understand and support each other more effectively.

As in the outlined example, reactive emotions that "protect" us from the vulnerability of our deeper emotions are often not particularly useful in our relationships and can lead to destructive or unhelpful behavior. In other words:

> I guard myself by not exposing my vulnerabilities, but I also prevent you from being able to really see me and respond to me.

A common problem found in many couples seeking assistance for their relationship is for one partner to report that the other is often critical and angry. When the deeper experience of the critical partner is uncovered, core sadness and loneliness in the relationship are revealed. Feeling alone in a relationship can be very painful, and when it triggers angry protest out of desperation ("You never spend Sundays with me anymore. We never go out like we used to!"), unfortunately the result is often to push the apparently distant partner even further away. Similarly, partners who withdraw typically reveal that fear of disappointing or failing, which is also very painful, underlies their problem-solving, placating and eventual withdrawal. Unfortunately, this approach will typically reinforce their partner's sense of alienation and evoke more criticism. And so the cycle will feed on itself until the partners begin to share their core sadness and fears in the negative dance, opening up the possibility of new experiences and responses.

> Partners usually find it easier to deal with each other's core emotions (e.g., sadness, fear) because they are more vulnerable. The expression of secondary reactions (such as irritable frustration, helplessness or anxious withdrawal) typically fuels negative cycles because they are more threatening.

See the list of reactive, secondary emotions that typically follow core, primary emotions next. Circle the reactive emotions that commonly characterize your interactions with your partner. Note that, often, these are the most prominent emotions in your negative interactions. We can flit quickly past our core emotions because they feel raw and vulnerable. Sometimes we are not even aware of them. Reactive emotions typically feel a little like the "default mode" or a person's "MO" (Modus Operandi) and they characterize the emotions that we *show* when we are interacting with our *guard up*. Are you familiar with any of the reactive emotions listed next? It may help to recall one or two recent times when you and your partner have been caught in your negative dance. Circle the ones that tend to pervade your interactions most commonly.

Common Reactive Emotions

Name: ________________	Name: ________________
Frustration	Frustration
Reactive or defensive anger	Reactive or defensive anger
Anxious	Anxious
Down	Down

Ashamed
Desperate
Helpless
Hopeless
Overwhelmed
*Numb
*Detached
____
____

Ashamed
Desperate
Helpless
Hopeless
Overwhelmed
Numb
Detached
____
____

**Yes, apparent* lack *of emotion is also a protective reaction to difficult core emotions. See Douglas Tilley's website for a worksheet on Understanding Your Negative Cycle and an expanded checklist in When We Are Not Getting Along: My Feelings, Thoughts, and Behaviors Checklist.*[16] *(www.douglastilley.com/Couple Concerns.htm)*

In close relationships it is particularly helpful for us to pay attention to our emotional experience and be able to track our shifting feelings. Accepting and understanding our core primary feelings (which will be discussed further in the next chapter) and getting a better understanding of our reactions to those primary feelings can help us to interact more effectively with our partners, family and friends. Rather than being governed by, or surrendering to our emotions mindlessly, an EFT approach helps to integrate emotions, intellect and will in a holistic way. As Les Greenberg and Sandra Paivio have suggested, "We need to integrate our heads and our hearts, being neither compelled by emotion nor cut off from it."[17]

Reflection 5.4 What do I feel and express in our negative dance?

Before we take a closer look at some of the common core emotions in your cycle, reflect for a few minutes on the predominant reactive emotions you express if you and your partner get caught in negative interactions. Could they be a reaction to a deeper core emotion? For example, do you sometimes feel frustrated anger in response to not feeling understood; anxiously withdraw in response to fear of disappointing your partner; numb out to avoid expressing your legitimate anger?

What reactive emotions do you notice yourself typically expressing in the negative cycle?

____
____

What is happening in your interaction with your partner when you express this reactive emotion? What is your trigger? It may be a particular phrase, action, look or tone of voice. *Remember that the reason for identifying triggers is to provide each other with important information on how you experience your interactions; it is not about blaming each other.*

Here are some common examples. You can indicate ones that fit for you or write your own.

______ When I hear you become louder and more persistent, I react with defensive anger.
______ When I sense that we are headed for conflict, I shut down/go numb.
______ When I don't know how to respond to you, I feel helpless and overwhelmed.
______ When your wall goes up and I can't reach you, I get frustrated.
______ When I see you close off or walk out of the room, I express reactive anger.

____
____
____

What do you think or say to yourself when you see or experience your partner's reactive emotions (e.g., "You don't care about me" or "It's pointless to talk, I'll never get heard!")?

____
____
____

What impact does your expression of reactive emotions (or non-expression of emotion) have on your partner?

____
____
____

How might this contribute to a negative cycle of interaction between you and your partner?

____
____
____

Complete this sentence together:

When I express my reactive emotion of ____________, you come back with a reactive emotion of ____________.

When I express my reactive emotion of ____________, you come back with a reactive emotion of ____________.

Patricia and William's cycle has been expanded to include their thoughts and reactive emotions as layers beneath their coping behaviors in their negative cycle.

Complete your own cycle together and then do the sentence completion following the example. It is similar to Conversation 2 of *HMT*.[18]

PATRICIA

What I do

Approach, convince, demand, probe, blame

What I think to myself

About me: "How come I can't get through to him?"

About you: "He always disappears on me!"

I react emotionally with

Reactive anger, frustration, desperation, anxiety

WILLIAM

What I do

Get logical, practical, defend, capitulate, distance, minimize

What I think to myself

About me: "Uh oh, what have I done now?"

About you: "She always needs to have her way"

I react emotionally with

Defensive anger, anxiety, feeling overwhelmed, feeling down, detachment

***How I feel inside**

Jittery

How I feel inside

Unsettled

***We will explore further in Chapter 6**

Figure 5.1 Patricia and William's dance with behaviors, thoughts and reactive emotions
Infinity diagram adapted from Scott R. Woolley, Ph.D.© and labeling adapted from Lucy Pascal, M.S.W.

Name:____________________

What I do

____

____

____

What I think to myself

About me: ____________________

____

About you: ____________________

____

I react emotionally with

____

____

Name:____________________

What I do

____

____

____

What I think to myself

About me: ____________________

____

About you: ____________________

____

I react emotionally with

____

____

***How I feel inside**

____

____

How I feel inside

____

____

***We will explore further in Chapter 6**

Figure 5.2 Our relationship dance with behaviors, thoughts and reactive emotion
Infinity diagram adapted from Scott R. Woolley Ph.D.© and labeling adapted from Lucy Pascal, M.S.W.

It is OK if you are not able to identify the core emotion yet. We will be exploring core emotions in depth in Chapter 6, which follows.

Example: When I feel lonely (*core emotion*), I typically react by getting frustrated (*reactive emotion*) with my partner because they "never" give me enough time and support (*thought*). When I am frustrated, I get critical (*behavior*). When I get critical (*behavior*), my partner defends back (*reactive negative behavior*). Maybe they are feeling hurt/blamed/attacked?

Name: ___________________
When I feel __________ deep down (core emotion), I typically react by feeling/thinking ___________ _______ ___________ ___________ (reactive emotions/thoughts). Then I typically do __________ (behavior) in our interaction. You respond by ________________ (reactive negative behavior), maybe you feel _____________.

Example: When I feel afraid of disappointing my partner (*core emotion*), I typically tell myself "I'll never get it right" (*thought*) and react by becoming irritable (*reactive emotion*), distant and logical (*behavior*). My partner responds by talking louder and pointing (*reactive negative behavior*). Maybe they are feeling hurt/dismissed/shut out?

Name: ___________________
When I feel __________ deep down (core emotion), I typically react by feeling/thinking ___________ _______ ___________ ___________ (reactive emotions/thoughts). Then I typically do __________ (behavior) in our interaction. You respond by ________________ (reactive negative behavior), maybe you feel _____________.

Make Time to Share with Your Partner

When you are ready, share your reflections with your partner and show interest in listening to their reflections. We encourage you to make space for each other; help each other out. It takes strength and "guts" to look at your reactions, acknowledge and "own" your part of the negative dance. Stay focused on the reflections and avoid wandering off topic onto complaints about your relationship or your partner. Make sure that you create opportunity for both of you to have time and safety to talk over your reflections. Please note that the reflections of chapters 5, 6 and 7 are not designed to help you solve all your difficulties in one or two conversations. Please be patient and continue your conversations with the later chapters that follow.

Remember to:

Listen with an
Open heart and mind.
Validate and acknowledge each other and
Express ideas softly, simply and slowly.

When you are listening, ask yourself, "What can I do to help my partner feel more comfortable sharing some of their emotions with me?" You may even ask your partner that question. Listen respectfully to them. It is OK if it is hard for you to understand your partner's emotional experience. Nevertheless, try to listen and learn. Be open to new information, even if that information triggers some uncomfortable feelings in you. You may need to say something like "I don't think I really understand what you are saying just yet, but I'd like to. Can you say a bit more?" These topics may also need more than one conversation, especially of one or both of you become tired. It is best if you can agree for it "to be continued" and suggest a time when you can talk further . . . and then ensure that you do.

Table 5.2 Trouble shooting guide for talking about emotions

WATCH OUT FOR NEGATIVE CYCLES! Be alert for any unhelpful interactions that may occur between you while sharing your reflections. You might like to self-check:

"Am I getting too pushy or critical of my partner? Is my partner holding back to feel safe from my judgment?"

"Am I so reluctant to participate in this exercise that my partner feels frustrated and alone, maybe contributing to their pursuit of me?"

If you notice something like this evolving, here are some suggestions to help you:

1. Stop talking about your reflections and sit quietly. Don't run away.
2. If either of you feels tense, take some deep breaths, and pause for a few moments.
3. Focus in on what has happened while you attempted to talk together. Comment quietly on what is happening now. For example, "Just at the moment, I'm feeling . . . uncomfortable/silly/ scared you might laugh . . ." OR "It seems like we are getting caught up in our old cycle/pattern. Maybe we'd better slow down?"
4. Try to put some simple words around what has just happened inside for you. (e.g., "Telling you about feeling afraid really upset me just then. I felt churned up in my stomach thinking about . . .")
5. If your partner discloses a vulnerable feeling like this, stay present: that is, don't change the subject, leave the room or start reading the newspaper. Let your partner know that you care about this feeling and are concerned for them.
6. It is unlikely you can undo the experience that triggered the difficult emotions for your partner but listening in a supportive manner will help a lot. You might say something like "I'm sorry this has churned you up (using your partner's own words to describe their distress). Let's slow down . . . is there anything more you'd like to say at the moment?"
7. If your partner has shared about their experiences in a way that triggers defensive feelings in you, pause and try to stay calm. Try to tune in to the deep feelings inside for you rather than just the surface reaction that prompts you to protect yourself. You might then be able to express the deeper feeling. For example, "When I hear you say . . . I feel hurt and blamed. I don't like that feeling."

Take a few minutes to talk over your experiences of disclosing. Thank your partner for participating in this exercise. Before closing your L-O-V-E conversations, ask yourself, "What was this like for me?" and your partner, "What was it like for you?" Share your responses openly with each other.

References

1. Bowlby, J. (1979). *The making and breaking of affectional bonds*. London: Tavistock.
2. LeDoux, J. (1996). *The emotional brain: The mysterious underpinnings of emotional life*. New York, NY and London: Simon and Schuster.
3. Ekman, P., Friesen, W., & Ellsworth, P. (1982). What are the similarities and differences in facial behaviour across cultures? In P. Ekman (Ed.), *Emotion in the human face* (2nd ed., pp. 128–143). Cambridge: Cambridge University Press.

4. Darwin, C. (1872/1955). *The expression of emotions in man and animal*. New York, NY: Philosophical Library.
5. Greenberg, L., & Johnson, S. (1988). *Emotionally focused therapy for couples*. New York, NY: The Guilford Press.
6. Greenberg, L., & Paivio, S. (1997). *Working with emotions in psychotherapy*. New York, NY and London: The Guilford Press.
7. Arnold, M. (1960). *Emotion and personality*. New York, NY: Columbia University Press.
8. Panksepp, J. (2009). Brain emotional systems and qualities of mental life. In D. Foscha, D. Siegel, & M. Solomon (Eds.), *The healing power of emotion: Affective neuroscience, development and clinical practice* (pp. 1–26). New York, NY and London: Norton.
9. Johnson, J., & Shulman, G. (1988). More alike than meets the eye: Perceived gender differences in subjective experience and its display. *Sex Roles, 19*, 67–79.
10. Sprecher, S., & Sedikides, C. (1993). Gender differences in perceptions of emotionality: The case of close heterosexual relationships. *Sex Roles, 28*, 511–530.
11. Blier, M. J., & Blier-Wilson, L. A. (1989). Gender differences in self-rated emotional expressiveness. *Sex Roles, 21*, 287–295.
12. Arnold, M. B. (1960). *Emotion and personality*. New York, NY: Columbia University Press.
13. Johnson, S. (2019). *Attachment theory in practice: Emotionally focused therapy (EFT) with individuals, couples and families*. New York, NY and London: The Guilford Press.
14, 15. Greenberg, L., & Paivio, S. (1997). *Working with emotions in psychotherapy*. New York, NY and London: The Guilford Press.
16. Furrow, J., Johnson, S., Bradley, B., Brubacher, L., Campbell, L., Kallos-Lilly, V., Palmer, G., Rheem, K., Woolley, S. (in press). *Becoming an emotionally focused therapist: The workbook* (2nd ed.). London: Routledge.
17. Greenberg, L., & Paivio, S. (1997). *Working with emotions in psychotherapy*. New York, NY and London: The Guilford Press.
18. Johnson, S. (2008). *Hold me tight*. New York, NY, Boston and London: Little, Brown and Company.

CHAPTER 6

MORE ABOUT EMOTIONS

What Are We Both Feeling?

As we have already mentioned, close relationships are steeped in emotions through conversations, celebrations, arguments, shared activities, working on problems together, and the list goes on. These and so many other interactions with close family and friends trigger emotional reactions in us every day of the year. *So too, we constantly trigger emotional reactions in others*. So, let's take a closer look at some of the commonly encountered positive emotions (happiness, joy and love) and difficult emotions (sadness, anger, fear and contempt). The exercises in this chapter will give you a chance to do some scuba diving, reflect more deeply on your core emotional experiences and consider how you and your partner express your deeper feelings.

Happiness, Joy and Love

When we feel happy there is a sense of "all's right with the world." Happiness is expressed on our faces through smiles and laughter; indeed, smiling is a universal signal inviting friendly interaction. At the end of fairy tales, there are usually lots of smiles and laughter, because the couple typically live "happily ever after." While it may be unrealistic to expect that committed couples will spend every minute of their lives together feeling euphorically happy, it is nevertheless encouraging to note that many couples, even after many decades together, report that their relationship has been the best part of their lives and that choosing their particular partner was the smartest decision they ever made.

Happy Couples

Professor John Gottman, after many years of investigating both happy and unhappy couples, reported that the relationships of happy couples do not necessarily all look the same.[1] Couples find different ways to make their relationship a success: some couples are validating, others are fiery, while others are conflict avoiding; all these types of couples can report satisfaction with their relationships. Validating couples give each other encouragement and support; fiery couples express lots of emotion, both negative and positive; and conflict-avoiding couples manage their relationship with minimal conflict, even if that means avoiding certain topics that are potentially conflict provoking.

Ingredients of Romantic Love

Despite there being different styles of relating, relationships that give couples happiness and joy typically involve three critical ingredients: intimacy, passion and commitment. In this "triangular theory of love,"[2] *intimacy* refers to opening up and confiding about your inner word, mutual understanding and concern

DOI: 10.4324/9781003009481-6

about the other; *passion* refers to affection, sexual vitality and fulfillment; and *commitment* is the ingredient that helps couples stay loyal and faithful in the relationship through hard times. Commitment becomes a motivating force for solving problems and healing ruptures. Researchers who study adult attachment propose a similar idea, suggesting that romantic love is an integration of attachment, care giving and sexuality.[3]

Other researchers have suggested that love can be divided into two types: passionate love (involving emotional intensity and sexual energy) and companionate love (involving respect, admiration and trust). Many people would hope that their romantic relationship could combine both the delights of passionate love and the security of companionate love.[4]

Whether we think of love as having two or three, or maybe more essential ingredients, there appears to be agreement among scholars that love is not a simple emotion. For example, most close relationship theorists would agree that love is multidimensional and involves emotions, thoughts, behaviors and motivations.[5] This comment points to the finding that love in committed couple and family relationships is not simply an emotional experience that waxes and wanes in response to circumstance. Love also involves intention, or will, to love, along with the emotional experience of joy in the presence of loved ones.

Close relationships scholar, Emeritus Professor Patricia Noller, once asked the question, "What is this thing called love? How do we define the love that supports marriage and family?"[6] Her review of the academic research on love and marriage over recent decades revealed that love certainly includes an emotional component that can also be thought of as an *attachment bond*, and also as an *attitude* that creates an environment in which the lovers and those dependent on them can grow and develop. The exact nature of this environment will depend on cultural factors, but in the West, at least, it is typically an environment of interdependence, equality and open communication. Professor Noller observed that both passionate and companionate love can be sustained throughout a lifetime; that love includes accepting differences and weaknesses; and that lovers need to nurture and nourish their love.

Reflection 6.1 How do we view love?

So how do you relate to these comments about love and happiness in couple relationships? What do you consider important aspects of a loving relationship?

____

____

____

How have your views on love been shaped by your religion, ethnic or family culture?

____

____

____

What do you and your partner do to nurture and nourish your love for each other?

____

____

____

Falling in Love

While there may not be a single definition of love, what we do know is that love makes us feel wonderful and moves us to create ties with people. Recent studies in neuroscience using functional Magnetic Resonance Imaging (fMRI) have investigated what happens when we are "falling in love," that is, in the early stages of feeling "madly" in love with a new partner. Results revealed that areas of the brain activated when participants thought about their beloved were those areas typically activated when people are influenced by euphoria-producing drugs such as cocaine or opiates. No wonder we feel so exhilarated! However, love (in the early stages) may indeed be blind, as the old adage suggests, because the fMRI results also revealed that the regions in the brain that decreased in activity during the love experience were those involved in critical thought and the experience of painful emotions,[7] perhaps explaining why we initially overlook our partner's flaws.

Further fMRI studies have investigated neural activity for long-term "in-love" couples. These partners (committed to each other for an average of 21 years) viewed photos of their loved partner while in the scanner and at least for some individuals, the results identified activity in the same reward/pleasure areas as for the newly-in-love couples just described. Areas implicated in attachment were also activated, which adds scientific validity to the concept that long-term romantic love includes emotional security as well as reward and pleasure, as described in Chapter 2.[8]

Love as Self-Expansion

Others have observed that love also includes a sense of expansion of the self.[9] For the person in love, life takes on a new meaning, and new possibilities emerge. In his renowned novel *War and Peace*, Leo Tolstoy describes the experience for Pierre Bezuhov as he falls in love with Natasha Rostov:

> A joyful, unexpected frenzy, of which he had thought himself incapable, possessed him. The whole meaning of life -not for him alone but for the whole world- seemed to him centered in his love and the possibility of being loved by her . . . He often surprised those he met by his significantly happy looks and smiles, which seemed to express a secret understanding between him and them. And when he realized that people might not be aware of his happiness, he pitied them with his whole heart and felt a desire somehow to explain to them that all that occupied them was a mere frivolous trifle unworthy of attention.[10]

Reflection 6.2 Happiness, joy and love

What are some memories of happy or joyous times with my partner?

____

____

____

Describe your idea of a happy time with your partner.

____

____

____

How do I express love to you/my partner? How does my partner express love to me?

___

___

___

Sadness

Experiencing Loss

Just as establishing a loving connection with another person stirs strong positive emotions in us, the loss of a close connection stirs strong feelings in us too. When that loss is irretrievable—when we know that nothing we do will bring back the lost love—we usually suffer emotional pain.[11] The loss of a valued relationship through death, divorce or unrequited love invariably causes sadness. There are many other losses in life that stir sadness, to varying degrees, for us as well. Consider for example, loss of health, faculties and functioning through aging, disease or accident; loss of home and country through immigration, displacement or war; loss of security through unemployment, economic downturns or organizational restructuring. These losses can be chronic and intense, challenging the stamina of the strongest individual or family.

Sadness also occurs from less tangible losses in a love relationship, such as when reality falls short of hopes and expectations. You may be reading this book because you feel disappointed and let down in your relationship. Most people view their close relationships as the most important part of their life. To lose the joy, harmony or closeness you once felt in your love relationship is indeed a profound loss that naturally evokes sadness. For other individuals, self-esteem can be lost, through disparagement, rejection or betrayal within their love relationship. It is especially poignant when the source of betrayal is someone close whom we thought we could trust.

There are other losses couples face that place considerable strain on them and make it difficult to take pleasure in their relationship. For many couples, a diagnosis of infertility is one such loss, resulting in significant heartache. For others, the rearing of children sometimes does not live up to expectations, resulting in frustration, sadness and disappointment. Losses, great or small, affect most of us at some stage in our lives.

Grief

Grief associated with significant loss has attracted the attention of many researchers, for not only is grief universally experienced, it can be intense, painful, disorientating and carries the potential to cause problems for our mental and physical health. One of the most influential figures in the field of grief and bereavement is the British psychiatrist, Dr. John Bowlby, who has been so influential in the development of attachment theory (described in Chapter 2). Bowlby placed grief in an evolutionary framework and suggested that as social beings our brains are hard wired to "retrieve" what has been lost. In terms of survival, it is in our best interests to stay close to the ones we love, the ones who care for us and protect our safety. Hence, when a significant person dies or moves out of our lives, for a time at least, we protest that loss and yearn to bring that person back.[12]

While we may think of tears or sobbing as the typical outward demonstrations of grief, Bowlby draws our attention to other reactions as well: it is normal to *protest angrily*, to long and to *yearn*, and, sometimes, even to *feel despair* about losing contact with a loved one.

- When you feel hurt in your relationship and cry out angrily, this is an example of "protest."
- When your heart aches and you express your pain by weeping outwardly or going into silent sadness, that is an expression of yearning.
- When you cling or placate, that might be a desperate attempt to hang on to each other.

These seemingly "immature" or "irrational" reactions to loss are understandable when we take an evolutionary perspective and view grief in its various manifestations as part of a natural attempt to retrieve our source of protection and safety.

Ultimately, however, the resilience of the human spirit silently draws the grieving person along to reorganization and recovery. While the "work" of adjusting to loss[13,14] is an individual journey, the support and kindness of others is nevertheless reported by most grieving people as a helpful part of their recovery process. Importantly, when we feel sad, we need to have that sadness respected. It does *not* help a sad person when well-meaning others try to help lessen sad feelings with platitudes like: "Oh, he was an old dog. You can get another!" or "It was only a miscarriage. You'll have more children." Similarly, it does not help in close relationships to dismiss the sadness of a partner, even if we can't understand the depth or significance of it. When feeling sadness people usually need acceptance of their feelings, compassion and comforting words or touch.

Recovery from relationship break up involves making sense out of how/why the relationship ended. If you are recovering from relationship break up and find yourself blaming yourself entirely for the end of the relationship, it will be helpful for you to pause and reflect on the bigger picture. Sometimes, relationships break up because of the particularly unhelpful behavior of one partner; more often, however, romantic relationships come to an end when two otherwise normal, nice and decent individuals come to realize that they are not able to meet each other's needs for intimacy and happiness. Placing all the blame and shame on either yourself or your ex-partner is unlikely to be helpful or accurate. Working through the reflections in this book and exercises that identify the layers of your cycle can help you to develop a balanced picture of how your relationship evolved to the point of separation.

Reflection 6.3 Sadness and loss

What experiences of loss or grief have I had in my life?

____
____
____

How do I feel sadness in my body (e.g., sinking feeling, heavy heart, tears)?

____
____
____

What sadness do I experience in my current relationship?

____
____
____

What do I typically do when I feel sad?

___

___

___

How do I express sadness to my partner?

___

___

___

What happens for my partner when I am sad? How does my partner typically react to me when I express sadness?

___

___

___

What sadness have I caused my partner? How do they typically react to feeling sad?

___

___

___

What do I feel now, recalling these experiences of sadness for either my partner or myself?

___

___

___

What helps me to cope with sadness, to heal from disappointment or loss? What comforts me?

___

___

___

What did I learn from this experience about my partner or myself?

___

___

___

Anger

"That Is so Unfair!"

Typically, an offence against "me" and "mine" provokes anger.[15] For example, anger frequently results from perceptions of unfair treatment,[16] or that the situation is contrary to what ought to be.[17] Consider, for example, how angry most people would feel if their partner leaves the relationship with no warning and no explanation. Neuroscientists observe that anger is associated with a narrowing of attention to exclude all but the anger situation, with exaggerated judgments of blame. Thoughts of "I'm right, everyone else is wrong" are common.[18] If you think back to the last time you felt really angry with your partner, you will probably recall feeling very sure that you were *right* or *justified* to be so angry; your partner was definitely wrong!

Puffing Up with Anger

A person who experiences anger (in contrast to fear and anxiety) often reports feeling stronger[19] with a sense that the situation is best handled with confrontation. In other words, anger makes us "puff up" to ward off threats.[20] Anger is also associated with muscle tension, feeling "hot and bothered," and wanting to express the feelings, either verbally or nonverbally.[21]

Avoiding Anger

Intense angry feelings can be uncomfortable for some people to feel and to express to loved ones. Some men may be apprehensive of being perceived as too aggressive or confrontational. Some women may be uneasy expressing anger because of societal views of anger as "unbecoming of a woman." A common result of these concerns is to *water down* expressions of anger by calling it "frustration" or "annoyance"; *dial it down* by analyzing the problem, problem-solving or minimizing the problem (e.g., It's not that bad); or *deny* it by simply denying angry feelings, joking or expressing another emotion instead, such as tears. Although not necessarily conscious, these are all strategies for avoiding anger. However, anger can help mobilize us to set healthy limits and establish boundaries, which is necessary at times.

Expressing Anger—"Too Hot or Too Cold"?

There is certainly a place for appropriately expressed anger in close relationships. However, we need to manage *how* we express anger, the intensity and the manner in which we deliver information about the source of our anger. When expressed thoughtfully, anger promotes the assertive expression of needs, and limits. Such an expression of anger can be healthy and feel empowering especially in relationships in which one partner has felt used, disrespected or unfairly criticized over time. Effective expression of anger is also typically preferable to partners than complete shut down or unbridled expression of anger. An effective expression of anger might be something like:

> "It is not acceptable to me when you ridicule me in public. I believe I deserve better than that." OR "I need you to give me a chance. I do not want to hear any more about the ways in which I failed years ago."

In fact, when these statements are said more firmly and assertively than angrily, they express *important information* to your partner about your basic needs for safety and respect, in contrast to just venting stressed or pent-up feelings, which so often occurs in relationship conflict.

However, problems can occur when anger is either expressed too freely or not freely enough. Researcher and therapist, Sandra Paivio, has commented that *over-control* of anger disrupts our attention, disorients us and causes us stress, whereas *under-control* of anger disrupts our interpersonal relationships.[22] Similarly, Linda Roberts, a close relationships researcher, has investigated what she calls "fire and ice in marital communication."[23] In some couple relationships where anger is expressed in a forceful or explosive way, partners on the receiving end of this fiery anger can feel severely burned. By contrast, in other relationships, one or both partners may express anger in a cold, silent or brooding way that creates an unbearably tense atmosphere lasting for days or even weeks. Robert's research confirmed the negative effect on wives of husbands' hostility, but also the negative effect on husbands of wives' cool withdrawal.

Reflection 6.4 Anger

How do I experience anger in my body (e.g., clenched fists; feel hot/cold; feel agitated and restless; feel pressured to speak)?

____

____

____

What typically triggers my anger?

____

____

What typically triggers my partner's anger?

____

____

What happens between us when either of us is angry?

____

____

____

Do I "bottle up" anger so much that I don't speak to my partner for days? If so, what is it like for me to be angry in this detached way? What does it feel like for my partner to experience my cool withdrawal?

____

____

Do I sometimes lose control of my anger, becoming explosive or out of control? If so, what does it feel like to be exploding? What is it like for my partner to receive this fiery treatment?

____

____

Do either of us try to minimize anger through intellectualizing, making jokes, blaming or crying instead? If so, what makes it difficult to express anger directly?

____

____

How else do my partner and I manage anger?

____

____

What helps us to calm down?

____

____

How would I *like* to manage my anger?

____

____

Fear

Fight, Freeze or Flight

The feeling of fear informs us of potential threat. Accompanying symptoms of fear and anxiety such as sweating, shaking, being speechless and feeling "jittery" indicate arousal of the body's autonomic nervous system[24] and prepare us to respond to the threat. When endangered, animals confront an adversary if they sense they can overpower or bluff their foe, but withdraw, flee or freeze if they sense that the opponent is too dangerous. The choice of responses, sensibly, may shift back and forth depending on the changing context. This is the "fight, freeze or flight" mechanism of self-preservation that also exists in close relationships. Although your partner is not an adversary, threat to the security of your relationship bond can evoke fear, or intense fear, such as panic. Here are some examples of attachment threats that plague distressed relationships. The fear that:

"I will let you down or disappoint you"
"I will evoke your anger"
"I'm unworthy of your love. I don't deserve you"
"You won't be there for me when I need you"
"You will eventually get fed up with me and leave"

Fear Versus Anxiety

Fear and anxiety are similar emotional experiences but are nevertheless distinct. Fear is usually a useful core emotion that occurs in response to a direct threat and when addressed, protects the relationship and then the fear diminishes. Anxiety has been described as an uneasy feeling of suspense or tense anticipation of something threatening.[25] You may have heard the expression, "free floating anxiety," which describes a sense that something is wrong or might soon go wrong, even though there is no specific evidence to indicate danger. Anxiety typically involves selective attention to potential threat; as Sophocles observed long ago: "To a man who is afraid, everything rustles." When specific relationship fears are not addressed directly and compassionately, anxiety tends to hang in the air perpetually. Anxiety like this does not serve a useful purpose and warrants attention to address its sources.

Coping with Attachment Threat

As mentioned in Chapter 3, some individuals do not feel secure in their close relationships. When partners feel the kinds of relationship threats described, it is difficult to feel secure. Attachment threats may be experienced because of unreliable or hurtful behavior in the relationship. However, it could also exist because of anxiety experienced in earlier relationships or societal oppression experienced by one or both individuals that is unintentionally reinforced by behavior in the current relationship.

Perhaps you may relate to one of the attachment threats described? Maybe you feel a niggling, underlying sense that your partner may not really want to be close to you, that ultimately, someday, the truth will be revealed that you are not truly lovable. It is likely that if you feel this way, you may be watchful and cautious in order to avoid "rocking the boat" in your relationship. Or perhaps your watchfulness may evolve into clinging or even picking a fight to get your partner's attention. Unfortunately, these watchful behaviors that typically express relationship anxiety and are meant to preserve the relationship can drive a partner away, resulting in the very thing that you feared in the beginning.[26]

When fear revolves around attachment threats there are two basic behavioral tendencies we typically see. As described in Chapter 3 and 4, some people cope by *turning down* their distress with avoidance or withdrawal, whereas other people make their distress more visible by *turning it up* in the form of protesting. People who turn down their distress typically do so by avoiding emotions or heated interactions and withdrawing from an interaction when feeling threatened. People who turn up their visibility tend to move toward their relationship partners when threatened by initiating contact and attempting to get through to them any way they can. For couples, anxiety is a troubling form of distress that can have problematic implications for the relationship. Fortunately, if the specific threat or fear that is fueling the anxiety can be identified, as in the examples outlined, anxiety can settle down. When people are able to express fears directly and experience their partners' sincere reassurance, the threat and attachment distress can diminish.

Reflection 6.5 Fear and anxiety

In what kinds of situations do I feel afraid? What/who typically triggers my fear?

____

____

____

Do I sometimes feel generally anxious or uptight without any *apparent* reason to be afraid? If I tune into myself deeply, is there an attachment threat fueling my fear?

____

____

____

What fears are typically triggered in my relationship?

____

____

When I feel fear or anxiety, what do I experience in my body (e.g., clenched stomach, shaky inside, whole body freeze, scattered thoughts)?

____

____

What do I tend to do inside myself and in our relationship?

____

____

____

What helps me to calm my fears/anxieties?

____

____

What happens for my partner when I feel afraid?

____

____

What do I notice when my partner is afraid?

____

____

What helps my partner to cope when feeling afraid? How can I help?

____

____

Do I ever feel fearful that I am not lovable and important to my partner? What do I do with that fear? How do I express it?

____

____

____

Staying on High Alert: The Aftermath of Trauma

Although an in-depth description of the neurobiology of fear is beyond the scope of this book, a couple of interesting points are noted. As indicated at the beginning of the previous chapter, emotions help us to survive. Potentially threatening changes in our environment trigger reactions in our body before our conscious mind can reflect on the threat. The amygdala, a part of the brain involved in the processing of danger and fear has close connections with the brain stem, the part of the brain that controls pre-programmed behaviors and automatic reactions. This explains why a hiker's foot pulls back at the sight of a possible snake before the person can consciously analyze if the object is a snake or a stick or a vine.[27]

Further, the responsiveness of the amygdala can be modified as the significance of the potentially threatening object/event is analyzed; this modification, however, takes time, which explains why we can still feel somewhat watchful and overly alert for a time after a frightening experience. Taking deep breaths and using calming self-talk is helpful; but these strategies usually need to be sustained for at least a few minutes to be effective. Sadly, individuals who have been exposed to traumatic experiences or abusive child-rearing environments, especially over a prolonged period of time or in intense amounts, often report feeling constantly watchful, jittery or "on edge." This is because the amygdala of these individuals has been overstimulated over a long period of time and remains on high alert for danger. The good news for these individuals is that treatment from a qualified professional and sustained support from a caring partner can help these symptoms to subside substantially.

Contempt

In Chapter 5 we noted that some emotions are clearly recognizable on the human face. These are happiness, sadness, anger, fear and surprise, and there is one more: contempt. Essentially, contempt conveys the message "You are inferior, worthless, or vile" and the expression of contempt is often perceived as arrogance. For some couples, contempt may take the form of mocking laughter, but only one person is laughing. The other partner is feeling ridiculed and put down. The face of a person expressing contempt typically shows a curled or raised upper lip and a lift to the head and face as though pulling back from a bad smell. Eye rolling can also express contempt,[28] as can scoffing comments.

Impact of Contempt in Close Relationships

Contempt in couple relationships is serious. Seeing contempt on a partner's face indicates significant relationship distress; in fact, contempt is a strong predictor of divorce.[29] As Professor John Gottman's research has demonstrated, all couples at times criticize or ignore their partners or get defensive, but in basically well-functioning relationships, contempt is very rarely observed. Expressions of contempt *indicate* as well as *cause* significant relationship distress. Hence, if you are aware of expressing contempt to your partner, take note and start work now to rid your relationship of contempt by examining the underlying reasons for it! Your relationship is not invincible; contempt can be very toxic and will quickly wear down good will and positive feelings and erode your attachment bond.

Disgust is closely related to contempt, and comes from a French word meaning, "distaste." Just as we spit out bad food, we also express disgust by rejecting offensive thoughts, values and practices.[30] Disgust (like anger) does serve a useful purpose at times because it lets us know when we are experiencing something violating to our body or sense of self (e.g., verbally, sexually or physically) and can help us create protective boundaries. Further, we note that it is not helpful when contempt or disgust are directed inward at the self (producing shame or self-loathing) or outward toward a partner in a disparaging way that leaves that person feeling inferior or worthless.

We encourage you to work actively at understanding your feelings and the situations that trigger contempt because context is important in determining the usefulness of our emotions. With close loved ones learn to express and discuss those underlying feelings (e.g., hurt, fear, sadness, anger, shame, hopelessness) rather than lapsing into harmful expressions of contempt. Also, the expression of positive emotions such as fondness, admiration and appreciation are antidotes to contempt.[31]

Reflection 6.6 Contempt

Have I ever felt anger at a violation and established a protective boundary by expressing contempt? How did I handle it?

____

____

____

How else could I have handled that experience so that I showed respect for myself and also the other person?

____

____

In my current romantic relationship, have I experienced contempt (e.g., rolled eyes, sarcastic putdowns, being mocked or a milder version such as feeling overly teased)? If so, what was that like for me? How did I feel? How did I then behave toward my partner?

____

____

____

Have I expressed contempt to my partner? If I look deeply inside, how did these feelings of contempt evolve for me in our relationship?

____

____

If I express contempt, my partner typically responds by

____

____

How do I feel now reflecting on these experiences?

____

____

Your Core Emotions Are Not Always Clearly Visible to Your Partner: What Emotions Do You Show?

It is natural for these core emotions of happiness, joy, love, sadness, anger and fear to emerge, sometimes mildly, sometimes intensely, and then dissipate as you move through your day. What do you do as your vulnerable (core) emotions emerge? Do you notice and tune into them as they occur? Do you allow yourself to go into and feel your emotions? Do you see your emotions as important to share with your partner?

> What you and your partner do with your vulnerable feelings actually creates the emotional tone and culture of your relationship.

Negative Cycles—Positive Cycles

The aim of this book is to help you develop a close and secure relationship bond through emotional sharing and responding. Sharing your core, softer emotions changes the tune of a conversation and can turn negative interactions into moments of intimacy. While it might seem hard just now for you to imagine, couples *can* turn their negative cycles around to create more positive interactions. We encourage you to keep working at building up your understanding of yourself and your partner. The next step in doing that is to look inside and explore the core emotions that underlie your own reactions and behavior in the negative dance. You can't express your deeper emotions to your partner if you are not in touch with them.

Let's look again first at Patricia and William's cycle to see if we can draw out their core emotions. When Patricia and William disagree, their disconnection evokes her *fear* of losing contact with him. The disagreement feels threatening to her and she tries to get them on the same page through persuasion, at first gently, but then more forcefully. Patricia also feels *sad* and *hurt* by the rejection she experiences when William brushes her off at the soccer field and later that evening when she tries to make contact with him. Of course, William does not see these vulnerable emotions in their cycle. What comes across to him is her frustration and anger. He then gets concerned and *afraid* that they are headed for a fight. William also experiences some *sadness* that he's disappointed her again and possibly some *anger* when he feels put down. Not surprisingly, when William becomes defensive or shuts down Patricia does not see this sensitive side and their connection remains tenuous. See how the layers of Patricia and William's cycle expand to include their core emotions. Following the arrows, you can see that when Patricia copes with her fears and hurts by protesting, William's fear and sadness are triggered and when he handles that by withdrawing, it further sets off Patricia's fears.

Can you imagine how it might go differently if Patricia and William openly showed their vulnerabilities? What could Patricia say if she lowered her guard, her reactive anger?

> "I realize that I feel worried when we disagree . . . *afraid* of the distance that creates between us, and I then get pushy to close the gap. I don't feel very good about being pushy, though." OR
> "I know that you were focused on the soccer game earlier today, but I just need to let you know that when you were curt with me, I felt snubbed. I'm still feeling a bit *sad* and rejected by that."

How do you feel toward Patricia when you imagine hearing these disclosures said softly, simply, slowly?

____

____

What would William say if he did not protect himself by defending his position or distancing from his feelings?

> "When we get into a power struggle like we are right now about the sofa, it seems like my opinion doesn't matter. It *hurts*. I feel *angry* and *sad*, so I usually retreat."
> OR "Sometimes when you approach me in confrontation, I actually do get *scared* that we're headed for a fight and I'll do anything to avoid that."

How do you feel toward William when you imagine hearing these disclosures said softly, simply, slowly?

PATRICIA

What I do

Approach, convince, demand, probe, blame

What I think to myself

About me: "How come I can't get through to him?"

About you: "He always disappears on me!"

I react emotionally with

Reactive anger, frustration, desperation, anxiety

WILLIAM

What I do

Get logical, practical, defend, capitulate, distance, minimize

What I think to myself

About me: "Uh oh, what have I done now?"

About you: "She always needs to have her way"

I react emotionally with

Defensive anger, anxiety, feeling overwhelmed, feeling down, detachment

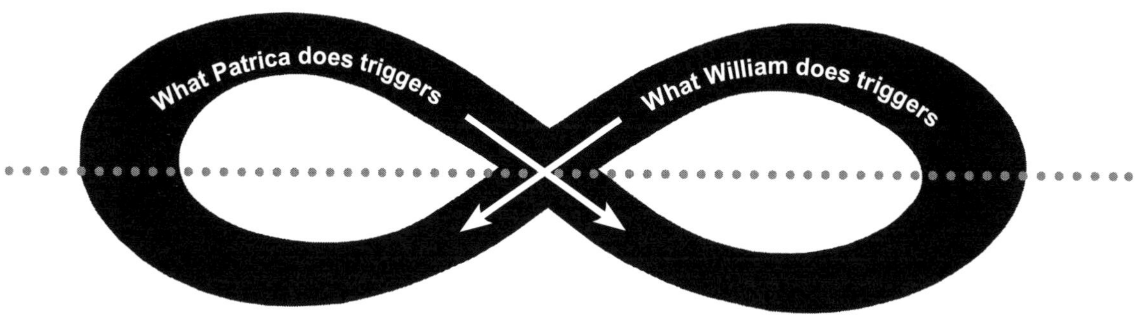

PATRICIA – How I feel inside

Afraid of disconnecting
Sad and lonely
Hurt from feeling rejected

WILLIAM – How I feel inside

Afraid of arguing or not meeting her expectations
Sad about feeling like a failure

Figure 6.1 Patricia and William's dance with behaviors, thoughts, reactive emotions and core emotions
Infinity diagram adapted from Scott R. Woolley, Ph.D.© and labeling adapted from Lucy Pascal, M.S.W.

Notice if these vulnerable disclosures of inside feelings relax and soften your responses to Patricia and William? Now you might like to reflect on how you express your core emotions of fear, anger or sadness. Are you and your partner able to talk about these deeper feelings openly? Or, do you get caught up in reactive emotions, or protecting yourself with negative behaviors?

For example, deep down, a partner in an insecure relationship might be feeling afraid and wonder: "Will she think less of me when I tell her about my mistake at work?" This fear might trigger the person to put up his guard ("I won't take that risk!"), which then might be expressed as an irritable remark: "I sure hope you aren't going to do your usual thing of telling me how I should have done it differently . . .!" In this example, the receiving partner hears an irritable remark and may feel attacked. The speaker has reacted by putting up a self-protective guard; it is very unlikely that the receiving partner will be able to see or respond to the partner's fear deep down. This interaction is heading down the path of a negative interaction.

How could this interaction go differently? It could start up with: "Honey? Do you have a minute? I feel embarrassed about something that happened at work today . . . I even feel on edge now that you might think less of me because of what I did." This is a very different opening to the example just outlined. In this alternative, the receiving partner is presented with the speaker's feelings of vulnerability, which is typically much easier to respond to than a prickly, self-defensive, or reactive comment. When your partner confides their softer core feelings, the implicit message is:

- You are important to me
- So important that I am willing to risk showing you parts of myself that I don't like
- You are the one I want to turn to when I'm struggling
- I need *your* love, empathy, support, encouragement.

As a general rule,

> Tell your partner openly about your *vulnerable, core emotions* rather than expressing self-protective reactions.

Reflection 6.7 Discovering our core emotions

Find a time and place where you can be quiet and reflective. Think of a recent time you and your partner got stuck in your usual negative cycle. It may help to write down some of the details.

Name: ____________________

Ask yourself: When I look deeper into what is going on for me in our negative cycle, what am I feeling at the core? ____

____

____

Name: ________________

Ask yourself: When I look deeper into what is going on for me in our negative cycle, what am I feeling at the core? ____

____

If feelings of frustration, irritability or numbness emerge, keep sitting with this question to see if you can drop down deeper. You know that you have hit a core emotion when it feels *vulnerable, new or fresh, from the heart or gut,* rather than predictable and on the surface.

You can replay the part of the interaction that had the most "heat" for you. Notice what you feel in your body: Where is there tension? Notice your heart beating, palms sweating, jaw tensing, stomach clenching . . . Tune into the rhythm of your breathing. Allow your attention to be drawn to any tension or strong sensation. Notice any emotions that emerge as you attend to that part of yourself.

If you sense an emotion surfacing, allow yourself to settle into it so that you can see what it is. Notice where you feel the emotion in your body and just make room for it. Give it permission to exist. Tell yourself it's okay. If your mind begins to wander to thoughts of work or other things, just gently bring your attention back.

Here are examples from our clients of common core emotions that underlie the protesting and withdrawing positions.

Protesting position	*Withdrawing position*
Sad about lonely, invisible	Sad about letting partner down
Sad and hurt about not feeling important	Anger about feeling disrespected
Afraid of abandonment, betrayal	Fear of rejection for constantly failing
Afraid of being rebuffed or dismissed	Afraid you will get "fed up" and leave
Hurt or shame when rejected	Angry about feeling controlled
Fear of not being lovable	Sad, ashamed about not feeling acceptable

If you have a felt sense of your core emotions in the negative dance, or in the recent interaction you are using for this exercise, go ahead and fill in your side of the loop. Can you share the core emotions you feel in your negative dance with each other now in a L-O-V-E conversation? If you are not getting a clear felt sense of your core emotions, do not worry. Set the exercise aside for now and try again later. Be patient and compassionate with yourself.

The more you and your partner can show acceptance now for being right where you are "at," no pressuring or discounting, the easier it will be to connect with your deeper emotions in the future.

Name: ____________________

What I do

____

____

What I think to myself

About me: ____________________

____

About you: ____________________

____

I react emotionally with

____

____

Name: ____________________

What I do

____

____

What I think to myself

About me: ____________________

____

About you: ____________________

____

I react emotionally with

____

____

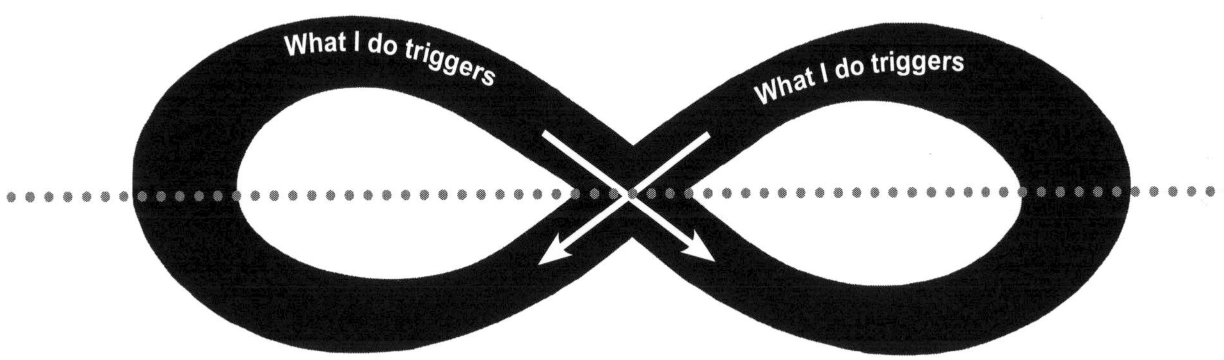

How I feel inside

____

____

____

How I feel inside

____

____

____

Figure 6.2 Our relationship dance with behaviors, thoughts, reactive emotions and core emotions
Infinity diagram adapted from Scott R. Woolley, Ph.D.© and labeling adapted from Lucy Pascal, M.S.W.

Reflection 6.8 How we impact each other

Think about the impact your emotions and behaviors have on your partner. How do your partner's emotions and behaviors impact you? It may help to do the sentence completion exercise together. There is a sentence completion set for each partner.

Name: ____________________
In my *core*, when I am ______________________ (e.g., afraid, sad, hurt, angry), but don't feel able to share openly, I *react* by expressing ______________________ (e.g., frustration, reactive or defensive anger, irritability, detachment). I typically *cope* by ______________________ (e.g., complaining, lecturing, going silent).
You then typically *react* by expressing ______________________ and *coping* by ______________________. I wonder what you are feeling in your *core*? ______________________
How do your vulnerable core emotions impact me? ______________________
____

Name: ____________________
In my *core*, when I am ______________________ (e.g., afraid, sad, hurt, angry), but don't feel able to share openly, I *react* by expressing ______________________ (e.g., frustration, reactive or defensive anger, irritability, detachment). I typically *cope* by ______________________ (e.g., complaining, lecturing, going silent).
You then typically *react* by expressing ____________________ and *coping* by _____________.
I wonder what you are feeling in your *core*? ______________________
How do your vulnerable core emotions impact me? ______________________
____

Name: ____________________
When I feel positive *core* emotions ______________________ (e.g., happiness, joy), I typically express/act with ______________________ (e.g., love, affection, openness, attentiveness, empathy). You then typically *respond* with ______________________ (e.g., joy, playfulness, relief, listening, disclosing your own feelings).
The more I interact by voicing my ______________________ (e.g., openness, encouragement, love, core feelings), the more you respond with ______________________ (e.g., smiles, relaxing, listening to me, sharing your own feelings with me).
How do your positive core emotions impact me? ______________________
____

Name: ____________________
When I feel positive *core* emotions ______________________ (e.g., happiness, joy), I typically express/act with ______________________ (e.g., love, affection, openness, attentiveness, empathy). You then typically *respond* with ______________________ (e.g., joy, playfulness, relief, listening, disclosing your own feelings.

The more I interact by voicing my ______________________ (e.g., openness, encouragement, love, core feelings), the more you respond with ______________________ (e.g., smiles, relaxing, listening to me, sharing core feelings with me).
How do your positive core emotions impact me? ______________________
____

Table 6.1 Eight tips for listening to your core emotions

1. Identify the trigger	Is the trigger inside (e.g., a thought: "I wonder if he'll show up on time," or perception: "She doesn't seem to care how I feel") or outside (e.g., a look, word or gesture from your partner) that caught your attention?
2. Do you lack emotion? Or have a lot of unsettled emotion?	Stop what you are doing, slow down, and turn your attention inside yourself. Take some deep breaths. If you *lack emotion*, shut down or go blank, pay attention to any sensation or emotion you are feeling inside. If you have *a lot of emotion*, keep breathing until you can center yourself and feel which emotion is most important to listen to. If you are having trouble, common areas to tune into are how your stomach, chest, shoulders, throat and jaws feel. Notice any areas that feel shaky, heavy, tense or clenched. Notice the rhythm of your breath and your heart rate. Notice if you go hot or cold. Tune into your posture and gestures. As you focus in on these areas, ask yourself what feeling is in there? Give yourself permission to feel it.
3. Keep it simple	Label the feeling simply and clearly: "I feel . . . afraid . . . sad . . . angry." (Naming an emotion helps to bring some clarity. Even obscure emotions such as "numb" or "upset" will get clearer each time you revisit them.)
4. Talk about yourself instead of blaming	Share about yourself, acknowledging the context without blaming: "I am feeling sad . . . because what you just said there hit me hard."
5. Keep reactive or defensive anger in check	Keep your *anger* in check, so that you are expressing the primary "soft" feeling underneath, rather than the protective "hard" feeling of anger on the surface. Venting will get you nowhere. It will be easier for your partner to respond constructively to your hurt or fear than to stony silence, criticism, blame or rage.
6. Manage over-control of anger with appropriate expression of feelings and needs	If you tend to *control your anger too much*, it will likely help you to express your needs and feelings more assertively. For example, "When you didn't include me in your plans, I felt hurt and angry. I'd like to be included in the planning. I need to be reassured that you want me to be involved in this project." Notice how this statement includes a clear statement of what the person *feels*, and also clearly indicates what is *needed* and/or *wanted*.
7. Face your fears	Wherever possible, try to face your *fears*, rather than avoid them . . . doing what you fear can be scary but very satisfying. In close relationships, talk to your partner about your fears. You may need to do this in small steps, such as starting with disclosing how hard (or scary) it is to even talk about your concerns. After you find that your partner is willing to listen, you can go on to disclose what is troubling you.
8. Lean into your sadness	When *sad*, it helps for us to tune in to what our bodies instinctively know is best to help us heal. Tears, for example, are Nature's way of bringing relief. Having a "good cry" changes the biochemistry of the brain, bringing comfort. At some point when it feels right, take the risk to share your sadness with your partner.

Sharing with Your Partner

When you and your partner are ready, set aside some time (or several times) to talk over your reflections. As your partner shares his or her core emotions with you, it is okay if you feel some doubt that your partner could actually be feeling these vulnerable emotions. Your doubts are very valid since you probably don't *see* vulnerability from your partner very often (or perhaps express it yourself). Nevertheless, it will help if you resist the impulse to dismiss the possibility that your partner's emotions are "real."

What you *see* when you're in the negative cycle is above the dotted line in the infinity loop of your relationship dance—how each of you cope and your reactive emotions. However, what about the portion that you can't see when you are in the negative dance (underneath the dotted line)? The exercises in this chapter focused on helping you go under the surface of your negative dance. As a couple, if you have the courage to put on your scuba diving gear and delve beneath the waterline, instead of snorkeling at the surface, you will discover the wonders lying at the bottom of the sea.

Remember the guidelines for talking with your partner: Use L-O-V-E conversations to get to know each other better:

- Take your time and listen respectfully
- Watch out for the negative dance and interrupt it: "Let's not get caught in the vortex"
- Thank each other for participating in the exercises
- Read on to understand more about you, your partner and relationship.

References

1. Gottman, J. (1994). *What predicts divorce?* Hillsdale, NJ: Lawrence Erlbaum.
2. Sternberg, R. J. (1986). A triangular theory of love. *Psychological Review, 93*, 119–135.
3. Hazan, C., & Shaver, P. (1987). Romantic love conceptualized as an attachment process. *Journal of Personality and Social Psychology, 52*, 511–524.
4. Berscheid, E., & Hatfield, E. (1978). *Interpersonal attraction*. Reading, MA: Addison-Wesley.
5. Greenberg, L., & Goldman, R. (2008). *Emotion-focused couples therapy: The dynamics of emotion, love and power*. Washington, DC: American Psychological Association.
6. Noller, P. (1996). What is this thing called love? How do we define the love that supports marriage and family? *Personal Relationships, 3*(1), 97–115.
7. Bartels, A., & Zeki, S. (2000). The neural basis of romantic love. *Neuroreport, 11*(17), 3829–3834.
8. Acevedo, B. P., Aron, A., Fisher, H. E., & Brown, L. L. (2012). Neural correlates of long-term intense romantic love. *Social and Cognitive Affective Neuroscience, 7*, 145–159.
9. Aron, E., & Aron, A. (1996). Love and expansion of the self: The state of the model. *Personal Relationships, 3*, 45–58.
10. Tolstoy, L. (1922–1923). *War and peace* (L. Maude & A. Maude, Trans.). The Literature Network. Retrieved January 18, 2014, from www.online-literature.com/Leo Tolstoy/war_and_peace/336
11. Bowlby, J. (1979). *The making and breaking of affectional bonds*. London: Tavistock.
12. Bowlby, J. (1969/1982). *Attachment and loss: Vol. 1. Attachment*. New York, NY: Basic Books.
13. Freud, S. (1913). Totem and taboo. In *Complete psychological works* (Vol. 13). London: Hogarth.
14. Worden, W. (2009). *Grief counselling and grief therapy* (4th ed.). New York, NY and London: Tavistock.
15. Lazarus, R. (1991). *Emotion and adaptation*. New York, NY and Oxford: Oxford University Press.
16. Fitness, J., & Fletcher, G. (1993). Love, hate, anger, and jealousy in close relationships: A prototype and cognitive appraisal analysis. *Journal of Personality and Social Psychology, 65*, 942–958.
17. Shaver, P., Schwartz, J., Kirson, D., & O'Connor, C. (1987). Emotion knowledge: Further exploration of a prototype approach. *Journal of Personality and Social Psychology, 52*, 1061–1086.

18. Clore, G. (1994). Why emotions are felt. In P. Ekman & R. Davidson (Eds.), *The nature of emotion: Fundamental questions* (pp. 103–110). New York, NY: Oxford University Press.
19. Shaver, P., Schwartz, J., Kirson, D., & O'Connor, C. (1987). Emotion knowledge: Further exploration of a prototype approach. *Journal of Personality and Social Psychology, 52,* 1061–1086.
20. Greenberg, L., & Goldman, R. (2008). *Emotion-focused couples' therapy: The dynamics of emotion, love and power.* Washington, DC: American Psychological Association.
21. Fitness, J., & Fletcher, G. (1993). Love, hate, anger, and jealousy in close relationships: A prototype and cognitive appraisal analysis. *Journal of Personality and Social Psychology, 65,* 942–958.
22. Paivio, S. (1999). Experiential conceptualisation and treatment of anger. *Psychotherapy in Practice, 55,* 311–324.
23. Roberts, L. J. (2000). Fire and ice in martial communication: Hostile and distancing behaviours as predictors of marital distress. *Journal of Marriage and the Family, 62,* 693–707.
24. Pinel., J., & Barnes, S. (2017). *Biopsychology* (10th ed.). Boston: Allyn and Bacon.
25. Rachman, S. (2019). *Anxiety.* Hove and New York, NY: Psychology Press.
26. Feeney, J. A. (2016). Adult romantic attachment: Developments in the study of couple relationships. In J. Cassidy & P. Shaver (Eds.), *Handbook of attachment* (3rd ed., pp. 435–463). New York, NY and London: The Guilford Press.
27. LeDoux, J. (1996). *The emotional brain: The mysterious underpinnings of emotional life.* New York, NY and London: Simon and Schuster.
28,29. Gottman, J. (1994). *What predicts divorce?* Hillsdale, NJ: Lawrence Erlbaum.
30,31. Greenberg, L., & Goldman, R. (2008). *Emotion-focused couples' therapy: The dynamics of emotion, love and power.* Washington, DC: American Psychological Association.

CHAPTER 7

THE ROAD TO SECURITY IS PAVED WITH GOOD INTENTIONS

How we interact in the world in general and in our relationships in particular is driven by multiple factors operating simultaneously. The last chapters have been focusing on emotions, helping you distinguish between different emotions (e.g., sadness, fear, anger) and different types of emotions (core or reactive). You have probably discovered that your negative relationship dance is fueled by how you both handle the core emotions as discussed in Chapter 6. But what sets off these core emotions? What evokes them? In this chapter we will be answering these questions and exploring another important dimension of your experience and your relationship.

We probably don't need to tell you that relationships stir up a lot of emotions. We believe that is because relationships are attachment bonds where we strive to meet our most basic human needs to be loved, cared for, and secure. From the bliss of falling in love, to the simple joy of being in one another's company, to tears of the first hurt feelings, emotions do not occur in a vacuum. There are fundamental relationship or attachment needs underlying your core emotions, such as the needs for security, closeness, to be seen and valued. As Sue Johnson says,[1]

> Attachment needs speak to the basic questions in our love relationships:
> If I call for you, will you come? Will you be there for me? Do you have my back?
> Will you confide in me? Will you keep me close?

Core emotions are evoked when we are *gratified* or *deprived* of our basic needs in our most important relationships. We all tend to feel positive emotions such as joy, happiness, delight and relief when our needs are being met. However, we tend to feel uncomfortable or experience specific negative emotions such as sadness, fear, anger and even shame when they are not being met. So, when you are having a strong core emotion in your relationship, it is an important reflection of your specific relational needs. For example, you might feel:

- Happy, after a tiring day, as you and your partner joke and laugh together, reflecting needs for levity and playfulness to balance the stresses of life
- Sad about harsh words spoken, reflecting the need for repair and comforting
- Angry about your character being attacked, reflecting a need for respect
- Fear of your partner getting fed up and leaving, reflecting needs for security and reassurance.

If you follow and listen to your core emotions, they will let you know what you need. In fact, if you trust them, your core emotions can be the GATEWAY to your relationship needs.

When you don't feel free to express emotional needs directly, or haven't discovered what your needs are, they may be expressed indirectly, confusing your partner. For instance, making a sarcastic comment to get your partner's attention. Knowing you can get your partner's attention is a very important need

DOI: 10.4324/9781003009481-7

in close relationships, most people would agree. Going about it by being sarcastic is likely to be not only confusing, but also counterproductive, potentially triggering you into a negative interaction.

If you look closely at the protesting and withdrawing behaviors in your negative cycle, there is almost always a meaningful *intention* behind them. That is to say, these difficult behaviors are your way of trying to restore a sense of connection, security or stability to your relationship—these are really *attachment intentions*. If you look closely for what is behind your behavior in times of distress in your relationship, you will discover what your intentions are. If you are like most couples, these intentions are rarely spoken of, but identifying your own intentions and expressing them to your partner can provide a bridge to help you find your way back to each other.

Finding the Attachment Intentions

Let's go back to the Patricia and William scenarios to discover the attachment intentions underlying their protest-withdraw dynamic. In the first vignette, Patricia is uncomfortable with their incompatible tastes and she's afraid that they won't come to an agreement. She pushes to forge a joint decision because she feels insecure when they are at odds with one another. Patricia tries to gain control over a disconcerting situation by becoming forceful. In the second vignette, she and William have an innocent misunderstanding that ensnares them into their negative dance. Patricia feels hurt when William brushes her off during the game. When she approaches him to talk about it later that evening, Patricia has already been sitting on her hurt for a while. She speaks of his tone being "inappropriate." Patricia is trying to make contact after almost a whole day of tension and feeling detached from William. She is also trying to get her hurt tended to, but it feels too raw to expose her hurt in a vulnerable way, so it comes out as an accusation. When Patricia and William are caught in their negative cycle, Patricia feels threatened by their loss of connection. When William goes silent or becomes logical, she feels shut out and essentially loses contact with him. *The attachment intentions behind Patricia's pursuing behavior are always to restore contact.* Her forceful method protects her from feeling too vulnerable in her hurt and fear; however, it also makes it difficult for William to see her softer feelings, which could cue him to offer the comfort and reassurance she is looking for.

Looking at William's side of their cycle, in the first vignette you can see that he feels overpowered and criticized in the way Patricia pushes harder when she feels insecure. He defends himself to a point, but eventually gives in to avoid an argument. William believes he needs to shut down in order to keep the peace between them. However, the pattern of accommodating comes at a cost to him, as he doesn't believe there is room for him in the relationship. The more William doubts that his feelings and opinions really matter to Patricia, the less inclined he is to share his inner world. In the second vignette, William puts up a wall when he experiences Patricia as complaining and disapproving of him. He becomes cool and rational because it seems like the only way he can gain control over his own anxieties and avoid a conversation that is threatening to spiral out of control between them. *The attachment intention behind William's wall is to keep the peace between them and protect him from difficult feelings*. However, when he puts up the wall, Patricia can't see how distressed William feels that he lets her down. It makes it very difficult for Patricia to respond compassionately to William's feelings of distress when she does not have access to them.

Drawing out the attachment intentions behind Patricia's protesting behaviors, can you see how they represent ways to make contact with William and get on his radar without becoming too vulnerable? On William's side, can you see how he attempts to minimize conflict and avoid Patricia's disapproval by shutting himself down and becoming rational? Here we have included the attachment intentions that complete all of the layers of the infinity loop depicting their relationship dynamic.

> Notice that protesting and withdrawing behaviors do a good job of masking our real attachment fears, insecurities and intentions.

PATRICIA

What I do

Approach, convince, demand, probe, blame

What I think to myself

About me: "How come I can't get through to him?"

About you: "He always disappears on me!"

I react emotionally with

Reactive anger, frustration, desperation, anxiety

WILLIAM

What I do

Get logical, practical, defend, capitulate, distance, minimize

What I think to myself

About me: "Uh oh, what have I done now?"

About you: "She always needs to have her way"

I react emotionally with

Defensive anger, anxiety, feeling overwhelmed, feeling down, detachment

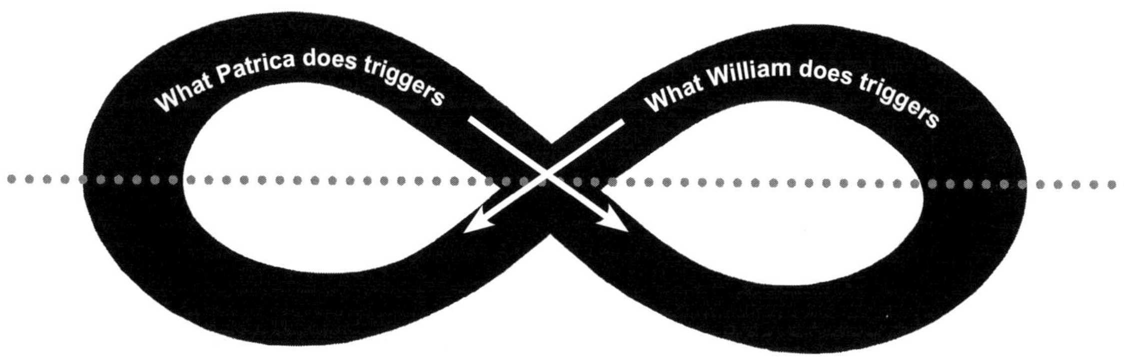

PATRICIA

How I feel inside

Afraid of disconnecting
Sad and lonely
Hurt from feeling rejected

What I need, what my intentions are

To make contact, create connection
To be seen, visible, reach you
To avoid hurt or rejection

WILLIAM

How I feel inside

Afraid of arguing or not meeting her expectations
Sad about feeling like a failure

What I need, what my intentions are

To create harmony, preserve the peace
To maintain our connection
To avoid the pain of disappointing you or getting rejected

Figure 7.1 Patricia and William's dance with behaviors, thoughts, reactive emotions, core emotions and attachment intentions

Infinity diagram adapted from Scott R. Woolley, Ph.D.© and labeling adapted from Lucy Pascal, M.S.W.

In our work with couples, we have noticed that when partners put their relationship wants and intentions out with reactive emotions or the behaviors of the negative cycle, it usually works against them. When William becomes distant in response to Patricia's attempts to make contact by pushing or becoming critical, it further evokes her fear that she can't reach him and she *escalates* her attempts in the only way she knows how. And as Patricia shows more frustration and anger, it will reinforce William's fear that he is disappointing her and that it is better for him to clam up so as *not to make things worse*. The more remote William becomes, the more it fuels Patricia's worry that she is losing contact with him, and so:

> The cycle feeds on itself through a series of emotional chain reactions and feedback loops that are distressing and painful to both partners.

You might be feeling discouraged right now and asking yourselves, is there any hope? How can we exit from these seemingly endless loops? If you can recognize that as a couple you are caught in a cycle that you *both* contribute to and are suffering from, then you can also *join together* to prevent getting hooked in. One of you might be able to see the bigger picture and gently invite the other to look at it with you. Therapists call this meta-communication (that is, communicating about your communication): "I think we're getting into the trap again. Let's slow this down . . . this is what's triggering me . . . what's triggering you?" Or you might decide to share some of the core emotions you've been tuning into: "I'm starting to feel *afraid* that you're not there" or "Right now I'm feeling *sad* because I feel like no matter how hard I try, I can't meet your expectations." *These disclosures bring your conversation below the waterline into tender emotions and desires that can draw you closer.* Working as partners instead of adversaries will begin to shift the emotional climate of your relationship in a positive direction. When you can share the parts of your experience that are more deep and vulnerable, it pulls for more compassion, caring and loving responses from your partner. Discovering the attachment desires and intentions underlying the negative cycle behaviors and emotions can also help you to see each other in a more forgiving light.

Reflection 7.1 Our attachment intentions

To look for the attachment intentions behind your behavior in the negative dance, begin by reflecting on the following (find a second set in Appendix A):

1. I get most triggered and distressed when I feel ______________________________ ______________________________ in our relationship.

2. What is missing for me most in our relationship is ______________________________ ______________________________

3. When I do my part of the dance, I am trying to ______________________________ ______________________________

4. My desire and/or intention is to ______________________________ ______________________________

The following is a list of common attachment desires and intentions, typically expressed by partners who protest and partners who withdraw. Circle the intentions that fit your experience or try them on and discover your own words to describe your intentions. In our negative dance, I am trying to:

Protesting Position	**Withdrawing Position**
Connect with you	Please you
Get on your radar	Avoid making a mistake
Get your attention	Avoid letting you down
Be seen and validated	Prevent conflict
Get you to respond to me	Keep the harmony between us
Avoid getting hurt	Cope with my own hurt or fear
______________________	______________________
______________________	______________________

Once your attachment desires and intentions become clear, take turns sharing them with one another. It can be helpful to tie in some specific examples from your interactions rather than discussing it in abstract ways. Remember to use the L-O-V-E conversation guidelines as you share together.

To complete the picture of your relationship dynamics, it is helpful to add in all the layers you have been exploring in this and the previous chapters. You can revisit a difficult conversation, and work through the layers of it together.

You can start by deciding on an incident from the past couple of weeks that is "typical" in your relationship to work through together. Pick one that was upsetting, but not your most sensitive one, and briefly describe it.[2]

You can find additional Our Relationship Dance work sheets (in Appendix B) to work through more sensitive conversations as you gain confidence. Initially it may be challenging to fill in all of the layers of your relationship dynamics. However, practice in working through difficult conversations and conflicts together will help you get to know not only the dance, but the softer core emotions and attachment desires that can draw you together.

Turning a Negative Interaction into a L-O-V-E Conversation

Once you have finished the worksheet together, you can go back and try "redoing" the interaction you described earlier. Can you revisit this incident, but this time as a L-O-V-E conversation? Look at each other and start with one person gently sharing . . . what *triggered* you in the interaction, your *core feeling* (e.g., sad about . . ., scared of . . .) that was evoked inside and the hidden *intention* behind your behavior at the time. Pause for a couple of minutes and take some time to notice and then share what it feels like to express yourself this way. Does it feel different? More scary or vulnerable? Is any part of it relieving? You might also like to ask your partner how it feels to hear your experience expressed in this new way you are trying out.

For the person listening, try to recognize that it is *a risk* to share more vulnerable emotions. Notice how your partner's disclosure might land differently inside of you. Does it evoke any feelings of care or compassion? If not, can you be curious and reflect on what might be blocking empathy for your partner right now? You might like to return to the Troubleshooting guide in Table 5.2 to give you some ideas of where your conversation might be breaking down. If you're feeling closer in this conversation, see if you can switch roles now and have the other partner do the same sharing exercise. It doesn't matter who goes first, as long as you both have an opportunity to give it a try.

Name: ______________________

What I do

____

____

What I think to myself

About me: ______________________

____

About you: ______________________

____

I react emotionally with

____

____

Name: ______________________

What I do

____

____

What I think to myself

About me: ______________________

____

About you: ______________________

____

I react emotionally with

____

____

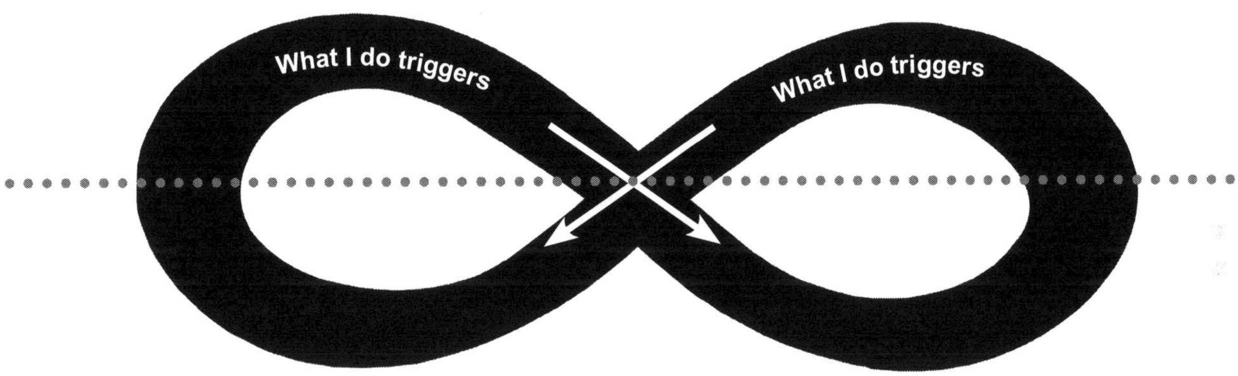

How I feel inside

____

____

____

What I need, what my intentions are

____

____

____

How I feel inside

____

____

____

What I need, what my intentions are

____

____

____

Figure 7.2 Our relationship dance with behaviors, thoughts, reactive emotions, core emotions and attachment intentions

Infinity diagram adapted from Scott R. Woolley Ph.D.© and labeling adapted from Lucy Pascal, M.S.W.

As you wind down, take a moment to notice anything that struck you as new or different during this conversation. Even if you are discouraged by the outcome of your interaction, try to focus on *anything at all* that felt new in the process. It could be that you were able to complete the conversation without someone ending it prematurely, or that you were able to stay calm throughout. It could be that there was a little softening in the air between you that was sensed but unspoken. Or it could be that it gave you a deeper understanding of each other. If you have been able to share something from your hearts together about the difficult interaction and feel a little softening and reconnection, no matter how small, that is truly worthy of celebration. Take a moment to congratulate yourselves or thank each other for participating. You can think of this conversation as a roadmap for mending and re-attaching after an argument or negative cycle has divided you. We hope you feel a sense that you are beginning to apply and integrate what you are learning in this workbook. As time goes on, the idea is that you will have some tools to return to difficult interactions with L-O-V-E conversations to work through them and reconnect.

As we draw this chapter to a close, we would like to encourage you to complete the sentences that follow that pull together and link the behaviors, emotions and attachment intentions in your typical relationship dance.

_______________ (Name)

In our negative dance, when I ____________________ (insert *behaviors*), deep down inside, I am really feeling ____________________ (*core emotion*), and I am trying to _______________ _______________ *attachment intention*).

_______________ (Name)

In our negative dance, when I ____________________ (insert *behaviors*), deep down inside, I am really feeling ____________________ (*core emotion*), and I am trying to _______________ _______________ *attachment intention*).

When you can easily complete the previous sentences, you will likely know your cycle like the back of your hand. The more familiar you are with the dance, the more quickly you will notice when you are slipping into it and the more able you will be to interrupt it by expressing your core primary emotions and attachment intentions. At this point we encourage you to take some time to go over previous exercises in any areas that still feel unclear to you. We also encourage you to practice working through the Our Relationship Dance work sheets until you can begin to share your core emotions and attachment intentions, initially to "redo" a difficult interaction and over time more spontaneously in your conversations as they start to go sideways. It's okay if you are not able to do it every time you get hurt. However, we invite you to notice how you are impacted when you *can* share spontaneously? Many couples begin to experience less friction and reactivity in their relationship. If you are noticing these changes, which often diffuse conflicts or reduce tension, it means that you are beginning to find ways out of the negative dance. You may be feeling more relaxed and in control of your relationship. You may be having deeper conversations. You may also be starting to see each other in a more benevolent light, and feel more open and generous toward each other. These welcome changes represent an important milestone in enhancing your relationship.

References

1, 2. Johnson, S. (2008). *Hold me tight*. New York, NY, Boston and London: Little, Brown and Company.

CHAPTER 8

SOCIALLY USEFUL EMOTIONS

Hurt, Shame, Guilt and Jealousy

So far, we have talked about the general function of emotions, considered how some emotions are reactions to other deeper emotions and briefly looked at the more core emotions of happiness and love, sadness, fear and anger. Now, in this chapter, we want to offer you support for dealing with some other emotions that may be more uncomfortable to understand and manage, more painful to bear, but which nevertheless serve a useful purpose in relationships. Some scholars refer to these emotions as "the dark side of close relationships";[1] it is undeniable that hurt, shame, guilt and jealousy can create intense emotional pain and trigger some unhelpful behaviors between partners. Nevertheless, these emotions have evolved over time to assist us to maintain social connections with others and tend to and repair relationship damage. Interestingly, relationship researchers have recently suggested these emotions may serve as *guardians* of our close relationships.[2] Toward the end of this chapter is a story about a couple who experienced some of the difficult emotions we will examine in this chapter. Their story shows how they found their way back to each other from the brink of divorce.

Hurt

Two Porcupines

Social psychologist, Professor Frank Fincham, describes two porcupines, huddled together in the middle of the night in the middle of Alaska. They desperately need to get close to each other for warmth; yet the closer they get to each other, the more at risk each is of being hurt by the other's quills. These two porcupines could be seen as a metaphor for the human condition in that our basic needs for closeness are also accompanied by the possibility of getting wounded.[3]

Notice, however, that we tend not to feel severely hurt by strangers or occasional acquaintances.[4] It is unlikely that we would complain about feeling hurt by the bank manager for rejecting our application for a loan or hurt by a shopkeeper for not opening a store on Sundays. We do, however, feel hurt if our partners or close friends reject our bids for closeness and understanding or don't make themselves available to help us in a time of need. It is in relationships of love and attachment that we are most vulnerable to hurt and also have the power to be most hurtful.

Hurt Feelings Are Comparable to Physical Pain

Hurt feelings *hurt*; indeed, recent neuroscience studies examining brain activity during episodes of social exclusion have found interesting parallels with physical pain studies. The same part of the brain

DOI: 10.4324/9781003009481-8

is active in experiences of social exclusion as in physical suffering.[5,6] It seems that hurt feelings are not specific to certain ages or cultures; clinical evidence suggests that hurt feelings are experienced in couple relationships across the life span and in different cultures.[7]

Participants in research studies of hurt in close relationships have reported experiencing a complex sequence of emotions in the aftermath of hurtful events,[8] such as sadness (e.g., at the loss of a relationship), anxiety (e.g., decreased security) and anger (e.g., at an unjustified attack). Change over time from one dominant emotion to another has also been described;[9] for example, sadness that gives way to anger, or conversely, initial anger that later gives way to sadness. Not surprisingly, unresolved hurt feelings tend to perpetuate spirals of negative interaction.[10]

Types of Hurtful Events

Close relationships scholar Dr. Judith Feeney has investigated the kinds of events people in committed relationships experience as hurtful. The hurtful events described by couples in her studies were associated with one of the following five categories of psychological hurt: 1) active distancing from the relationship (e.g., a partner expressing lack of interest or threatening to terminate the relationship); 2) passive distancing (e.g., being ignored by a partner or excluded from their plans); 3) criticism; 4) infidelity; and 5) deception (which included breaking of promises, being lied to or having confidences betrayed).[11]

Infidelity

Infidelity is usually a source of intense hurt for couples. Participants in Feeney's study rated infidelity as the most serious hurtful event, with reports of more hurt feelings, powerlessness, stronger belief that the hurt was intended and long-term negative effects on both the betrayed person and the relationship. Although we typically think of infidelity as involving a sexual relationship, intense emotional connection with a third person can also cause hurt and damage to the relationship bond. Further, serious adverse consequences from "cyber affairs" have also been reported,[12] with the injured partners emphasizing that being lied to was a major cause of their distress, and that cyber affairs were as emotionally painful to them as offline affairs.

In many romantic relationships, sexual exclusivity, that is, having sexual contact and commitment to one and only one partner at any given time, is an important expectation, and seen as an indicator of love.[13] However, non-traditional models of love are becoming more commonly practiced and recognized culturally and in the scientific and self-help literature. For example, some couples open their relationship up to multiple sexual partners typically after having negotiated parameters and limits such as always practicing safe sex and no emotional involvement with other sexual partners.[14] Still other partners practice consensual nonmonogamy in which relationship security is not limited to two. If you are wishing to explore polyamory, we encourage seeking the guidance of a self-help book that specializes in this area, such as Jessica Fern's *Polysecure*.[15] As Fern points out, significant preparation is recommended in navigating the transition from monogamy to polyamory, which creates irreversible changes individually and relationally, involving experiences of growth and loss. Ongoing communication of needs and expectations, as well as staying within the shared vision as it has been mutually defined will facilitate conditions for security in polyamorous relationships.

Reflection 8.1 Hurt

In my current relationship with my partner, when have/do I experience hurt? What happens? What do I feel? How do I then act toward my partner?

____

____

____

How have I/do I hurt my partner's feelings? How does my partner react? What effect has this event/these events had on our relationship?

____

____

____

What attempts, if any, do we make to repair the damage? How successful have those attempts been?

____

____

____

Please note that when you and your partner share your reflections, it is quite likely you may have differing "versions" of the same hurtful events. Partners tend to tell the story of a hurtful event from their own perspective. This is to be expected. Try hard to listen to your partner without jumping in with "corrections," justifications or to tell your own version of the story. Try to learn something new about your partner from listening to their feelings and experience. *The goal of this exercise is not for the two of you to* agree *on the events, but to hear and understand your differing experiences.*

Suggestions for dealing with hurt feelings will be offered in Chapter 10, Relationship Injury: How Can We Repair the Damage?

Guilt and Shame

As we think back over our interactions with partners, close friends and close family members, most of us recall clearly what it is like to feel guilty or ashamed about what we have done, or maybe failed to do. When we feel guilt or shame that is commensurate with the misdeed, we can use these feelings to help us make amends and change our behavior to prevent future hurt. Consider the following: "What we are and what we see ourselves as being seems to be constantly under construction and reconstruction, with the architects and remodeling contractors largely being those with whom we have close interactions."[16] How does this apply to you in your relationship? Are you willing to let your partner tell you when you have caused hurt or harm? Do you try to change your behavior to reduce the pain you cause your partner? For example, if your partner tells you that angry shouting is frightening, are you willing to express your anger less forcefully or loudly? Alternatively, are you willing to reduce your own pain by being straightforward and telling your partner which behaviors are hurtful? For example, if your partner frequently criticizes your mother, are you willing to tell them clearly, but respectfully, how much that hurts you? Oftentimes, partners are quick to let each other know if they are not pleased with the other's actions or lack of actions. However, some may go about that in ways that feel like a demolition, rather than remodeling. Sometimes, attempts at modifying yourself or your experience with your partner are constructive; other times it is not. Let's look more closely.

Guilt as a Motivator for Relationship Repair

Given that most people in close relationships feel at least some responsibility to care for and attend to the needs of their partners, causing harm (whether intentionally or unintentionally) is likely to create at least some guilt feelings in the partner who offends. Guilt in this sense can be very helpful, for it motivates us to take action to repair the damage. For example, when an offending partner expresses guilt and remorse to the person who has been hurt, the hurt person often feels reassured that the offender is *attending* to the relationship.[17]

Individuals vary in their responses to interpersonal wrongs; for example, some readers may react to everyday relationship hurts as serious violations, while others may appear unaffected by serious wrongdoing. Further, some people refuse to take responsibility for acts they clearly committed; others feel more than their warranted share of responsibility for events.[18] These variations usually link to differences in temperament, quality of earlier family environments, how interpersonal transgressions are viewed in your culture, experiences of discrimination and marginalization, and overall psychological wellbeing.

Guilt Versus Shame

Guilt is the emotion we feel when we know we have done something wrong. When we confess a wrongdoing, learn a lesson how to do it differently next time and change our behavior as the result of feeling guilty, then our experience of guilt has been constructive. The emotion of shame can also serve a useful purpose when it helps us realize we have behaved outside of a group norm or acted against our own moral values; for example, having betrayed or abused a partner.

However, when anger, disappointment or disgust with the whole self is intense and sustained over time, the experience of *shame* usually becomes unproductive. As one man recounted after having an affair: "I feel like I should club myself with a baseball bat." This man was *stuck* in unproductive shame, which took the form of self-loathing. It was so hard to believe that he could help his wife to forgive him, that he avoided her as much as possible, making the couple's road to recovery much longer and more painful. Unhelpful shame, such as this example, usually involves an overwhelming sense of being small and worthless in the eyes of others and is often accompanied by a desire to escape or hide from the situation. Some individuals unfortunately carry a chronic sense of shame from the way that they were reared (for example, from being the recipient of contempt, unfair criticism, humiliation or harsh punishment).[19] Sadly, such individuals report feeling unlovable and *flawed* to their core. Shame is often expressed with downcast eyes and drooping head. A shamed person may describe "losing face," blushing, "going hot" and having a pounding heart. Maybe you will recall feeling like this at some stage of your life?

As well as negative consequences for the person feeling deeply ashamed, shame can also lead to negative consequences for relationships. It can consume the person feeling ashamed so much that it prevents them from fully hearing and responding to their partner, who may be feeling sad, hurt or let down. Shame can hijack emotional connection by preventing a person from responding to any of their partner's needs. For example, partners with profound shame may protect themselves from feeling it by denying, blaming, retaliating or even raging, which is rarely helpful in close relationships.[20] Sometimes the distinction between guilt and shame is not really clear and the two emotions appear to overlap; the person feels a mix of guilt and shame; there is regret at what has been done along with feeling the self is essentially bad.

Thus, in summary,

> **It is valuable, even if at times painful, when feeling guilty or ashamed, to reflect responsibly on our actions, grow personally and repair damage to our relationships through sincere apology and consistent efforts to change our offending behavior (or lack of behavior).**

Showing concern for the impact of our actions on others, humility in admitting our mistakes and motivation to make repairs strengthens our relationships. By contrast, the negative impact of hurtful incidents is often made much worse by unproductive shame such as defensive denial, refusal to take responsibility and moving the blame onto someone else.

Before exploring the exercises on guilt and shame, let's look at Fredericka and Monty; a couple whose relationship had an intensely negative tone, fraught with some of the emotions we have introduced in this and previous chapters. We mention them now because they have inspired in us a trust that emotions such as guilt and shame can serve a purpose but need to be understood and navigated constructively. Through the transforming power of working with the social emotions of hurt, shame and guilt, couples *can* find love again. Chapter 10 will delve more deeply into the healing of relationship injury.

Fredericka and Monty: A Story About Finding Love Again

Fredericka, a German translator working in a home-based office, and Monty, a physicist also from mixed European descent, arrived in therapy on the brink of divorce after an initial meeting with their respective lawyers. They admitted that after pursuing individual therapy separately and a course of couple therapy that was unsuccessful, this was their last hope at attempting to make their relationship work. Their initial motive to work on their relationship was primarily for their children, aged 11 and 13 years, and a 17-year-old daughter from Fredericka's previous marriage. Monty and Fredericka agreed that their relationship had felt empty and loveless for years, including no demonstrations of physical affection and intimacy for over a decade. Unfortunately, that was the extent to which they could agree. Monty described Fredericka as prone to contemptuous angry tirades during which she would become incredibly disparaging of him. The household operated under a shroud of tension with himself and the children tiptoeing around to avoid the next outburst. Indeed, Fredericka acknowledged that she had fallen into a profound depression that had an irritable quality to it and was apparently resistant to treatment. Fredericka believed her depression was fueled by Monty's detachment and coldness. Her inability to access him came through in her spiteful description of him as "incapable of feeling." Yet it pained her to witness how effortlessly he joined with the children.

The Negative Cycle

This couple presented with marital distress and depression diagnosed by Fredericka's family physician. It is not uncommon for partners living in chronic distress in their relationships to experience symptoms of general psychological problems as well. These may include depression, anxiety, insomnia, stress and burn out, low self-esteem and even some physical symptoms, to name a few. This reflects how interconnected relationship functioning is with our general wellbeing.

FREDERICKA

The protesting partner who focused on tasks rather than feelings

Behaviors

Fredericka expressed her distress in angry tirades; She focused on tasks and "To Do" lists as proof of his love

Thoughts

"Relationships don't last. Monty is incapable of feeling. I don't have any impact on him"

Reactive emotions

Depressed and anxious about feeling helpless; Contempt for Monty hiding and keeping her at a distance

MONTY

The withdrawing partner with Fredericka, but closer with the kids

Behaviors

Monty detached from Fredericka emotionally; He and the kids tip toed around her irritable depression; He defended himself rationally and was critical of her

Thoughts

"Fredericka needs me to be strong and competent. My feelings and concerns will burden her. I need to protect myself from her anger"

Reactive emotions

Emotional numbness obscured desperation and exhaustion

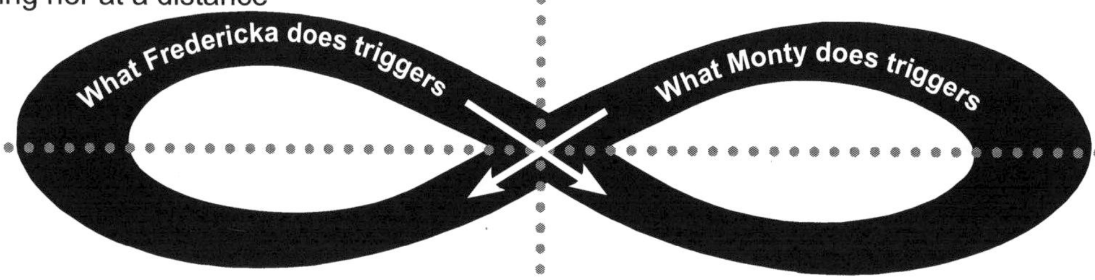

Core emotions (Fredericka)

Sad and lonely; Emptiness in the relationship; Shame for her angry outbursts; Panic that she was losing another man in her life

Unmet attachment needs (Fredericka)

To feel safe and secure in the relationship; Reassurance that she is lovable to Monty and that he is there for the long haul

Core emotions (Monty)

Hurt and attacked, fearful of Fredericka's anger; Sad that he couldn't make her happy despite his best efforts

Unmet attachment needs (Monty)

To feel truly known and loved by Fredericka; For there to be room for his feelings and needs in their relationship

Figure 8.1 Fredericka and Monty's relationship dance

Looking more closely at the dynamics of Fredericka and Monty's relationship helped them understand how their chasm evolved and how it maintained Fredericka's depression. Fredericka felt very alienated from Monty and their children. Her contemptuous outbursts were an attempt to get her distress through to him because she saw him as immovable and felt that she had no impact on him whatsoever. Another way Fredericka tried to get a response from Monty was by presenting him with a weekly "To Do" list of household maintenance and repair jobs. Monty liked the hands-on work and ability to please Fredericka in some way and she was temporarily settled by his completion of the list as a reflection of his love. However, as you might imagine, it was a hollow substitute for real connection. Underneath her angry tirades was a very sad, lonely person, pained by the image of herself as a dragon, which she saw in her family's eyes. Monty detached from her and aligned with the children to buffer himself from the impact of Fredericka's anger. Contrary to her experience, Fredericka *was* having a profound impact on Monty. His response to disengage from her helped him cope with how destroyed he felt every time they argued bitterly. Unfortunately it only reinforced Fredericka's experience that she had no way of getting a response from her husband, which fueled her pain and depression.

Previous Attachment Experiences

Fredericka and Monty had relatively happy childhoods and positive relationships with parents and siblings. Central to Fredericka's experience of relationship was her union at age 20 to her first husband who died in a sky-diving accident after only two years of marriage. She was devastated by this sudden loss and overwhelmed with being a young mother raising a child on her own. Her beliefs about the permanence of relationships were crushed. Essentially, it hurt so much to lose her young sweetheart that she decided not to allow herself to love that deeply again. Furthermore, she tried to make her life safe and predictable, even affecting her choice of a partner years later.

When she met Monty, Fredericka was looking for a predictable, steady person for herself and her child. She was initially comforted by their stable life and Monty's emotional containment. However, when Monty dealt with problems by withdrawing into himself and keeping her outside of his inner world, it evoked the feeling that she was losing another man in her life.

On Monty's side, early in their relationship he turned inward because he saw Fredericka as having suffered enough. He did not want to further burden her with his own issues and he minimized his needs. They laid down the pattern of Fredericka organizing and controlling their lives and Monty being the "rock" trying to provide predictability and stability, not leaving much room for a deep emotional connection between them.

Over time the panicky feeling that Fredericka was losing another man would morph into escalating, angry, desperate attempts to get a response from Monty. When these attempts proved unsuccessful, contempt and depression set into their lives. After Fredericka's depression was diagnosed, Monty became more convinced that there wasn't room for his own concerns in their relationship. He continued to keep his concerns locked away and focused his attention to shielding himself and the children from Fredericka's irritability.

Changing the Music, Changing the Dance

Fredericka and Monty presented for therapy in a highly conflictual state. Early sessions escalated quickly with Fredericka becoming loud and blaming and Monty adopting a defensive position in which he rationalized his actions, counter blamed and denied feeling anything at all. In sessions, the more Monty denied feelings, the more Fredericka ramped up her attempts to get through to him. After one particularly upsetting exchange, Monty looked worn out and disheartened. When the therapist reflected his state, Monty broke down in despair, opening up about how pained he was with the current state of their marriage. Fredericka stared in disbelief as Monty shared for the first time how much he hurt when she attacked him. He acknowledged that he hid behind an impenetrable wall of calm to protect himself, but he felt torn up inside. Fredericka's disbelief moved to a realization that her angry tirades really did have a profound impact on Monty and she moved from reactivity to compassion to shame. She also shared that Monty's self-sufficiency made her feel incredibly anxious because it shut her out of his world and confirmed that she was not needed. It was enlightening for Fredericka to hear that she was having an impact on him; this new experience was quite a contrast to her previous interpretation that his calm exterior meant he did not care about her distress.

These disclosures of their core emotions in their negative dance were a turning point in their relationship and it began to improve. There was a break in the tension between them. Fredericka reported feeling calmer and was more respectful; Monty relaxed and became more communicative than before. Their conflicts decreased and interactions shifted toward a positive working relationship, bringing great relief to the household. In EFT terms they had de-escalated their negative cycle, which then provided a foundation to create deeper emotional closeness and intimacy.

Embracing Attachment Needs

The relief Monty experienced when he first opened up to Fredericka gave him a taste of the potential connection between them. Maybe they did not have to be so alienated? Maybe Fredericka could become a source of support to him? Monty decided to give it a try. He began by expressing his immense sadness (*core emotion*), built up over years of not being able to satisfy Fredericka despite his hard work around the house. He confided, with some embarrassment, that his self-worth had taken a beating from being afraid of her anger and his perception that he was not a good husband. He reassured her he would not disappear emotionally in the future and he asked her to open her heart to him instead of railing against him when she needed him. He also shared that he was sad, lonely (*core emotion*) and tired of being self-sufficient. Monty said explicitly that he needed Fredericka, her love and comfort, and he asked her to help him make room for his feelings in their relationship (*attachment need*).

The process then shifted to Fredericka; it was now her turn to dig deeply into her inner world and work through her own blocks to intimacy. It was difficult (shameful) initially for Fredericka to hear how hurt and devastated Monty had been by her angry attempts to reach him. However, her desire to "be there" for Monty helped Fredericka use her shame as a motivator to focus instead on being receptive to his disclosures. She shared her shame and regret honestly, which he received graciously, creating some repair between them. Interestingly, Fredericka found that being needed by Monty gave her a sense of purpose in their relationship, which proved to be key in improving her own self-image and lifting her depression. Fredericka made the connection that her attempt to protect herself from getting hurt in the past, by vowing not to love deeply again, had played into her feelings of loneliness and depression in this relationship. She experienced sorrow (*core emotions*) about how deprived she had felt over the years and then she turned to Monty and revealed a mixture of emotions. She began with expressing a desire for a close bond (*attachment need*), moving beyond the utilitarian way she had approached him for attention in the past—the To Do lists. Fredericka also shared how exciting and incredibly scary (*core emotions*) it was for her to hope their relationship could be the best of both worlds: a place of intimacy and shelter. She asked for Monty's patience and reassurance as she took steps to depend on him emotionally (*attachment need*).

Although Monty was immediately compassionate to Fredericka's struggle, it took some time for this couple to navigate how to balance their needs so that Monty did not just set himself aside as in the past. However, they found their way by taking small steps and checking in with each other regularly, continuing these bonding moments. Little by little, their perseverance paid off. Their attachment bond and trust strengthened; the heavy weight lifted. Monty and Fredericka found joy in each other's company again, and even became affectionate and playful with one another. There was once again laughter in their home.

Let's look now at feelings of guilt and/or shame you may have in your own relationship.

Reflection 8.2 Guilt and shame

In my current relationship with my partner, when have I experienced guilt? What happened? What else did I feel? How did I then behave? What helped?

Have I felt chronic or unproductive shame in my life? Who triggered for me the feelings of being worthless, small or of little value? *This may be a painful reflection for you; take it slowly and be gentle with yourself.*

What did I want to do (e.g., hide away or retaliate with anger)? What happened then? What happens for me now as I recall those feelings?

Do I ever feel shame in my couple relationship? What evokes the feelings of shame?

What does my partner say or do that triggers feelings of shame in me? How do I typically behave? What impact does that have on my partner? Is it helpful?

Do I provoke feelings of shame in my partner? What is that like for them? Is it helpful? What am I really trying to achieve when I act in a way that makes my partner feel shamed?

Chapter 10 will further the reflection on relationship repair.

Table 8.1 Tips for dealing with guilt and shame

If you feel bad about something that you have done to your partner (or failed to do), it may help to:	
1. Find your courage	Create some time and space to reflect. Gather your courage to be honest with yourself.
2. What are you feeling guilty about?	Check in to see if you are feeling guilty about something you have done, such as causing hurt and pain, or unproductive shame about the flawed person that you perceive yourself to be at the core. *Where possible, try to draw out of your reflections a clear sense of what you* did *that was unhelpful, unkind, or thoughtless.* "I now regret that I did . . . (did not . . .)" rather than getting stuck in a bad feeling about who you *are*. Write a list if there are numerous deeds you feel badly about.
3. No blaming or minimizing	*Resist the temptation to relieve your bad feelings by blaming someone else or minimizing the significance of the event.* Stand up tall and acknowledge your mistake(s).
4. No shaming	*Recognize unproductive shame for what it is: anger and contempt turned inward on the self.* Reflect on where these shaming messages came from. Consider what it might be like to stop pouring anger and derision on yourself. Ask yourself: "Am I ready to focus now on how to *repair* what has been done and *prevent* future problems from recurring?"
5. Focus on repairing	*Consider how you could repair the damage.* What would you like to say to your partner? When offering an apology, make sure it is sincere, simple and stays focused on the event(s) you set out to talk about. Let your partner see your humility and genuine remorse. Keep the focus on your feelings of regret and guilt; when talking with your partner express your desire to make amends. *MAKE IT CLEAR THAT YOU HAVE CONCERN FOR THE PAIN YOU HAVE CAUSED*
6. Be patient for forgiveness	*Accept that you do not have the right to demand that your partner forgives you.* You could *ask* your partner to forgive you; remember, however, it may be too hard for your partner to do so right away. You may have to wait for your partner's forgiveness. (Further discussion about forgiveness will follow in Chapter 10.)
7. What does your partner need to forgive you?	*Ask what you can do to help your partner feel better and forgive you.* Show interest in your partner's responses but don't try to force him or her to feel or do something that does not feel authentic. Show your humility, curiosity and respect.

Jealousy

Romantic jealousy typically occurs when our relationship is perceived as being threatened, whether real or imagined. Events that trigger jealous feelings vary from person to person and couple to couple. These triggers might include events such as smiling at, flirting with or touching a third party, through to talking about or meeting up with ex-partners or other people who could be considered "eligible" as future partners. As noted earlier in regards to the hurt of infidelity, online relationships have more power to trigger distress in your partner than some Internet users would want to acknowledge. Thus, we encourage you, if you engage in online activities such as cybersex, viewing pornography and flirting, to accept that these activities may trigger jealousy and other intense negative emotions for your partner. Recent evidence has also highlighted the potentially negative impact of Social Networking Sites in evoking mistrust and jealousy.[21]

Positives and Negatives

Jealousy, in small amounts and thoughtfully expressed, may be considered useful to relationships. The natural urge of jealousy is to protect the relationship by preventing third-party intrusion. So, a "stab" of jealousy may remind you how important your partner is, not to take your partner for granted, and how essential it is to guard the relationship from intrusion.[22] Jealousy, however, is not always limited to a simple stab. A range of destructive consequences have been found in response to jealous feelings, including fearful or angry rumination, depressive withdrawal, obsessive surveillance, verbal aggression and even physical violence.[23,24] Jealousy, especially when it triggers strong feelings of fear and anger, can take couples down a destructive path. This kind of jealousy can be viewed as an expression of insecurity in the couple's bond, both from the standpoint of the partner feeling jealous, as well as the partner engaging in behaviors that spark jealousy.

If your relationship is vulnerable to jealousy, it's time to stop and reflect. Ask yourself what is this really about? Am I prone to feeling jealousy or triggering it in my relationship? Is the jealousy I feel to do with insecurity or instability in our relationship today or related to the past? Sometimes, jealousy today is tangled up in events of yesterday. For instance, if you were betrayed in a previous relationship, it would be natural for you to be watchful and sensitive to any "hints" of betrayal in future relationships. In another case, a woman whose father had multiple affairs and who herself had experienced the unwanted attention of a number of older men in her work place, found it hard to trust her husband when he became a business executive. Her jealousy aroused impatience in her husband because, from his perspective, her suspicions were groundless.

If you are aware that your earlier life experience has influenced your current ability to trust your partner, it will be useful to try to tease apart and keep distinct your previous experience and your current partner's behavior. It will also be helpful to *let your partner know of your sensitivities*. If you are a partner to someone who is prone to jealousy, *think about what you can say or do that will give your partner assurance of your commitment* to your relationship. The more you are able to give your partner reason to trust you, the more they will be able to overcome the insecurity and fear that can be associated with jealousy.

Reflection 8.3 Jealousy

In my current relationship with my partner, have I felt jealous? What evoked my jealousy?

____

____

What else did I feel? How did I then cope and behave? What impact did that have on my partner?

____

____

____

What helped me feel better or made me feel worse?

____

____

____

Does my partner experience jealousy related to my interactions with other people? How does my partner typically behave when feeling jealous? What has my partner told me about those feelings?

____

____

____

What have I done that has triggered jealous feelings for my partner?

____

____

If I look closely at my motives, was I trying to send my partner a message through my triggering behavior? If so, what emotions inside of me were being expressed through my behavior?

____

____

What have we found helpful as a way of dealing with jealousy in our relationship?

____

____

See Chapter 9 for the story of Brad and Janine, a couple who struggle with the issue of jealousy and find a way to create security together.

The following table suggests some tips for handling jealousy in romantic relationships.

Table 8.2 Tips for handling jealousy in romantic relationships

1. Prevention is best	In loving relationships, partners do not deliberately provoke pain in the other. If you know your partner is prone to jealousy, talk it over so that you know clearly what events they find hard to handle. With this understanding you can choose actions that do not provoke distress. For example: "I'm OK with you talking about your 'ex', but I don't like it when I hear *after the fact* that you have met up with them for lunch." You might decide as a couple that if you do intend to see your ex, you will always tell your partner first of the arrangement. Collaborate together to work on good outcomes (e.g., "What would be helpful for you? What can I do to ease your concerns?").

2. Jealousy means you care	*If your partner has a tendency to feel jealous,* try to frame this in your mind as a reflection of how very important you are to your partner. If they didn't care what you did and whom you spent time with, your relationship might not be considered very valuable to your partner.
3. What are you feeling?	*If you feel a stab of jealousy, pause and note it.* Check what is happening to evoke your feeling. Slow down and acknowledge other feelings related to the jealousy. Is this a stab of jealousy that reminds you of how important your partner is? Or do feelings such as hurt, insecurity or inadequacy get triggered intensely?
4. Slow down and check your assumptions	*If you feel jealous and notice that you are starting to get tense,* angry or otherwise distressed, work at staying as calm as possible. Take some deep breaths to slow down your thoughts and actions. Remind yourself that you may have misinterpreted the situation. Ask, without implied blame, to discuss and clarify the situation.
5. Acknowledge your jealous feelings	*If you decide to talk to your partner,* keep the focus on your experience rather than accusing him or her of bad behavior. Otherwise the conversation could easily spiral down in a cycle of attack/defend. So go carefully and keep your focus on sharing your vulnerable feelings rather than blaming. For example, "When I heard you laughing on the phone with your ex tonight, I felt quite a stab of jealousy. I know you don't like hearing me say this but I would rather tell you about it than brood endlessly over it." Here the experience of jealousy is honestly expressed without accusations. Give your partner a chance to respond supportively.
6. Keep your reactions in check	*If your partner is telling you about jealous feelings, it can trigger strong reactions inside of you.* You may feel unfairly accused or attacked, and very frustrated if you have been accused often before. You can help diffuse jealous feelings by acknowledging the difficult feelings your partner is having (even if they are not grounded in reality). *If you have given your partner cause to feel jealous in the past* (e.g., through flirting, using Internet porn, or having secret communications with ex partners), then you will need to actively help your partner recover from these hurts, as mentioned earlier in this chapter.
7. Staying on alert	Following negative relationship events such as affairs, hurt or jealous partners are often somewhat embarrassed to report that they continue to engage in *"surveillance" behaviors* (e.g., checking their partner's mobile phones or whereabouts). While this is understandable in the aftermath of a betrayal, prolonged use of these strategies will likely result in frustration for your partner and will be counterproductive for you. It is better to share your fears and insecurities and have your partner comfort you.

Sharing with Your Partner

When you and your partner are ready, set aside some time (or several times) to talk over your reflections.

- Use L-O-V-E conversations to get to understand each other better
- Take your time when expressing your feelings. Listen respectfully to what your partner has to share
- Watch out for negative interactions that could erupt from talking about these sensitive topics
- Read on to understand more about you, your partner and relationship success.

References

1. Guerrero, L., & Andersen, P. (1998). *The dark side of close relationships*. Mahwah, NJ: Lawrence Erlbaum.
2. Panalp, S., Fitness, J., & Fehr, B. (2018). The role of emotion in relationships. In A. Vangelisti & D. Perlman (Eds.), *Cambridge handbook of personal relationships* (pp. 256–270). Cambridge: Cambridge University Press.
3. Fincham, F. (2000). The kiss of the porcupines: From attributing responsibility to forgiving. *Personal Relationships, 7*, 1–23.
4. L'Abate, L. (1997). *The self in the family: A classification of personality, criminality, and psychopathology*. New York, NY: Wiley-Blackwell.
5. Eisenberger, N., Lieberman, M., & Williams, K. (2003). Does rejection hurt? An fMRI study of social exclusion. *Science, 302*, 290–292.
6. Panksepp, J. (2003). Feeling the pain of social loss. *Science, 302*, 237–239.
7. Akiyama, H., Antonucci, T., Takahashi, K., & Langfahl, E. S. (2003). Negative interactions in close relationships across the life span. *Journals of Gerontology: Series B: Psychological Sciences and Social Sciences, 58B*, 70–79.
8. Leary, M., & Springer, C. A. (2001). Hurt feelings: The neglected emotion. In R. Kowalski (Ed.), *Behaving badly: Aversive behaviours in interpersonal relationships* (pp. 151–175). Washington, DC: American Psychological Association.
9. Feeney, J. A. (2000). *Hurt feelings in couple relationships: Exploring the emotional experience*. Paper presented at the 10th International Conference on Personal Relationships, Brisbane, Australia.
10. Adler, R., Rosenfeld, L., & Towne, N. (1992). *Interplay: The process of interpersonal communication*. Fort Worth: Harcourt Brace Jovanovich College Publishers.
11. Feeney, J. A. (2004). Hurt feelings in couple relationships: Towards integrative models of the negative effects of hurtful events. *Journal of Social and Personal Relationships, 21*, 487–508.
12. Schneider, J. (2003). The impact of compulsive cybersex behaviours on the family. *Sexual Relationship Therapy: Special Cybersex, 18*, 329–354.
13. Buss, D. M., & Shackleford, T. K. (1997). From vigilance to violence: Mate retention tactics in married couples. *Journal of Personality and Social Psychology, 72*, 346–361.
14. Roloff, M. E., & Cloven, D. H. (1994). When partners transgress: Maintaining violated relationships. In M. Roloff & D.Clovehn (Eds.), *Communication and relational maintenance* (pp. 23–43). San Diego: Academic Press.
15. Fern, J. (2020). *Polysecure: Attachment, trauma, and consensual nonmonogamy*. Portland, OR: Thorntree Press.
16. Aron, A. (2003). Self and close relationships. In M. Leary & J. P. Tangney (Eds.), *Handbook of self and identity* (pp. 442–461). New York, NY and London: The Guilford Press.
17. Vangelisti, A. L., & Sprague, R. J. (1998). Guilt and hurt: Similarities, distinctions and conversational strategies. In P. A. Andersen & L. K. Guerrero (Eds.), *Handbook of communication and emotion: Research, theory, applications and contexts* (pp. 123–154). San Diego, CA: Academic Press.
18. Vangelisti, A., & Crumley, L. (1998). Reactions to messages that hurt: The influence of relational contexts. *Communication Monographs, 65*, 173–196.
19. Greenberg, L., & Goldman, R. (2008). *Emotion-focused couples therapy: The dynamics of emotion, love and power*. Washington, DC: American Psychological Association.
20. Tangney, J. P. (1995). Self-relevant emotions. In M. Leary & J. P. Tagney (Eds.), *Handbook of self and identity* (pp. 384–400). New York, NY and London: Teh Guildford Press.
21. Muise, A., Christofides, E., & Desmarais, S. (2009). More information than you ever wanted to know—does Facebook bring out the green-eyed monster of jealousy? *Cyber Psychology and Behavior, 12*(4), 441–444.
22. Pines, A. (1992). Romantic jealousy: Five perspectives and an integrated approach. *Psychotherapy: Theory, Research, Practice and Training, 29*, 675–683.
23. Babcock, J. C., Costa, D. M., Green, C. E., & Eckhardt, C. I. (2004). What situations induce intimate partner violence? A reliability and validity study of the "proximal antecedents to violent episodes (PAVE)" scale. *Journal of Family Psychology, 18*(3), 433–442.
24. Wigman, S. J. A., Graham-Kevan, N., & Archer, J. (2008). Investigating sub-groups of harassers: The roles of attachment, dependency, jealousy, and aggression. *Journal of Family Violence, 23*, 557–568.

CHAPTER 9

REBUILDING OUR BOND

If you have been reading and following the reflective exercises up to this point, we hope you have a fuller understanding of the dynamics of your relationship. Chapter 2 and 3 developed the idea that your relationship is an attachment bond to meet your needs for intimacy, security, and support. Chapter 4 helped you notice how you cope and act in the dance that both triggers you and further ensnares you and your partner into negative interactions. Chapters 5, 6 and 8 focused on helping you tune into and share your emotional worlds, first by identifying the reactive emotions that drive your negative cycle (e.g., reactive or defensive anger, anxious controlling, panicky shutting down, resigned helplessness or depression), and distinguishing them from the core emotions that help you diffuse it (e.g., sadness about the hurts, fear of not measuring up or being abandoned). You probably noticed that when you express those softer core emotions, they evoke more compassion from your partner. We also hope that reading and sharing your reflections about particularly sensitive emotions such as hurt, guilt, shame and jealousy in Chapter 8 brought you closer. In Chapter 7 you likely discovered that there is a reason for the negative behaviors in your interactions that relate to you and your partner's fears in the relationship (e.g., losing the connection, making a mistake, disappointing yourself or your partner). You will probably have discovered aspects of yourself and your partner that have been hidden away for a long time. You may be aware now that your partner is afraid of disconnecting from you or evoking your disappointment. You may also be aware that your partner can feel desperate at times and intends to reconnect or freezes in those moments when the two of you get caught in the negative dance to avoid making things worse. We hope that these realizations have helped you to see the benevolent intentions in undesirable actions.

Recognizing your feelings and understanding the dynamics of your relationship probably enables you to see yourself and your partner in a more compassionate light. Many of our clients have expressed that they are tuning into themselves and each other more deeply than before, seeing the vulnerable emotions that are beyond their guards of self-protection. Recognizing the bid for connection that underlies a complaint, or the fear of inadequacy that drives a person to withdraw, offers a new lens from which to view your partner and relate to them. As this lens helps you see new aspects of your partner (their doubts, fears, or insecurities), it likely pulls for different responses in you than the old negative cycle. In this chapter we help you to build on these new ways of experiencing and relating to each other. We will revisit those vulnerable emotions, help you to go deeper with them so you can tap into your basic needs and longings in this relationship, share and respond caringly to each other.

How Do You Know You Are Ready to Go Deeper?

Typically, if a couple is able to grasp the dynamics of their relationship and understand how their own and their partner's actions, intentions, reactive emotions, and core emotions fit together to ensnare

DOI: 10.4324/9781003009481-9

them in negative interactions, the level of conflict and tension between them diminishes. We believe this decrease in conflict or tension occurs because self-reflecting and expressing while being open to your partner's disclosures helps you experience the relationship differently, and, in turn, gain a new perspective on each other. We hope that working through the exercises together in the previous chapters has helped you see each other in a new light so that you can feel a sense of calm, warmth and stability in your day-to-day lives.

You might be wondering what additional work there is to do, because the atmosphere between you feels so much better. Most couples feel that diffusing their conflict is a major milestone in their process. Although it provides relief from some negative feelings and experiences, and partners get along better, it does not in itself deepen the relationship. Put simply, the absence of negative provides a platform for going deeper but does not necessarily create a more intimate or secure connection. Partners need to bring more of their vulnerable emotions and needs into their conversations to deepen the bond between them.

It is natural to feel cautious or nervous about revisiting those softer core emotions, delving deeper and becoming closer. However, if you feel dread about it, perhaps it is a valid indicator that your relationship is not quite ready. Readiness to go deeper is usually contingent on a growing sense of emotional safety, less friction or tension, and a real sense of partnership and goodwill developing between you. You can think of this as a prerequisite. It might be helpful to slow down and first do a check on some typical indicators that the negative dance is no longer in control of your relationship. A reduction in the frequency and intensity of your negative dance is the prime indicator of readiness to delve deeper. As you might imagine, you need to feel a certain amount of confidence that taking these emotional risks will not make things worse between you or spiral you down into the negative cycle again.

Reflection 9.1 Relationship stability checklist

Check off the following indicators of relationship stability as they apply to you and partner.

1. ___ I believe we each have our own part to play in the sequence of steps in our negative interactions.
2. ___ The nickname for our negative cycle is ____________________
3. ___ I can describe my part in the negative dance as ____________________
4. ___ I can describe my partner's part in the negative dance as ____________________
5. ___ I know these things I do or don't do (behaviors) that trigger my partner

   ____
6. ___ I know that these behaviors from my partner trigger me

   ____
7. ___ I know that these reactive emotions of mine fuel our negative dance

   ____
8. ___ I know that these reactive emotions of my partner's fuel our negative dance

   ____

9. ___ I know these core emotions are stirred up for me in our negative dance

____

10. ___ I know that these core emotions are stirred up for my partner in our negative dance

____

11. ___ We have strategies for interrupting or diffusing the negative dance, such as

____

12. ___ It seems like we can be more flexible during disagreements.

13. ___ We are now more able to share our feelings.

14. ___ I believe our problems are caused by the negative dance we *both* contribute to and suffer from.

15. ___ We are no longer blaming each other as much in conversations.

16. ___ I understand that my benevolent intention in the negative dance is

____

17. ___ I understand that my partner's benevolent intention in the negative dance is

____

18. ___ We are arguing less than we were in the past.

19. ___ We feel more relaxed in each other's presence.

20. ___ Our relationship feels more stable than before.

21. ___ When we do get caught in the negative cycle, we are able to recover more quickly than before.

Look in Appendix A for a Second Copy

If you are checking most of the items listed, you are likely ready to move onto deepening your bond. If you are not able to check most of the items, notice if your unchecked items relate to behaviors (items 1 to 6), emotions (items 7 to 13) or the intentions you are ascribing (items 14 to 17). Items 18 to 21 reflect the typical outcomes of increased awareness in the areas of behaviors, emotions and attributions. Revisit Chapter 4 to gain a better understanding of behaviors that trigger your negative cycle, Chapters 5 or 6 for help distinguishing between reactive emotions that fuel the negative cycle and core emotions that diffuse it and Chapter 7 to discover the benevolent attachment intentions underlying your actions in the negative cycle.

A Roadmap for Building a Secure Bond

Once you have established that there is enough stability in your relationship, the next phase along this journey is to deepen and strengthen your attachment bond; that is, to create a *secure* attachment bond.

In this next stage, partners who typically withdraw in the negative cycle, learn to come forward and bring their concerns, fears and insecurities to their partner instead of shutting them down and being alone with them. They discover that when they confide their uncertainties, it can provide a huge sense of relief and breaks down the isolation they've been living. When a partner can show their hurts and fears rather than distancing, the other partner can see their vulnerability and respond compassionately. Withdrawing partners can feel more whole and in charge of their life as they actively take part in expressing themselves in their relationship and directly asking for what they need to feel securely attached.

Partners who adopt a protesting position in their relationships often have a sense of what they need and yearn for. In this part of the process they discover how to put their needs across in a more vulnerable way that invites responsiveness. For people who pursue, it is showing their soft underbelly that draws their partner close. Again, it can really break down the sense of abandonment and loneliness to take the risk to be vulnerable and find that you can depend on your partner to come close and be there for you.

We would now like to introduce you to Janine and Brad whose story illustrates how a couple can take these steps of risking emotionally to rebuild their attachment bond. We will start by describing their relationship at the beginning of therapy and some of their relevant life experiences. We will then describe their negative dance and highlight how they managed to gain control of it. Finally, we will show you how they risked sharing their attachment fears and needs to transform their relationship bond into a warm, loving, secure haven.

Janine and Brad: Creating Security Together

The Problem

Janine and Brad were a delightful cisgender heterosexual Australian couple of British ancestry who presented for help with their relationship. Underneath their attractive, successful exterior lay deep wells of struggle and suffering. For Brad (a tall, good-looking sales manager), Janine was beautiful, intelligent and desirable to him, but there was nevertheless a nagging sense of unease that she did not give as much of her heart and soul to their relationship as he did. He never felt really sure that she was with him 100 percent. Some nights he even lay awake worrying about whether she might leave him one day; this would occur especially after they had been out together in the evening. When they were out at parties, Janine would be a bit flirtatious, nothing outrageous, but nevertheless flirtatious enough to deeply disturb Brad.

Furthermore, every conversation about her party behavior ended in fighting; these fights would result in days of strained and painful silence between them. Both hated the fighting, the silences, the feeling of distance that would be evident between them. But . . . both also felt locked into their individual perceptions of the problem; each felt right and justified to be angry. Both felt wedded to their own construction of reality, and could not let go of their individual positions long enough to really understand what was going on for the other.

For Brad, Janine behaved inappropriately when they were out and he wanted her to stop. He also deeply resented any suggestion from her that he was being jealous, possessive, controlling, overly sensitive or difficult. Hearing each of these adjectives directed toward him, resulted in Brad feeling belittled and small (though Janine did not know this), which led to angry rumination that went on for days. They had fought bitterly many times over Janine's choice of every one of these words. For Brad it was unbearably painful, even to the point of sometimes evoking stormy tears for him, to hear her suggest that this problem was all in his mind.

Janine (an attractive school teacher), on the other hand, was amazed at Brad's reactions and frankly could not see what all the fuss was about. His criticism of her after parties became predictable, exhausting and downright annoying. She warmly acknowledged that he was a wonderful man, someone she loved and admired, but she had to admit that this issue was very hard to bear. Further, she could not really understand why he mulled over the question of her commitment to their relationship. "I've always been my own person. I need my individuality; I don't know what you are worrying about?" would be the gist of her comments in response to his complaints, expressed over and over again in wearying conversations that never really got resolved.

The Negative Cycle

After Janine and Brad had worked with their couple therapist for a while, they came to understand an important piece of information; namely, *what happened at parties was important, but what was more important was* what happened between them *when they tried to talk about what happened at parties*. Janine and Brad were able (after much hard work and efforts to listen to each other) to realize that they were caught in a predictable, painful and negative cycle of interaction that kept going around and around. Essentially, it went like this: the more Brad criticized Janine for her "flirting" and the more he questioned her commitment to their relationship, the more she felt controlled, frustrated and angry. The more controlled, frustrated and angry Janine felt, the more she tried to deal with these feelings by denying the need for his concerns about her party behaviors and her commitment to the relationship, resulting in more hurt, anger and suspicions for Brad. The more hurt he felt, the more he pursued and criticized. Thus, a feedback loop was now firmly in place, with each partner feeling caught and unable to move. Brad and Janine were stuck.

This negative dance (or feedback loop) was telling a story, a story of very painful emotions and unmet attachment needs. Their negative cycle had become self-sustaining, because the more this couple struggled with their problem, the more hurt and frustrated each became. The negative cycle of interactions both expressed and fueled their attachment distress.

Previous Attachment Experiences

To understand Brad and Janine's distress in more depth, their therapist asked some questions about their experiences in earlier close relationships and learned that Brad had been married previously, with a son whom he loved dearly. Fourteen years into the marriage, his wife unexpectedly had an affair and left him, taking their son with her, and demanding large amounts of money for his maintenance. Brad was so shocked and surprised; he admitted that it took him years to accept what had happened. Brad had also experienced adversity in his growing-up years; his father was a heavy drinker and was inconsistent in interactions with Brad. Some days he was friendly, almost demanding of Brad's time and company; other days he was intoxicated, unreasonable and violent. Brad's mother did her best, but she was often helpless and afraid. For Brad, there had never been a close relationship in his life that felt really safe. To be watchful and alert for danger was the only way he knew how to survive.

Janine, on the other hand, had also been married before, to a man who left her for another woman. The eventual separation was amicable enough, but it did nothing to build up her confidence in men or marriage. Her parents had also had a very unhappy marriage and, sadly, her mother had died of a chronic disease when Janine was in her teens. Janine reported, "I learned early to look after myself, to make my own fun and to go my own way."

In the light of earlier comments in this book about the development of security or insecurity through experiences in close relationships, it is not hard to see how Brad and Janine had ended up in

JANINE
The Withdrawing Partner

Behaviors
Janine avoided conversations about their relationship and defended herself when Brad accused her of flirting

Thoughts
"He mulls over everything little thing. I don't get what all the fuss is about!"

Reactive emotions
Frustration with all the questions and accusations; Annoyed by feeling controlled

BRAD
The Protesting Partner

Behaviors
Brad raised his issues of concern about their relationship by confronting her and accusing her of flirting

Thoughts
"She doesn't get how much I hate her flirting. She doesn't care how upset I get"

Reactive emotions
Frustration and brooding anger about accusations of jealousy; Anxiety she would suddenly leave

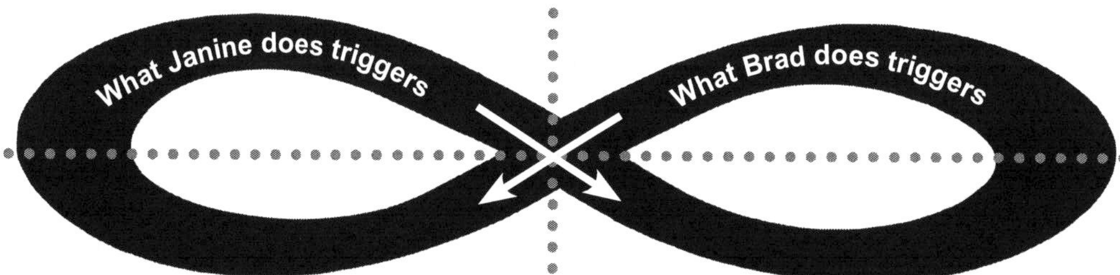

Core emotions
Fear of being controlled or overwhelmed by Brad's needs

Unmet attachment needs
To feel loved and safe in the relationship, with space to be herself

Core emotions
Fear she was less invested in their relationship than he was; Hurt that she didn't understand him

Unmet attachment needs
To feel safe and secure that he mattered to Janine and was loved by her

Figure 9.1 Janine and Brad's relationship dance

so much emotional distress. You can probably see anxiety in Brad's experience and behavior. He felt uneasy that Janine might let him down; that she might cause him harm, and yet he wanted her so much to be close and to love him unconditionally. He felt ambivalent. The unpredictable and at times violent experiences of his childhood, combined with the unexpected collapse of his marriage had *understandably* left him in serious doubt about his worth as a person and the safety of close relationships. "Other people let you down, they always do" was his sad conclusion about relationships. Unfortunately, his angry rumination and hostile remarks about Janine's behavior was getting perilously close to bringing about the very thing Brad feared most, that she would leave him.

You can probably also see discomfort with closeness in Janine's way of being in romantic relationships. Although she felt reasonably confident about herself and was not plagued with doubts that Brad would leave her, Janine nevertheless felt overwhelmed and crowded by Brad's need for closer connection, for more reassurance and expressed commitment. For Janine, it was *understandable* that she felt this way; the adults in her life with whom she had had close ties had let her down, certainly not always deliberately, but, nevertheless, in ways that left Janine acutely aware that other people are not always willing or able to be reliable, nor is it wise to depend on them entirely. The safest person to depend on is yourself had been her ticket to psychological survival.

Embracing Attachment Needs

Brad and Janine both brought to this relationship unmet attachment needs. For Brad, although he may not have realized it consciously, he nevertheless desperately needed to feel loved, reassured, important and safe. Similarly for Janine, she too needed to feel safe and secure, that a partner could be there for her in a supportive and reliable way, and that closeness did not have to mean surrendering an individual identity. Secure attachment bonds lead to flexible and comfortable space between two partners. The distance between these two people did not feel quite right, and it certainly was not flexible. For Brad, there was a perception of too much distance; for Janine, there was not enough. Brad pursued for more closeness, while Janine withdrew for more space.

Janine's behavior at parties and reticence to give Brad frequent verbal assurances of her commitment touched a deep place of pain for him; this pain could be thought of as his unmet attachment needs. Touching this sensitive place evoked core feelings of fear and unworthiness in him, to which he reacted by experiencing reactive emotions of anger and desperation. His anger was expressed in critical comments and defensive remarks. Essentially, in an attempt to control his own deep pain and unmet attachment needs, Brad was desperately trying to control Janine's behavior.

Similarly, for Janine, Brad's criticism and pursuit touched a deep place of unease for her (her unmet attachment needs for safety and security), which evoked a core fear of being engulfed and controlled, to which she reacted by becoming either aloof and ultra reasonable ("There is nothing for you to be worrying about!") or angry and defensive ("For goodness' sake, just stop trying to possess me!"). Thus, in attempting to change how she felt, Janine was actually trying to change Brad, by seeking to diminish his concerns and fears.

What this couple was experiencing is what so many distressed couples experience; namely, reactions to unmet attachment needs in one triggering reactions to unmet attachment needs in the other. Brad and Janine were not lacking in sexual attraction, ability to share household jobs, capacity to enjoy friendly outings, or communication skills to talk about day-to-day problems or their dreams and hopes for the future. Rather, they were struggling with intense fear of being unworthy and abandoned, and grasping for some sense of security. Unfortunately, their reactions in the negative dance brushed up against the painful sensitivity of their unmet attachment needs.

Changing the Music, Changing the Dance

Sue Johnson, the developer of EFT for couples, says that *emotions are the music of the attachment dance*. Emotions move us to reach for what we need; sometimes, however, emotions overwhelm us, leading to further distress for our partners and ourselves. Understanding, validating and meeting the attachment needs of our partners changes the music and as the music changes, so too does the dance.

Brad and Janine were very successful in changing their music and their dance. Painstakingly at first, but later more easily, they succeeded in slowing down their reactions to each other and instead created a place to listen with more openness to the troubling experiences of their pasts and the ongoing pain in their hearts. Instead of seeing each other as the enemy, they came to understand that their negative cycle of interaction was really their enemy. They learned to be more aware of what was driving their own reactions and also what impact their reactions were having on each other. Little by little, they helped each other to stop their previously predictable interactions, to step off their well-worn path, to take some risks to engage in new interactions and thus create a new and positive relationship.

With some help from their therapist, each partner was courageous enough to look into the other's face and quietly and clearly express attachment fears and longings. In learning to understand and effectively express their own vulnerable feelings (in place of frustration and anger), they realized that they no longer needed to concentrate on controlling or changing the other. In this new place of safety that they created for each other, they were able to soothe each other's pain, reassure each other's fears and support each other's longings.

Brad was able to talk about how he felt at parties when Janine was flirting; how he was swept back into feeling like the watchful boy who might be hurt at any moment. Janine, no longer hearing criticism and attack, was now able to hear this information and see her partner in a whole new light. He was vulnerable now, no longer a controlling and intrusive force to resist. Brad listened with new ears to Janine's description of how caged and cramped she felt to have him pressing for more commitment and closeness. She was able to express her love and devotion to him, but this time it was accompanied by a quiet and heartfelt request for him to trust her, that she had no intention of ever letting him down. Brad, no longer feeling so anxious and watchful, felt reassured that Janine was in this relationship for the long term; and further he was able to see her as distinct and separate from both his ex-wife and his father.

Toward the end of their therapy, they found new solutions for their old problems. They were able to comfortably discuss the next party and how they would manage it *together*; they found new solutions for old problems with his son, and her career. They had learned to tune into each other and express their attachment needs. Janine and Brad were now listening to new music; they had created a new dance! A phone call at 18 months' follow-up indicated that they were going from strength to strength.

As with Janine, for partners who typically withdraw, this stage is a process of *coming forward, engaging, showing yourself and your needs, putting two feet into the relationship*. For partners who typically protest, like Brad, it involves taking the risk to *express feelings and needs from a soft, heartfelt place, and showing your vulnerability*.

The moving story of Brad and Janine can remind us that reaching for and responding to each other's needs can *transform your relationship bond*. It can become a place of safety and security where you can *lean into each other. Together you have the ability to create a safe place to land with each other and know that you always have each other's back*.

Relationship Bonding Conversations: Going Deeper into Core Emotions and Needs

Setting the Stage

We have two main recommendations as you enter into this part of the process that focuses on expanding and deepening your emotional awareness. First, we suggest that your conversations follow a particular rhythm in which one partner does the majority of self-reflecting, sharing, and expressing, while the other partner listens intently without interrupting or expressing their own perspective (recall the tips for L-O-V-E conversations). For the expressing partner, it provides the time and space to unfold your experience more fully. For the listening partner, this spaciousness takes the pressure off the need to respond right away, jump in to provide solutions or other actions that may interrupt your partner's sharing. So, initially, the process will feel lopsided, with one person in an expressing role and the other in a listening role. However, the roles will then reverse in future conversations; so that ultimately both of you feel you can share your full experience and be heard.

Second, if one of you has typically taken the role of initiating conversations in the past (typically this would be the person who adopts a pursuing or protesting position), it is best if the other one (typically in the withdrawing position) begins the conversation at this stage. The rationale is that getting this conversation off on a different foot by the person who is less likely to initiate (regardless of which three relationship cycles you identify with) explicitly creates an opportunity to shift the old dynamic into a new dance. In time, we expect that you will both feel comfortable to initiate these conversations and that they will unfold in a natural, fluid way. They will become a source of intimacy and closeness.

For Partners in the Withdrawing Position

As the expressing partner it is very important to be mindful of focusing your reflections on yourself and expressing *your own feelings*, experiences, and needs; it is not about blaming your partner or making them responsible for your suffering or your happiness. In fact, by doing the work to tune into yourself at a deep level, you are taking ownership of your emotions and doing your part to actively shape the relationship. For some, it will feel like putting your whole self into the relationship for the first time.

Let's take some time now to look at the long-term effect of negative cycles, which includes both your partner's way of trying to reach you, perhaps with anger and criticism, and your response of withdrawing, avoiding, defending or giving in. Most people find that there is a significant emotional cost to themselves after years of the negative cycle playing out over and over. There can be a tendency to be so watchful of not letting down your partner that you ignore your own feelings and lose touch with them. This may even be a pattern you established long before you met your current partner but continues into this relationship. You may keep quiet about certain opinions or feelings and accommodate because you don't feel emotionally safe to express them. So better to keep things smooth between you and your partner. But the cost is that you aren't seen. Perhaps it doesn't feel like there is room for your feelings and needs if your partner is often bringing their issues to you. Or bringing them to you in a way that seems more urgent than your own.

Also, it is painful to get the message that you are disappointing your partner and getting it wrong. Or to feel that you are somehow not enough to meet your partner's needs. Thus, shutting down can be a way of protecting yourself from this painful message and the feelings of inadequacy that can come from it. We recognize that shutting yourself down and avoiding certain topics may have felt like the best solution at the time. However, the cost to doing so is that you are alone with these painful feelings that will continue to sit inside of you until you get a chance to express them, be heard and feel cared for. This next conversation is a way to create the space to give voice to feelings you may have locked away. It also gives your partner the opportunity to know and understand you better, so they can respond to your needs in the relationship and help you feel more secure.

Some key questions to ask yourself are: What has it been like for me to walk around in this relationship feeling . . .

- so afraid of being inadequate or a disappointment to you?
- afraid of your disapproval or anger?
- so ashamed of making a mistake that I'd rather not put myself out there?
- like I have to silence myself, so I don't burden you?
- sad and lonely because I don't think I deserve you?
- hurt because no one has ever really accepted me?

As you read these statements slowly, notice and allow any emotions that emerge as you ask yourself the question. Try to turn the volume down on any internal voices that tend to move you away from your feelings by minimizing, explaining away, analyzing, invalidating or telling you this is useless. Notice and acknowledge reactive emotions that creep in but try to move through them and continue looking for more core, vulnerable emotions. If you touch into core vulnerable emotions, turn the volume up on them. It is common to experience sorrow about how lonely and painful it has been for you to carry around these difficult emotions about your relationship. It might sound something like this:

> This fear can be so paralyzing for me at times. I want so much to be a good partner and I try really hard at it, so when I keep getting it wrong, it is very painful. I walk around in this relationship feeling worthless to you and that is so devastating.

Just make room for whatever core emotions emerge and try to meet them with compassion. If you stay with your emotions long enough, there is often a turning point in accepting your feelings as legitimate and a conviction to be more true-to-yourself. A feeling something like "I deserve to feel good about myself in this relationship" emerges. As you stay with your process, notice if your emotions begin to shift toward self-acceptance. It might sound something like this:

> I have felt like such a failure and when I think about that I feel incredibly sad. When I stop to think about it, I realize how demoralizing it has been for me to feel so small. I begin to feel some anger, at myself, for letting myself get so low. I don't want to live like that anymore . . . like I'm not good enough.

Continue to stay with your emotions as they ebb and flow and notice if they point you to what you need to feel better in this relationship. The path to your deeper relationship needs is through your core emotions. Follow your emotions and see where they take you. Ask yourself:

What would help me with this feeling of ________________________ (e.g., failure, inadequacy, loneliness, worthlessness, insecurity that you don't truly accept me or don't really want me)? What do I long for from my partner to feel secure?

Common Attachment Needs Expressed by Our Clients[1]

Identify two or three that ring most true for you:

- To be accepted for who I am
- To be affirmed by you

- For you to reflect good things about me
- To feel close to you
- To feel valued and important to you
- To feel cherished
- To feel loved by you
- To feel like I add value to your life
- To feel acknowledged and appreciated for my efforts
- To feel reassured that you really want to hear my feelings
- To know you are there for me
- To feel true partnership in life together
- To feel safe with you
- To feel taken care of
- To be comforted, hugged or held.

If you imagine expressing your needs to your partner, an example of how it could sound is:

> I think I really need to show myself in our relationship more, so I don't end up feeling like I'm second to you. That feels risky for me, but I'm willing to risk it because it feels so much better to be true to myself. When I do that, I really need to know that you will accept me for who I am. I know that we do things differently, and that's OK, but it doesn't mean that I'm 'less than.' I need some reassurance from you that you want the 'real' me—not just the person who pleases you.

The following guided reflection offers prompts to support you through the process we have described.

Reflection 9.2 Guided reflection for partners in the withdrawing position

____

(name)

1. How has the negative dance hurt or taken a toll on you? Be specific.
   Take time with this question and allow yourself to check in and notice what you feel inside. (Possible examples include physically carrying tension in specific parts of your body, losing touch with yourself, how your mood might be affected, or your self-confidence being eroded.)

   ____

   ____

2. If you have dealt with challenges at work, with family, or in your relationship on your own, how has that been for you?
   What have been the benefits of handling things on your own?

   ____

   ____

3. What have been the downsides of handling things on your own?
   For example, have you ever felt overwhelmed, anxious, depressed or alone?

   ___

   ___

4. What kinds of experiences and feelings in your relationship have been difficult to share with your partner? What has been hard about sharing with your partner—what did you fear might happen?

   ___

   ___

5. What negative messages or beliefs have you internalized *about yourself* that have created insecurity and made it hard to show yourself fully?
   (For example, I feel like I am not good enough for you. I am a complete failure no one would ever want me. Or any vulnerability is a sign of weakness and will turn you off or open me up to hurt.)

   ___

   ___

6. What fears have you internalized *about your partner or relationship*?
   (For example, I am afraid you will eventually get fed up with me and leave. You will be burdened by my issues. Or you don't really want me or at least not all of me.)

   ___

   ___

7. What support or reassurance do you need right now from your partner to help you be able to bring more of your true self into this relationship? What do you long for?
   a) What do I need right now in our relationship to help me feel more secure within myself?

   ___

   ___

   b) What do I need right now to help me feel more secure with you, emotionally safer or closer to you?

   ___

   ___

Can you look at your partner now, meet their eyes and share your reflections and longings? It's okay if you are nervous about this conversation. Perhaps you could start by expressing that first, sharing what your fears are about this conversation and what could help you get started.

___

Instructions for the Listening Partner

As you sit in the listening role, try to adopt the perspective that your partner is sharing valuable information about themself with YOU. Consider that the desire to confide in you is a reflection of how important you are to your partner. *The fact that your person struggles with some difficult emotions in your relationship is the result of the negative dance; it is* not *the result of you being a bad person or partner.* It is so important to hold onto this frame as you listen to your partner's expressions. Also try to bear in mind that for most people, this kind of sharing can feel scary, vulnerable, exposing and even shameful. It can also feel liberating and relieving.

Let's review how L-O-V-E conversations go:

Listen to all that your partner has to say without interrupting or setting the record straight. Listening in this way allows your partner to fully unfold their experience and get to those deeper emotions and attachment needs.

Open your heart and mind to create safety for your partner to risk showing the parts of them that seem weak or unlovable. True intimacy involves being able to bring your whole self into the relationship.

Validate and acknowledge your partner's emotions. Simply knowing that you are absorbing what you're hearing and caring about it is heartening for your partner who is risking opening up to you.

Express your thoughts and feelings softly, simply, slowly. Give this experience plenty of time and space. Find some way, no matter how small, to reach back and respond to your partner. Consider what you want to say.

When You Let Me in This Way, I Feel . . .

- Drawn toward you
- Touched inside
- Needed by you
- Compassionate
- Sad for how you've struggled in our relationship
- Warm inside
- Like I can finally see you for the first time in a long time
- Close and connected to you
- A bit disappointed or sad that I haven't had a chance to see and respond to these vulnerable parts before
- Admiration of you for going to these difficult emotional places
- Hopeful that we can be more open and closer in the future.

It is now time to turn to your partner and in your own words share how you are impacted by their words. *Don't forget to respond to your partner's needs.* Can you offer the reassurance, acceptance or other needs your partner has expressed? If yes, you can go ahead and do so now. If not, acknowledge that you are struggling and take some time to sort out what is happening. Share when you are ready.

Debriefing Your Experience

Have you had a bonding experience, shared a sweet moment, felt intimacy? We suggest that you take a few moments to debrief how you each experienced this conversation. Most couples report feeling closer and more connected. If you are not feeling this way, how would you have liked it to go differently? Share your perspectives on this gently, as you may still be feeling a bit vulnerable and exposed from your conversation.

In the next section partners who are typically in the protesting position will shift to tuning into themselves and disclosing their deeper emotions and needs. We will guide you in unfolding your experience and expressing it, however, *it is best to take a break now* and not do it right after the intensity of the work you just completed.

For Partners in the Protesting Position

Let's now take a look at how the negative cycle has affected you and your feelings of security over the years as it played out repeatedly. In response to your partner's withdrawal or defensiveness, you have likely felt as if you have to work hard to get a response from them. This may have cultivated vigilance in you for signs that the relationship is losing closeness or, worse, coming apart. Out of desperation you may have poked, protested or even picked a fight to try to get your partner's attention or to get some acknowledgment that there was a problem. If your partner seemed disengaged, you may have felt as if you need to take more than your share of the load in caring for your relationship and family "It's all on me." It may have engendered the sense that your partner isn't there for you in times of need, which can be jangling, frightening and feel like abandonment in the moment. This dreadful feeling can be amplified if you didn't grow up with caregivers who attuned to your needs and were there for you.

Most of us wish to feel cherished by our partner, so to have to struggle to get your partner to engage with you can also be a profoundly sad, painful and rejecting experience. Over time it can evoke doubts about yourself and fears about whether you are lovable or attractive enough: "If I was interesting enough, attractive enough, special in some way why would I have to work so hard for your attention?" So, partners in the pursuing position often live with a lot of tears and fears. Fear and vigilance around: "Will you be there for me?" and fears concerning my own desirability: "Am I too much, too needy? Maybe no one would want me." Being able to express your fears and doubts to your partner and receive their reassurance can be the healing balm that sooths these insecurities.

Some key questions to ask yourself are: What has it been like for me to walk around in this relationship feeling . . .

- invisible to you?
- like I have no impact on you?
- unwanted by you?
- afraid of being rejected?
- sad and lonely because I don't think I deserve you?
- fearful of being abandoned?

As you read these statements slowly, notice and allow any emotions to emerge as you ask yourself the question. Turn the volume down on any internal voices that rush in to say there is something wrong with you if you are feeling this way, you are too needy, tell you this is hopeless or otherwise invalidate your feelings. Also avoid diverting responsibility for your emotions onto your partner (i.e., avoid any statement of this nature: "I'm feeling this way because you . . .") Acknowledge these thoughts and then set them aside to let yourself go into your core emotions. Notice and acknowledge reactive emotions that creep in but try to move through them and continue looking for and attending to more core, vulnerable emotions. If you touch into softer core emotions, turn the volume up on them. It is natural to experience sorrow about how lonely and painful the difficult aspects of your relationship can be. An example might be: "I walk around in this relationship feeling so hurt and rejected when I can't reach you. I know you usually see my anger, but underneath that it is so very sad for me to feel so invisible to you."

Like waves, emotions are constantly shifting, ebbing and flowing. How does it feel to begin to touch these softer feelings that are usually hidden by the negative dance? For protesting partners there is usually a huge leap of faith in risking to trust that if I let you into my sore places and expose my deepest insecurities, you will catch me. If you stay with your core emotions long enough, there is often a tipping point when the cost of staying self-protective and lonely outweighs the risk of trusting. With that leap of faith comes a turning point that sounds something like "I can't bear this empty existence anymore. I have to risk letting down my guard and try to trust it will be OK." As you stay with your process, notice if your emotions begin to shift toward wanting to put down your guard and letting your partner see the vulnerable emotions that lie underneath. It might sound something like this:

> This is scary to say, but when I sit here and feel how it has really been for me, I realize how desperately lonely I am, and I am hit with a huge wave of sadness. Then I get panicked there is something wrong with me and no one would ever want to take care of me. That is a very vulnerable feeling for me. That goes way back for me, but it gets triggered so easily in our relationship.

Continue to stay with your core emotions as they shift and notice if they take you to what you need and yearn for to feel better in this relationship. The path to your deeper attachment needs is through your emotions. Lean into your emotions and see where they take you. Ask yourself: What would help me with this feeling of ________ (e.g., fear that I'm unlovable, I'll be abandoned, fear/shame that I'm too much, too needy, insecurity that you won't want me or be there for me when I turn to you)? What do I long for from my partner?

Go back to the list of relationship needs and identify two or three that ring most true for you. If you imagine expressing your needs to your partner, an example of how it could sound is something like this:

> I know I need to turn to you and show my needs in a more vulnerable way instead of demanding and that will make it easier for you to respond to me. The thought of doing that feels incredibly scary and exposing, so I really need your reassurance that I am lovable to you and that you really *want* to be there for me. I need to know that if I reach for you, you'll reach back and hold me.

The following guided reflection offers prompts to support you through the process we describe here.

Reflection 9.3 Guided reflection for partners in the protesting position

____

(name)

1. How has the negative dance created pain or insecurity in you? Be specific.
   How/where have you felt this in your body? Take time with this question and allow yourself to check in and notice what you feel inside. (Possible examples include physically

feeling anxiety in specific parts of your body, feeling unable to settle yourself, how you feel energetically, or how you view yourself.)

2. If you have dealt with challenges at work, with family, or in your relationship on your own, how has that been for you?
   What have been the benefits of handling things on your own?

3. What have been the downsides of handling things on your own?
   For example, have you ever felt overwhelmed, anxious, desperate or lonely?

4. What doubts or fears have you internalized *about your relationship or your partner* being there for you?
   (For example, I'm afraid you will be turned off by my feelings. I'm afraid you don't really want me to need you because no one has ever taken care of me. Or people always abandon me, I'm sure you will too eventually. Relationships don't last.)

5. What doubts or fears have you internalized *about yourself*, your own lovability or your own needs for security?
   (For example, it hurts so much to imagine, but I must be hard to love—I'm too much, too angry or too needy; not attractive or intelligent enough. I'm afraid with the person that I am, no one could truly love or cherish me.)

6. What kinds of experiences and feelings in your relationship have been difficult to share with your partner in a vulnerable way? What has been hard about letting your partner see your vulnerabilities or insecurities—what did you fear might happen?

7. What support or reassurance do you need right now from your partner to help you be able to share your true insecurities and vulnerabilities with them? What do you long for?
   a) What do I need right now to help me feel more secure with you, emotionally safer or closer to you?

b) What do I need right now in our relationship to help me feel more secure/better about myself?

Can you look at your partner now, meet their eyes and share your reflections and longings? It's okay if you are nervous about this conversation. Perhaps you could start by expressing that first, sharing what are your fears about this conversation and what could help you get started.

Instructions for the Listening Partner

As you sit in the listening role, try to adopt the perspective that your partner is sharing valuable information about themself with YOU. Notice if your partner has struggled to fight their fears to show these vulnerable feelings and needs. It is difficult to expose parts of yourself that you don't find appealing, especially if your life experiences have taught you not to expect to be seen and loved. It is so important to hold onto this frame as you listen to your partner's expressions. Remember, these disclosures can feel scary, vulnerable, exposing and even shameful. You don't have to fix anything or make it better. All you need to do is sit with your partner through this conversation with an open, caring heart.

Find some way, no matter how small, to reach back and respond to your partner. Consider what you want to say. You may wish to refer back to the examples in the L-O-V-E conversation suggestions earlier in this chapter. It is now time to turn to your partner and in your own words share how you are impacted by how they reached for you. *Don't forget to respond to your partner's needs.* Can you offer the reassurance, closeness or other needs that were asked for? If yes, you can go ahead and do so now. If not, acknowledge that you are struggling and take some time to sort out what is happening. Share when you are ready.

Debriefing Your Experience

You have now completed a powerful conversation that usually helps partners engage and feel more strongly bonded. You might be feeling a little raw. We suggest that you take a few moments to debrief how you each found this experience. Most couples report feeling closer and more connected. If you are not feeling this way, how would you have liked it to go differently? Remember that how we express our emotions and relationship needs are shaped in part by experiences in our family of origin, culture and social position. Might some of your differing expectations be better understood by exploring this possibility together? Consider reviewing your responses to the Reflections in Chapter 3 and Reflection 5.2, exploring together how your life experiences shed light on how this conversation went. Share your perspectives on this gently, as you may still be feeling a bit vulnerable and exposed from your conversation.

We want to reassure you that as couples continue with these conversations, they become more natural, and partners develop a deeper understanding of each other over time.

However, if you have become blocked in either expressing your softer emotions and longings or truly responding to your partner's disclosures, there may be a deeper rupture in your relationship that needs to be processed separately. You can explore this possibility in the next chapter. Alternatively, there may be other factors that are making it hard to open up vulnerably or be emotionally responsive to your partner who is reaching out to you. For example, a history of abuse, attachment trauma in your family or through discrimination and oppression which can understandably complicate the trust and closeness these conversations typically engender. You may need to reach out to a therapist to support you in rebuilding your relationship bond.

Over many years with many couples, we have seen these intimate conversations become an antidote[2] to the old negative pattern of interactions. Notice that if you typically withdraw in the negative cycle, the conversation pulls you to engage with your partner and share feelings and needs more fully. If you typically protest or become demanding when you are hurt, the conversation helps you put your needs across in a softer way. These shifts involve putting your most raw and vulnerable needs across differently, so that you send a clear distress call, signaling your partner to respond lovingly. The impact of these conversations may feel gradual or dramatic, but as you continue to share in this way, they begin to reshape your relationship into a secure bond. A bond in which you discover a new positive cycle and ways of relating, where you can reach for and be responsive to each other. Where you can feel truly accepted, embraced and precious to your partner!

References

1. Johnson, S. (2008). *Hold me tight*. New York, NY, Boston and London: Little, Brown and Company.
2. Furrow, J., Johnson, S., Bradley, B., Brubacher, L., Campbell, L., Kallos-Lilly, V., Palmer, G., Rheem, K., Woolley, S. (in press). *Becoming an emotionally focused therapist: The workbook* (2nd ed.). London: Routledge.

CHAPTER 10

RELATIONSHIP INJURY

How Can We Repair the Damage?

Throughout this book we have frequently referred to the fundamental importance of close relationships for individuals' health and wellbeing. We honor the emotional bond that is established between partners in close relationships: Each partner can provide comfort (a safe haven) and encouragement (a secure base) for the other . . . BUT . . . Getting close also carries some risks. Getting close carries the possibility of being hurt or causing hurt, and most people would agree that *hurt feelings hurt*! By now, after engaging in the guided reflections in earlier chapters, you and your partner may have identified some times when hurtful events have occurred in your relationship. These events call for repair, and yet, sometimes, repair can feel difficult to accomplish. When hurtful events are not addressed and successfully resolved, hurt can fester and erode a couple's emotional bond; our purpose then in this chapter is to give more careful consideration to repairing injuries, small and large, that can occur in close relationships. We would like to help you approach the repair process in small and manageable steps.

Before we consider more serious hurts in close relationships, it is helpful to acknowledge that supposedly "little" hurts can also hurt. Sometimes one partner's thoughtless remark to the other or an oversight leaving one partner excluded can stab. When these seemingly small hurtful events occur frequently, confidence in the love and loyalty of the relationship can diminish. Essentially, none of us like to be devalued or overlooked, especially by the ones we love. The more our partners mean to us, the more vulnerable we are to feeling hurt if they come across as uncaring or dismissive.

In an Australian study of hurt feelings in couple relationships, community couples in the early years of commitment were recorded for five minutes while they talked about how they dealt with hurtful events in their relationship. Interestingly, 63 percent of more than 100 couples noted that the *timing* of a conversation to resolve the hurtful event was important.[1] Some couples agreed that resolving the event quickly was helpful, while others indicated they did better with some time to get calmer before talking. It can be harder when one partner likes to talk soon, and the other partner wants time before talking. These couples especially need to gather as much patience and tolerance as they can, in order to find a path forward where both partners feel heard and cared for.

Affairs and Other Hurtful Events

The Brisbane couples described a range of hurtful events in their relationship. Here are some examples:

- "She came back from overseas and announced she didn't think she wanted to continue with our relationship. I was gutted."
- "I had horrible morning sickness. I was lying in bed and my husband accused me of doing this to get out of housework."

DOI: 10.4324/9781003009481-10

- "We were at a party and my fiancée publicly criticized the way I was telling a story. We had a huge fight on the way home."
- "He said he was taking his daughter to a coffee shop for her birthday. I later found the bankcard receipt for an expensive restaurant, and also learned that he had invited his 'ex' as well!"
- "I went to my daughter's place for a few weeks to help her with the new baby and returned to find he had started a relationship with a woman from church!"[2]

Notice how two of these couples spontaneously added comments about the immediate consequences of these events; for one, there was a visceral reaction: "I was gutted"; for the other, serious conflict erupted: "We had a huge fight on the way home." These reactions are not uncommon and can lead to ongoing distress both personally and interpersonally.

One partner's involvement with a "third party" can certainly create serious personal distress and relationship damage. Despite the strong norm against extramarital sex in monogamous relationships, national studies of heterosexual couples in the USA found that nearly one-quarter of husbands and one in ten wives have had extramarital sex at some point during their marriage.[3] Perhaps you have picked up this book because you and your partner are trying to repair the damage caused by an affair. Perhaps you are wondering "How will we ever get over it?" or maybe "How did it even happen?"

While there may be a range of reasons why affairs occur (such as low self-esteem, boredom, lack of closeness or sexual fulfillment and family-of-origin modeling of affairs as the norm), the risk of an affair occurring has been found to increase by 28 percent when individuals report that they are "very" happy in their marriage as opposed to "extremely" happy.[4] This is an interesting finding and points to the importance of couples making their relationship the number one priority in their lives: High relationship quality becomes a barrier to infidelity. When couples feel really close and secure, there is much less room for a third party.

Infidelity Hurts

Usually, sex with a third party is a source of intense hurt and typically results in significant interpersonal conflict and distress. Exceptions to this experience would be for partners who practice consensual nonmonogamy with an explicit arrangement of sexual openness in their relationship or for partners who mutually acknowledge that they are not whole-heartedly committed to each other. However, for many couples, infidelity is associated with intense pain for the hurt partner. As mentioned earlier, in Chapter 8, infidelity was rated as the most serious hurtful event, with long-term effects on both the hurt partner and the relationship.[5] Other researchers have identified that betrayal from infidelity frequently arouses intense negative feelings and thoughts, and triggers impulses toward retaliation.[6]

Not surprisingly, research has also revealed that individuals report feeling more guilt when they have perpetrated a betrayal (such as infidelity) than other forms of negative interpersonal behaviors.[7] Further, guilt and fear of repercussions from discovery often motivate partners to engage in deception (sometimes elaborate and prolonged) about sexual liaisons. Unfortunately, many hurt partners have reported that deception hurts as much as the actual affair, maybe even more so, resulting in serious breakdown of trust. "How will I ever trust my partner again?" For most couples, the aftermath of the affair is turbulent, even chaotic, as *both* partners are grappling with intense negative feelings.

Resolving Hurtful Events

Over a hundred couples (in satisfying relationships) who participated in the Brisbane Hurt Feelings project were asked how they had successfully resolved hurtful events like the ones listed. They reported that it helps for the partners to:

- Be truly motivated to resolve the issue
- Engage in positive, constructive discussion
- Consider each other's views and feelings
- Do something practical to demonstrate that remorse is sincere, and the relationship is of value.

In particular, these couples commented that it helps if the *partner who was hurtful* can:

- Listen to the one who feels hurt
- Try to understand their perspective and truly appreciate the damage caused
- Acknowledge the hurtful behavior and
- Apologize.

It also helps if the *hurt partner* can:

- Aim to stay as calm as possible when expressing feelings
- Express feelings clearly
- Keep the size of the event in perspective and
- Listen to the partner's perspective who caused the hurt feelings.[8]

Our work with distressed couples has shown us that it is usually hard work to get a relationship back on track after the disturbance of an affair. For many couples the discovery of an affair triggers a crisis. It helps to acknowledge that the reaction to an affair often feels like a crisis because it *is* a crisis: many relationships don't make it after an affair is disclosed. However, many couples *do* make it through the crisis and these couples typically have put a lot of effort into the repair process. Many of these couples have told us that after the resolution process they feel closer than ever before.

Here are some more suggestions for dealing with an affair:

- Partners need to be tested for sexually transmitted infections.
- In considering telling other people (including children) you need to balance the need for authenticity and support with the risk of causing collateral damage.
- If you are the hurt partner, it is understandable that you may want to know details of the affair; however, finding out extensive details (for example, about explicit sexual activities or exactly how the affair was kept secret) can be re-traumatizing and typically is not helpful to the recovery process. It *is* helpful however, for the individual who had an affair to acknowledge their partner's desire to know more and be willing to answer questions about basic information, feelings and state of mind at the time of the affair. It will be helpful if these questions are asked respectfully, rather than as a harsh interrogation.
- Rage reactions are very understandable but if prolonged usually add to the size of the problem that you and your partner are struggling with. Your rage is a reaction to legitimate anger in response to a betrayal and intense pain, shame, fear and sadness. In the long run, it will be more productive to talk about the hurt, fear and sadness and use your core anger to set appropriate boundaries.
- If you are the one who had the affair, you may believe that it was justified because you were so unhappy in the relationship. However important it will be to address your sources of unhappiness in the relationship, justifying yourself and/or blaming your partner will make it difficult for your relationship to heal.
- It is unhelpful to suggest your partner should be able to "get over" the affair as if this is something they can do on their own. It is only through expressing their pain to *you and feeling that you are present, deeply affected and remorseful* that trust can rebuild over time.

Lasting Recovery from Affairs

Often couples discover after they have worked through the initial painful crisis of the affair and its aftermath that something was missing or going wrong in their relationship. In some way, there was room for a third party to get between them. This is noted, not to shift responsibility away from the partner who was unfaithful, but to draw attention to an important part of the recovery process.

To create lasting recovery from an affair, couples need to attend to what was going on in the relationship and for the person before the affair occurred.

For some couples, this may involve resolving issues around criticism or control; for others it may mean revising unrealistically high expectations, addressing issues related to self-esteem or overcoming fear of showing vulnerability or weakness; some couples may need to work at creating more opportunities for emotional connection and closeness, while others may need to seek medical or psychological help for problems with their sexual relationship. Whatever the problem, it needs to be acknowledged and worked on; the alternative of ignoring the identified problem leaves the couple's relationship vulnerable to future risk.

Retaliation Versus Repair

The tendency to respond to personal injury with either retaliation or avoidance is understandable—these reactions are self-protective strategies which at times can be useful for survival, especially when the threat or danger is physical. Furthermore, most people would admit to gaining some satisfaction from revenge at least once in their lives. However, that satisfaction is often short lived, as Charlotte Bronte observed in her novel *Jane Eyre*:

> Something of vengeance I had tasted for the first time; as aromatic wine it seemed, on swallowing, warm and racy: its after flavour, metallic and corroding, gave me a sensation as if I had been poisoned.[9]

Retaliating, getting even, sulking or holding out on your partner may be temporarily satisfying for you if you have been hurt; these reactions, however, may lead to not-so-temporary negative consequences for your relationship. As most couples have discovered, over-control of emotion (icy avoidance or "the silent treatment") or under-control (fiery retaliation) can escalate problems very quickly. How then can you find a way to repair damage that will benefit you both? Constructive communication, open disclosure and tending to painful emotions are all helpful aspects of the repair process; ultimately, however, if you have suffered after experiencing a hurtful event, you will eventually have to grapple with the question of whether you want to forgive and/or whether it is safe to forgive your partner.

Forgiveness?

Traditionally, forgiveness is recommended as a way to heal interpersonal difficulties; forgiveness, however, is usually easier to talk about than to do. If we are to consider forgiveness as part of a possible relationship-repair strategy, we need to be clear about what forgiveness is, and what it is not. Robert Enright,[10] an American psychologist who has spent many years investigating forgiveness, notes that forgiveness is a *choice*, that is, it is not something that we have to do, but it is an option we can choose. Table 10.1 also displays some more of Enright's thoughts.

Table 10.1 Clarifying forgiveness

Forgiveness is *not* the same as . . .	condoning (condoning often means putting up with bad treatment in silence, or convincing ourselves we deserve the bad treatment, or pretending that a partner's actions were excusable)
	forgetting (forgiveness doesn't cause amnesia, but it may change the way we think about the past)
	calming down (anger may diminish over time, but that isn't the same as actively choosing to forgive)
	pseudo-forgiveness (such as saying "I forgive you" but not meaning it)
	reconciliation (forgiveness happens in the mind and heart of an individual, whereas reconciliation happens between two people; sometimes individuals forgive the offender but choose not to reconcile with them)
Forgiveness is also *more* than . . .	accepting what happened (we can "move on" from hurt, but still feel coldly indifferent)
	feeling neutral toward another

Other investigators comment that forgiveness is not an act, but a process;[11] it takes time[12] and involves giving up our need to see others only in terms of our own needs, wishes and longings.[13] Forgiveness can therefore be thought of as a helpful process, which happens over time, where the hurt person becomes less motivated to retaliate or avoid (even though that may be justified), and more motivated by goodwill.[14] This might involve stepping back and taking a broader perspective or a willingness to look at the events in a more nuanced manner, as is evident in the following comment.

A group of South African psychologists offer further thoughts about forgiveness: "Mature forgiveness is an integrated, realistic view which contains both good and bad aspects of the self and others."[15] For couples struggling to resolve hurtful events this would mean recognizing that you are not characters in a fairy tale where you are either totally good or dreadfully bad. *Both* of you are involved in this story and *both* of you are human. Neither is perfect. Both of you have good qualities and both are capable of acting badly. If you are the hurt partner, in forgiving, you are essentially taking a bigger view of all concerned; the good and the bad aspects of yourself and your partner are both acknowledged.

Archbishop Desmond Tutu also from South Africa, writes that forgiveness does not mean being spineless or weak, never feeling angry, neither does it mean a subversion of justice, or simply trying to forget. In *The book of forgiving*,[16] Desmond and Mpho Tutu reflect on their own family's traumatic experiences and offer reflections, meditations and supportive exercises that facilitate healing.

Benefits of Forgiveness

Despite the understandable difficulties in forgiving, there are potential health benefits from letting go of hurt and anger. Essentially, in letting go of anger, resentment or grudges, we are letting go of the impulse to get "pumped up" ready for a fight. When our bodies are preparing for conflict, blood pressure and heart rate increase, and if this physiological arousal is chronic over time, your health can suffer. Letting go of grudges results in measurable decreases in physiological arousal.[17]

Forgiveness also offers benefits for the welfare of relationships. Investigation into characteristics of long-term heterosexual marriages has identified the benefits of forgiveness for relationship wellbeing and longevity.[18] In this study, a large group of couples who had been married for 20 years or more were asked to identify the most important characteristics they or their partners possessed which contributed to their long-term relationship. The ten most frequently suggested characteristics were reported. Not surprisingly, couples suggested qualities such as commitment, respect, sexual fidelity and desire to be a good parent. Also included in the "top ten" was *willingness to forgive and to be forgiven.* Both for individual health and peace of mind, and for the benefit of the relationship, forgiveness can be a great thing to do . . . but is it easy to accomplish? . . . Maybe for some . . . maybe not for others.

What Helps Couples to Forgive?

It is not surprising that an apology for wrongdoing assists the forgiveness process. This could be because genuine apology may *help the hurt person have softer feelings for the offender;*[19] an apology may indicate that the wrong doer has suffered, and therefore has been at least been somewhat punished;[20] an apology may imply *intention not to repeat* the offence which lessens fear of repetition;[21] or when victims take the offenders' perspective they may be conscious of times when *they themselves have been offenders*, leading to discomfort.[22] Whatever the reasons, a genuine apology for misdeeds and asking for forgiveness indicate a step of goodwill toward an injured partner.

If you have been hurt and feel reluctant to forgive, it may be that you are feeling afraid of being hurt again. Hurt partners often, and understandably, ask, "How do I know that my partner is not going to do that to me again?" Please take note of what we are going to say next:

The best person to help a fearful partner reduce fear of the future and make a decision to forgive is the person who caused the hurt.

This idea often comes as a surprise to partners who have been hurtful because they (wrongly) assume that forgiveness is all up to the hurt person. When partners who have been hurtful sincerely acknowledge what they have done and clearly understand and own up to the impact of their actions, they are able then to offer an apology that is sincere and meaningful.[23] This might sound something like:

> I get it now how much I have hurt you. I don't think I really understood for a while, but now I see that I have hurt you so much. I want you to know that I feel absolutely terrible about that. It is hard to find words to say how sorry I feel, but I hope that one day you will be able to believe how sorry I am.

Such an acknowledgement of the harm you have done is a crucial step in assisting your injured partner to begin to trust you again.

Other research with couples following betrayal has found that partners who caused the hurt reported that extensive effort was required to demonstrate to their partners that they were "truly sorry," that their relationship was of primary importance to them, and that they were worthy of forgiveness.[24] Constructive efforts to repair the situation for this group of couples included regular demonstrations of thoughtfulness or kindness, seeking counseling for drinking or gambling problems and resolutely ending extramarital liaisons. As part of one treatment study,[25] people who acted hurtfully were recommended to write a letter to their injured partners which clearly expressed *regret* (what the regret was about including understanding of how hurt had been caused), *responsibility* (taking ownership for their role in the injury) and *remedy* (describe what will be done now to help the partner to heal from the hurt). After receiving and absorbing the letter of apology, hurt partners were then encouraged to write a letter in reply which indicated that they were in the *process of resolving and forgiving* the hurtful event, what they had been *able to resolve/forgive,* what they still *could not let go of/forgive* and *what they presently needed from their partners* to help them to let go of the hurt/anger and forgive.

Reflection 10.1 Exploring our hurts

What does this chapter mean for our relationship?

What injuries (small or large) in our relationship call for repair? There may be many incidents that come to mind. The one I choose to work on today is

____

When I felt hurt . . .

What exactly caused me hurt? (State clearly what the event meant for you.)

____

____

____

Are there any aspects of that hurtful event that still cause me to feel hurt? What other emotions are involved for me (e.g., anger, sadness, fear)?

____

____

____

What can I forgive? What can't I forgive? What do I need from my partner at this point? What would help me to let go of the hurt?

____

____

____

Has my partner apologized or acknowledged their part in my hurt? (Does my partner even know I was hurt?) What might be potential barriers or obstacles to my partner's apology/acknowledgement in relation to the outlined incident/s? Might my reactions be keeping alive the conflict and distress between us?

____

____

____

What do I see as potential barriers or obstacles to my letting go of hurt and forgiving in relation to the outlined event/s? What might help me overcome these obstacles?

____

____

____

Forgiving the Unforgivable

Resolving Attachment Injuries

Very serious hurts that injure a couple's attachment bond are referred to in EFT as "attachment injuries."[26] Such injuries are not every day, minor hurts; this term refers to events that so damage a couple's emotional bond that the relationship now feels utterly insecure. The injured partner may make an existential decision not to trust or count on their partner in the future; that is, "I am alone in this relationship and I have to take care of myself," which colors the relationship from that moment on.

These events require intensive repair efforts to heal. Maybe you are reading this book because an event in your relationship has very seriously damaged the emotional bond between you and your partner. This might have been an episode of infidelity, but it might also be other events where you felt your partner let you down at a crucial time of need: for example, some events reported to us that created a heightened sense of vulnerability and need for support included obstetric complications associated with having a baby, losing a parent, having a critically ill child or undergoing chemotherapy.

When the vulnerable person was either too afraid to ask for support or if support was asked for but not provided, deep hurt and a rupture in the attachment bond resulted.

You might still be feeling hurt, and not only hurt, but frustrated, angry, and maybe even overwhelmed because of the difficulty you have experienced in trying to talk about this with your partner. Perhaps the pain still feels very raw. The following story provides an example of a couple with longstanding marital difficulties that included an injury to their attachment bond when their first baby was born. We include it to illustrate how serious such injuries can be, but also to offer hope by reporting the progress that they made in healing the injury.

Georgie and Sylvester

Georgette, or Georgie as she preferred to be called, and Sylvester, were a cisgender, heterosexual Dutch couple, whose parents had emigrated from the Netherlands to Australia following World War II. They had outwardly been very successful, making money, raising healthy children and establishing a nice home and garden. However, they experienced a lot of recurring and distressing conflict, which finally brought them to couples therapy when they had been married for 22 years.

One of the events that had negatively impacted Georgie's view of Sylvester and her marriage was her experience when their first baby was born. Here's some of their story: Georgie's labor began in the early hours of a Monday morning when Sylvester was starting a challenging new project at work. From his point of view, the timing could not have been worse. He felt frustrated and angry that he was torn between his family and work responsibilities and let Georgie know his feelings as they drove to the hospital. As Sylvester was driving and complaining, Georgie tried not to react too much and instead concentrated on relaxing her body during contractions and staying as calm as possible.

Once she was admitted to hospital, Sylvester felt torn between supporting Georgie and meeting the expectations of his work colleagues; hence, he spent quite some time in the hospital coffee shop talking to colleagues on the phone about the new project. He returned briefly to Georgie every hour or so and fortunately was present for the baby's birth. From Sylvester's perspective, he had done his duty: he had driven his wife to the hospital, visited from time to time across several hours and witnessed his son's birth.

For Georgie, things had not gone as she'd expected or needed. As her contractions got stronger, she felt increasingly distressed and more nervous about how she was going to cope with this sort of pain for hours. However, she felt she should not "make a fuss" and did not clearly ask him to stay with her. As the hours in the delivery suite dragged on and Sylvester persisted in going away to phone his colleagues, Georgie felt terribly alone. In the film they had watched at their prenatal education classes, the father-to-be was sitting with his wife throughout her labor, rubbing her back and holding her hand. "Where is *my* husband now?" wondered Georgie. Her disappointment was deep; she felt painfully let down, hurt and alone. "I realized that I could not depend on him to put my needs first, ahead of his work, even when I was having our baby!"

A few weeks after the baby's birth, Georgie expressed her anger and disappointment to Sylvester. He was utterly amazed that she was so "upset" and quickly pointed out how everything had turned out well; the nurses had been great and looked after her, the baby was beautiful and healthy, and she had made a good recovery. He was unable to understand her distress and put it down to post-natal "nerves." When Georgie became angry that he was dismissing her perspective, Sylvester reacted defensively and left the house. Georgie sat at home alone with their baby and sobbed. At that moment, she made a decision to not ever need Sylvester so much again. Twenty years later, she reported to their therapist, "I made up my mind that day, that if we had any more babies, I would ask my mother to come with me to the hospital. I did not want to ever again feel so let down. He clearly was not capable of giving me support."

For Georgie, her attachment bond with Sylvester had been seriously injured; her assumption that he would always be there for her when really needed was shattered. This event was no everyday hurt or upset, like when he forgot her birthday or made critical remarks about her mother. During the hours of labor to give birth to baby Mark, she had needed Sylvester's comfort and support more than she had ever needed it before—he had not been there for her—and soon after, he was unwilling to hear her emotional pain about the event and acknowledge his part in it. For Georgie, things had gone from bad to much worse.

In the years that followed, Georgie rarely made reference to this event, but when she did, her voice sounded hard and cold. It was as though the old wound had opened unexpectedly creating stabs of pain again. Invariably in these moments, Sylvester would bristle in irritation, tell her to get over something that had happened so long ago, and then he would walk away. However, this injury would not just "go away" and the couple's relationship became defined by a sense of betrayal and reluctance to trust for Georgie ("Don't ever need him too much because he won't be there") and a sense of inadequacy for Sylvester ("I am never, ever, good enough for her").

Recovery from Attachment Injuries

The injurious event needs to be considered in the light of the *attachment bond* between you and your partner; that is, the emotional bond between you both has been so damaged that your relationship now feels insecure. You have more than likely lost confidence in your partner, no longer feel you can really trust them and are likely to be stuck in ongoing conflict or helpless withdrawal.

Professor Sue Johnson and her colleagues offer helpful suggestions for these types of injuries that may speak directly to your current struggle and pain.[27,28,29] Here is what they have to say:

By this point in the conversation/s, partners who experienced an injury are hopefully opening up, feeling and expressing the poignancy of their pain around the event rather than their outrage. Similarly, partners whose actions were hurtful can now hopefully see their injured partners as vulnerable and in need, rather than "unreasonable" or "always complaining." Further, by this point, hurtful partners are also hopefully getting a clear sense of how important they are to their person and that their support

Table 10.2 Steps in the healing process for the hurt partner

Suggestions from Professor Johnson and colleagues regarding what injured partners need to identify:	Examples of what Georgie said to Sylvester
What was lost in the hurtful event:	"I realized that I could not depend on you to put my needs first, ahead of your work, even when I was having our baby!"
The negative and even hopeless feelings that followed:	"I felt very, very alone, and wept."
How they have tried to protect themselves:	"I made up my mind that day, that if we had any more children I would ask my mother to come with me to the hospital. I did not want to ever again feel so let down."
Then . . .	
Shattered assumptions about safety in their relationship need to be named:	"I decided that you were not capable of giving me support when I needed it most."
It helps for the couple to recognize how their negative cycle of interactions has developed around the hurtful event or has been fueled by it:	"The angrier and more resentful I felt and acted, the more guilty and withdrawn you became, leading to more frustration and loneliness for me and ultimately more criticism of you."
And how they have attempted to mend the damage:	"I know you've said you were sorry, but then you would ask me, 'How much more do you want?' When you spoke like that, I would crumple inside and feel: 'He doesn't get it. It's like my feelings don't matter at all."'
Painful as it can be to acknowledge, it helps to name how hopes and longings for closeness have been suppressed:	"I gave up even talking about it to you anymore. What was the point of longing for what I believed I couldn't have?"

is uniquely helpful and profoundly valued by their partners. *How deeply partners engage with their own softer core emotions and respond to each other distinguishes couples who recover from attachment injuries from those who do not.*[30] Once couples are on the path, these reparative conversations open the way for hurt partners to risk reaching out and hurtful partners to experience genuine remorse, take responsibility for their actions and offer sincere apology. When an apology is stripped of excuses, elaborate explanations and self-defence—when the person apologizing can grasp the full weight of their hurtful actions and express the associated shame and/or remorse—the hurt partner typically feels differently about the injury and can move to feeling more compassionately toward the other partner. The way is now opened for forgiveness to occur and trust to be rebuilt over time. Table 10.3 offers a summary of how hurtful partners can help the repair process.

Resolution for Georgie and Sylvester

After a number of sessions in which Georgie and Sylvester grew to understand and manage their negative cycles of interactions and their emotional needs, Georgie indicated that she needed to talk about

Table 10.3 Suggestions for partner who has been hurtful to aid relationship repair

It will help for you to

- Listen carefully to your partner's experience and expression of hurt
- Allow yourself to be moved by their pain
- Accept your importance to your partner. If you were not important to your partner, they would not be so hurt
- Put aside defensiveness and take responsibility for your actions (or lack of actions)
- Let your regret/remorse find expression in sincere words that convey your awareness of the pain you have caused. Be humble and let your partner see your sadness or shame
- Ask your partner how you can bring comfort or healing.

something that had happened a long time ago. Instead of expressing her anger and despair about the events associated with Mark's birth, as she had done in the past, this time Georgie was able to express her hurt and sadness. When Sylvester listened, really listened, with mouth closed and heart open, to Georgie's clear but sad recounting of the impact on her of his actions during the birth of their son Mark, he felt ashamed.

For the first time in 20 years, he let go of his pride and let himself acknowledge aloud to her how bad he had often felt about the way he had ignored her need for support and care on that Monday so long ago. With tears and remorse clearly evident on his face, Sylvester sincerely apologized. "I feel ashamed and sad that I let you down all those years ago. I can't imagine the pain you were suffering. I should have been beside you. I am sorry beyond words. I have no right to expect that just because it is in the past, it is OK and you can forgive me." They sat together in sober silence for a time.

To Sylvester's surprise, Georgie then straightened up in her chair, looked visibly more relaxed and stated, "You have no idea the relief it is to hear you admit that you *did* let me down. It is so helpful to hear you say that!" Later, when Sylvester asked her humbly how he could help her to feel better, she quietly said:

> You really don't have to say any more today. For years it has felt as though that wound in my heart was just *patched*, not really healed. Working together on our relationship these past months, and especially today, hearing you acknowledge your part in my disappointment and sense of betrayal has helped me so much. I feel that gaping wound can really heal now.

After another long pause and shedding soft tears, Georgie added quietly, "I know I will be able to forgive you in time. Already it feels like a weight has lifted." At that moment, Sylvester looked like a heavy weight had lifted from him as well.

We note that for some couples, *after* the impact of hurtful behaviors have been fully acknowledged and sincere apology has been offered and accepted, further conversations may occur that help partners better understand what influences were operating for the hurtful partner at the time of the injurious event. For example, in Georgie and Sylvester's case, they were able to talk together about Sylvester's many years of feeling compelled to achieve at work, to value financial success (almost at any cost) and the experiences of his childhood that had shaped these tendencies. He was able to acknowledge to

Georgie how academic success had been the only way he got his parent's attention and praise; he had started off in their marriage determined he was going to prove to Georgie how incredibly successful he could be. He had earmarked the management of the project that started the day of Mark's birth as a key opportunity for demonstrating his potential for success.

At the end of this chapter, there are guided reflections to help you and your partner work together on any past events in your relationship that may have caused either or both of you great emotional pain. We hope this chapter and your collaborative work on the reflections will help you to heal the injury.

Two Final Notes

When is Forgiveness Not Appropriate?

No one has a right to *demand* forgiveness of a partner who has been wronged. It is ultimately a choice, not a duty for a hurt person to forgive. In particular, perpetrators of abuse or violence do not have a right to demand forgiveness from their partners, because doing so may leave the victim vulnerable to further harm. For example, it is concerning to know that when women forgive their violent partners, they are more likely to return to those relationships.[31] While we have already emphasized that forgiveness is not the same as condoning or forgetting,[32] "premature" forgiveness[33] may function as condoning, and therefore will be *un*helpful if violence in the relationship has not be addressed.

If you live in an abusive or violent relationship, we urge you to seek professional help as soon as possible to assist you and your partner to address the serious issues that erode your wellbeing and safety. Change can happen. Problems can be overcome. Couples can transform their relationships. However, you need to start by establishing safety and respect.

What About Forgiveness of Self?

Any discussion of forgiveness needs to include at least a brief consideration of forgiving oneself. If you have high amounts of empathy for the person you have hurt, you may tend to have low amounts of empathy for yourself.[34,35] Conversely, if you are quick to forgive yourself and forget about the consequences of your own behavior, you may tend not to be very sensitive or empathic toward the person you have hurt.[36] So, feelings of guilt can be healthy and helpful, particularly if we become motivated to apologize and make dedicated attempts to repair relationship damage;[37] feeling acutely aware of the harm we have caused can also motivate us to "mend our ways." In this sense, forgiving oneself should not be rushed.

However, at some point, after you have expressed sincere remorse, demonstrated a willingness to change, and done your part wholeheartedly to make amends, forgiveness of self could be viewed as "morally appropriate."[38] Especially if partners have indicated a willingness to forgive, self-condemnation long term is unlikely to be useful. As has been mentioned before, forgiveness is a choice, and requires a change of heart. Forgiving oneself can be a healthy step in bringing closure to a difficult chapter in your relationship. Just as when we forgive others, self-forgiveness may be assisted by seeing ourselves in a larger context (a whole person rather than just one deed), recognizing our strengths as well as our weaknesses, asking, "For how long do I need to keep punishing myself?" and reflecting on what personal meaning or learning has been gained from the mistake and the suffering.

Reflection 10.2 Attachment injuries

If Reflection 10.1 opened up awareness for you of more serious injury, take some time to go deeper by reflecting on the following questions.

What was lost in the hurtful event?

____
____
____

What were the negative, helpless or hopeless feelings for me that followed?

____
____
____

How have I tried to protect myself since that event occurred?

____
____
____

What assumptions about safety in our relationship were shattered that day?

____
____
____

How have our negative interactions developed since that event?

____
____
____

How have we attempted to mend the damage caused?

____
____
____

What hopes and longings for closeness have I suppressed?

____
____
____

Before talking to your partner about these reflections, we suggest that you reflect on whether it is safe to share your reflections. You might like to revisit the checklist in Chapter 9 (Reflection 9.1) to review your readiness to talk about a topic that is loaded with potential "raw spots."

Reflection 10.3 Talking it over

What is it like for me to contemplate talking to you, my partner, about events from our past that still cause me hurt? What would I like to say?

___

___

___

How can I express those thoughts and feelings in a way that will be clear but not hurtful and destructive to our relationship?

___

___

How can I start the conversation in a way that is not harsh?

___

___

What do I need to do to express my hurt clearly without getting caught up in outrage and venting?

___

___

Do I have concerns about such a conversation?

___

___

If so, it will help to look back over earlier chapters on the negative cycle and reactive versus core emotions. Think about what you have learned about your emotions, how you express them, your part in any negative cycles of interaction. Think some more about using the simple guidelines for L-O-V-E conversations: listen to each other with an open heart and mind; validate and acknowledge each other; express thoughts and feelings simply, softly and slowly.

It may help to begin such a conversation by expressing your concerns about the process, rather than going straight into the content of what you want to say. For example, "I'd like to talk to you about something that is important to me, but I feel uneasy, a bit scared that I'll lose my cool. This is hard for me, but I also don't want it to be bad for you. I've made notes from the reflections in The Two of Us workbook to help me stay on track. Is this an OK time for us to talk or would you rather I wait until . . .?"

Reflection 10.4 If I have hurt my partner

What exactly caused my partner hurt? What other emotions are involved for my partner (e.g., anger, sadness, fear)? What specifically did I do/not do that was hurtful?

____

____

What does my partner need from me now? What would help tend to the hurt?

____

____

Are there any barriers or obstacles to my offering a sincere apology to my partner in relation to the outlined incident/s? What is it like for me to anticipate apologizing to my partner?

____

____

____

What do I see as potential barriers or obstacles to my partner forgiving me in relation to these event/s?

____

____

What would I like to do for my partner or say to my partner now?

____

____

____

If offering an apology, stay focused on what you REGRET, take RESPONSIBILITY for your role in the injury and talk about how you hope to REMEDY[36] the hurt caused. Avoid defending yourself or making excuses. It may help for you to write out what you want to say and then read the letter to your partner or give it to your partner to read.

Important as it is to offer apology and seek forgiveness, remember that forgiveness cannot be engineered or forced. While waiting for forgiveness, work on reducing negative behaviors (such as criticizing, excessive drinking, gambling or flirting) and work on increasing positive behaviors such as kindness, listening and supporting with family responsibilities. In particular following affairs, it is usually very helpful to be open and honest about your whereabouts and activities while away from your spouse. This will help rebuild their trust in you.

Reflection 10.5 Debriefing about the reflections and conversations with my partner

What has it been like for me to engage in the reflections of this chapter?

____

____

What was helpful?

____

____

What still feels unfinished?

____

____

What was it like to talk to my partner?

____

____

What was it like listening to my partner express their vulnerable feelings?

____

____

How did I feel expressing my vulnerable feelings?

____

____

Was there anything that felt too hard to talk about with my partner?

____

____

If any of these reflections open up issues for you individually or as a couple that feel too hard to handle on your own, we encourage you to seek some professional help. Find a counselor, therapist, pastor or doctor in your local area who is willing to work with you to find a way through these difficulties.

References

1. Feeney, J. (2009). When love hurts: Understanding hurtful events in couple relationships. In A. Vangelisti (Ed.), *Feeling hurt in close relationships* (pp. 313–335). Cambridge: Cambridge University Press.
2. Feeney, J., & Fitzgerald, J. (2012). Relationship education. In P. Noller & G. Karantzas (Eds.), *The Wiley-Blackwell handbook of couples and family relationships* (pp. 289–304). Malden, MA: Wiley-Blackwell.
3. Laumans, E. O., Gagnon, J. H., Michael, R. T., & Michaels, S. (1994). *The social organization of sexuality*. Chicago: University of Chicago Press.

4. Treas, J., & Giesen, D. (2000). Sexual infidelity among married and cohabitating Americans. *Journal of Marriage and the Family, 62*, 48–60.
5. Feeney, J. A. (2004). Hurt feelings in couple relationships: Towards integrative models of the negative effects of hurtful events. *Journal of Social and Personal Relationships, 21*, 487–508.
6. Rusbult, C. E., Kumashiro, M., Finkel, E. J., & Wildshut, T. (2002). The war of the roses: An interdependence analysis of betrayal and forgiveness. In P. Noller & J. Feeney (Eds.), *Understanding marriage* (pp. 251–281). Cambridge: Cambridge University Press.
7. Kowalski, R. M., Walker, S., Wilkinson, R., Queen, A., & Sharpe, B. (2003). Lying, cheating, complaining, and other aversive interpersonal behaviours: A narrative examination of the darker side of relationships. *Journal of Social and Personal Relationships, 20*, 471–490.
8. Feeney, J., & Fitzgerald, J. (2012). Relationship education. In P. Noller & G. Karantzas (Eds.), *The Wiley-Blackwell handbook of couples and family relationships* (pp. 289–304). Malden, MA: Wiley-Blackwell.
9. Bronte, C. (1847/1992). *Jane Eyre* (p. 38). Oxford: Oxford University Press.
10. Enright, R. (2001). *Forgiveness is a choice*. Washington, DC: APA Life Tools.
11. Fincham, F. (2000). The kiss of the porcupines: From attributing responsibility to forgiving. *Personal Relationships, 7*, 1–23.
12. Worthington, E. L., Sandage, S., & Berry, J. (2000). Group interventions to promote forgiveness: What researchers and clinicians ought to know. In M. McCullough, K. Pargament et al. (Eds.), *Forgiveness: Theory, research and practice* (pp. 228–253). New York, NY: Guilford Press.
13. Pingleton, J. (1989). The role and function of forgiveness in the psychotherapeutic process. *Journal of Psychology and Theology, 17*, 27–35.
14. McCullough, M., Worthington, E., & Rachal, K. (1997). Interpersonal forgiving in close relationships. *Journal of Personality and Social Psychology, 73*, 321–336.
15. Kaminer, D., Stein, D. J., Mbanga, I., & Zungu-Dirwayi, N. (2000). Forgiveness: Toward an integration of theoretical models. *Psychiatry, 63*, 344–357.
16. Tutu, D., & Tutu, M. (2014). *The book of forgiving*. London: William Collins.
17. vanOyen Witvliet, C., Ludwig, T., & Vander Laan, K. (2001). Granting forgiveness or harboring grudges: Implications for emotion, physiology and health. *Psychological Science, 12*, 117–123.
18. Fenell, D. (1993). Characteristics of long-term marriages. *Journal of Mental Health Counselling, 15*, 446–460.
19. McCullough, M., Worthington, E., & Rachal, K. (1997). Interpersonal forgiving in close relationships. *Journal of Personality and Social Psychology, 73*, 321–336.
20. Ohbuchi, K., Kameda, M., & Agarie, N. (1989). Apology as aggression control: Its role in mediating appraisal of and response to harm. *Journal of Personality and Social Psychology, 56*, 219–227.
21. Weiner, B. (1995). *Judgements of responsibility: A foundation for a theory of social conduct*. New York, NY: The Guilford Press.
22. Takaku, S. (2001). The effects of apology and perspective taking on Interpersonal forgiveness: A dissonance-attribution model of interpersonal forgiveness. *Journal of Social Psychology, 141*, 494–508.
23. Makinen, J. A., & Johnson, S. (2006). Resolving attachment injuries in couples using EFT: Steps toward forgiveness and reconciliation. *Journal of Consulting and Clinical Psychology, 74*(6), 1055–1064.
24. Fitness, J. (2001). Betrayal, rejection, revenge and forgiveness. In M. Leary (Ed.), *Interpersonal rejection* (pp. 73–103). Oxford: Oxford University Press.
25. Greenberg, L., Warwar, S., & Malcolm, W. (2010). Emotion-focused couples' therapy and the facilitation of forgiveness. *Journal of Marital and Family Therapy, 36*, 28–42.
26. Johnson, S. M., Makinen, J., & Millikin, J. (2001). Attachment injuries in couple relationships: A new perspective on impasses in couple therapy. *Journal of Marital and Family Therapy, 27*, 145–155.
27. Johnson, S. (2008). *Hold me tight*. New York, NY, Boston and London: Little, Brown and Company.
28. Johnson, S. M., Makinen, J., & Millikin, J. (2001). Attachment injuries in couple relationships: A new perspective on impasses in couple therapy. *Journal of Marital and Family Therapy, 27*, 145–155.
29. Makinen, J. A., & Johnson, S. (2006). Resolving attachment injuries in couples using EFT: Steps toward forgiveness and reconciliation. *Journal of Consulting and Clinical Psychology, 74*(6), 1055–1064.
30. Zuccarini, D., Johnson, S. M., Dalgleish, T. L., & Makinen, J. (2013). Forgiveness and reconciliation in emotionally focused therapy for couples: The client change process and therapist interventions. *Journal of Marital and Family Therapy, 39*, 148–162.

31. Gordon, K. C., Burton, S., & Porter, L. (2004). Predicting the intention of women in domestic violence shelters to return to partners: Does forgiveness play a role. *Journal of Family Psychology, 18*, 331–338.
32. Enright, R. (2001). *Forgiveness is a choice*. Washington, DC: APA Life Tools.
33. Walrond-Skinner, S. (1998). The function and role of forgiveness in working with couples and families: Clearing the ground. *Journal of Family Therapy, 20*, 3–19.
34. Macaskill, A., Maltby, J., & Day, L. (2002). Forgiveness of self and others and emotional empathy. *Journal of Social Psychology, 142*, 663–665.
35. Zechmeister, J., & Romero, C. (2002). Victim and offender accounts of interpersonal conflict: Autobiographical narratives of forgiveness and unforgiveness. *Journal of Personality and Social Psychology, 82*, 675–686.
36. Sandage, S., Worthington, E., Hight, T., & Berry, J. (2000). Seeking forgiveness: Theoretical context and initial empirical study. *Journal of Psychology and Theology, 28*, 21–35.
37. Leith, L., & Baumeister, R. (1998). Empathy, shame, guilt and narratives of interpersonal conflicts: Guilt—prone people are better at perspective taking. *Journal of Personality, 66*, 1–37.
38. Carpenter, T., Carlisle, R., & Tsang, J. (2014). Tipping the scales: Conciliatory behaviours and morality of self-forgiveness. *The Journal of Positive Psychology, 9*, 389–401.

CHAPTER 11

STORIES OF CHANGE

Now we would like to share with you the stories of a few couples who have sought our assistance for their relationship difficulties. We have changed a number of details to protect their identities, but have retained key points of their day-to-day problems. We have also included some details of their attachment histories to illustrate how their earlier life experiences played a part in influencing how they felt and interacted in their close relationships as adults. Self-awareness, commitment and willingness to risk something new helped these couples to restructure their relationship. As you will read, they changed the music and the steps of their relationship dance, with very satisfying results. We hope that these stories of change will encourage and inspire you to work for change in your relationship.

Angela and Denise: Finding Belonging

In Chapter 4, we introduced you briefly to Angela and Denise, a cisgender lesbian couple. You may be surprised to hear that they learned to unlatch from their angry reactive cycle and form a secure and mutually supportive relationship. Here is how they did it.

The Negative Cycle

These women were competitive. They both had successful careers in business and advertising and they both liked to feel in charge. When they disagreed over almost anything, it was only a matter of moments until one or other was getting angry and defensive. When the blaming started, it escalated quickly, with many uncomplimentary verbal exchanges flying back and forth. Fights would invariably lead to hurt feelings, anxiety and angry tears for Angela and sullen silence for Denise.

Their main triggers were around interactions with Denise's extended family. Denise's parents and four brothers were frequently expressive about their conservative religious and political values. Although Denise had technically been "out" for over 20 years, her family consistently denied their daughter's sexual orientation. When Denise was around her family, she appeared to handle her sexual orientation with denial as well which was incredibly injurious to Angela. At these family functions, Denise was careful never to touch Angela, speak affectionately to her nor in any way let it be seen that they were a couple, essentially acting out in the relationship oppression she had internalized from her family and community. As a result, Angela felt excluded, unimportant and very hurt. She would say little and endeavor to keep the peace during these events, but afterwards, her hurt and anger would spill over into provoking and caustic remarks about Denise's family. Angela's intention in picking a fight with Denise was to see if she was still capable of getting Denise's attention. Denise would bristle with annoyance and fire back, "If you just tried to understand what I have endured from my family over the years, you would not carry on like this!"

DOI: 10.4324/9781003009481-11

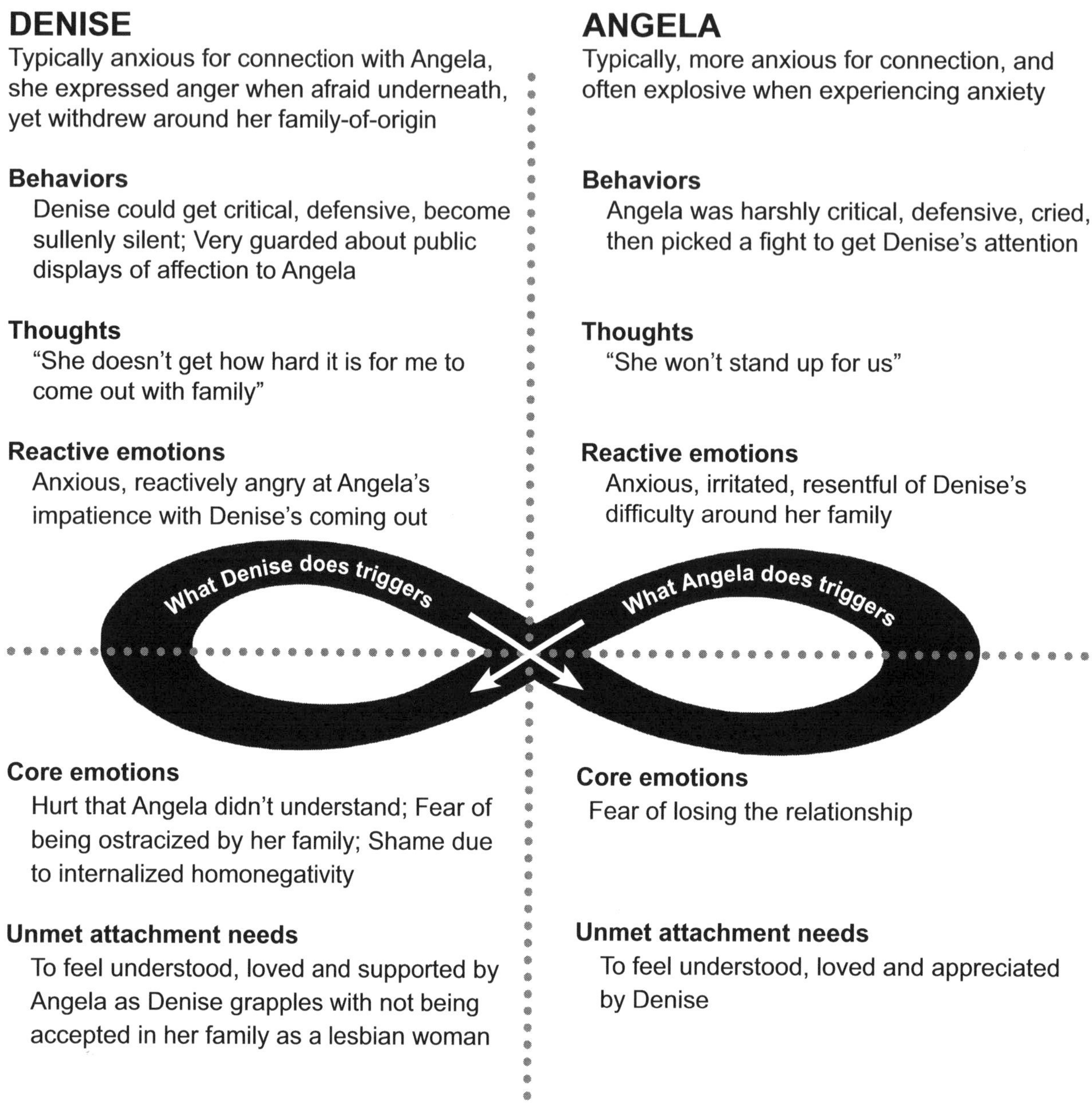

Figure 11.1 Denise and Angela's relationship dance

The problem came to a head when Denise was involved in a car accident. For the first few days there was doubt if she would survive, and she later spent many weeks in a rehabilitation unit to regain her mobility. Angela was distraught with fear and anticipatory grief. To make matters worse, Denise's family were deeply resentful of Angela's presence at the hospital and verbally attacked her one evening in the hospital car park. Angela decided then that she did not want to see any of these people ever again, and she conveyed this decision to Denise when she came home from hospital. To Angela's dismay, Denise replied with, "If you don't come with me to family functions, then we have no relationship!" The fight that followed so demoralized this couple that they realized they needed help. They presented for therapy and sadly reported the years of painful interactions that had plagued their relationship.

Previous Attachment Experiences

During the therapy process, the couple talked about their experiences in their developmental years, including the struggles to accept their sexual orientation and come out. Denise described her family as volatile and unpredictable. Sometimes they could be kind and helpful, but other times they were critical and harsh. It seemed like all her family members were sure they were right and most conversations took the form of her father or brothers "holding forth" rather than listening to each other and exchanging ideas. For as long as Denise could remember, her mother was often unwell with depression and anxiety; from time to time she would remind Denise that she was not the daughter she had hoped for, that she was a source of disappointment and embarrassment. Denise's adolescence had been infused with feelings of guilt, doubt and fear. In her early twenties she had married a man in the hope of pleasing her family; the relationship was unsatisfactory to both partners and they divorced soon after.

Angela's family life had been very different. She was an only child; her parents had an unhappy marriage and had fought repeatedly. During her childhood her father drank a lot and her mother suffered with depression. They were so absorbed in their own problems and unhappiness that they did very little to ever make Angela feel important or special to them. She lived predominantly in a world of her own, feeling lonely and small. When she finally talked to them about her sexual orientation, they didn't seem to react much; Angela wondered, "Maybe they don't really care who I am or what I am!"

Neither Denise nor Angela had ever experienced nurturing love or a feeling of emotional security. Neither had ever felt like they truly belonged to their family and were important to them in an accepting and respectful way. Both had unmet attachment needs to feel loved and worthwhile. For both these women, conflict in their relationship touched raw places of vulnerability and resulted in self-protective reactions of blaming and criticizing.

Changing the Music, Changing the Dance

In the course of therapy, Denise and Angela were able to quickly grasp their negative cycle of interactions; all too well they understood how fast they could trigger each other and escalate into arguments. Both expressed sadness that their relationship had deteriorated to this place; both expressed remorse for the way that they had hurt each other over the years. Both, however, expressed caution in picturing that they could ever change.

Embracing Attachment Needs

The turning point came when they reflected on Denise's accident. As Angela tearfully described her fear and grief when she thought that Denise might die, Denise listened in disbelief. She admitted it was hard to believe that she could mean that much to anyone. She expressed her gratitude to Angela for the support she gave her in her rehabilitation, the way in which Angela's love had helped Denise to persevere when the road had seemed so long.

Angela went on to say, quietly but clearly, how hard it was for her to be ignored by Denise around her family, how painful it was to feel so unimportant, of so little value, so small. For the first time ever, a conversation about Denise's family occurred that did not escalate into blame and criticism. Carefully, the couple listened to each other's vulnerable feelings. They were able to stand back from their knee-jerk reactions and help each other understand what was going on inside. Angela was able to tell Denise that she needed to feel special to her, that she wanted so much to feel sure of her importance to Denise.

Cautiously Denise began to reveal the grief and hurt that she had experienced in her family of origin. "However, I am terrified to imagine my life without my family; for all their faults I don't seem to know how to stand up to them and ever disagree with their opinions or demands." Denise went on to disclose how afraid she had felt all these years that the truth of their relationship would blow up at a family gathering. She expressed shame at hearing just how bad Angela had felt, how poorly she had treated her, and the harm it had caused her. With a flushed face, a pounding heart and a shaky voice, she asked Angela for forgiveness. Together the couple expressed their love and commitment to each other and their determination to find a better way to relate to each other.

The road was not immediately smooth for this couple after these important conversations. For Denise, learning to work with her love for Angela and yet also cope with her family's demands and her own needs for her family's approval took some effort and time. However, she and Angela were in a new place now, and they continued to talk about their vulnerabilities and their needs; they learned to react less and listen more. Together they discussed new ways to manage their interactions with Denise's family. Over time, their positive interactions and expressions of support and love strengthened each other's sense of felt security in their relationship; gradually, Denise also grew to feel more sure of herself and her own worth as a lesbian woman.

Some months later when a great job opportunity for Angela came up in another part of the country, Denise encouraged her to accept it. They started to plan with excitement a new life with more freedom and opportunity to make friends with other people in the LGBTQ+ community. They were creating for themselves more freedom from conventional values and a new chance to make their relationship the central part of their lives. A new chapter had begun, and both were now optimistic about what their future held.

Yuko and Michael: Weary of Pursuit

Michael and Yuko's therapy began with a panicky phone call to the couples' clinic by Michael indicating that he was afraid his wife was about to leave him. He was unsure about his wife's willingness to participate in therapy and felt quite desperate about the possibility of his marriage dissolving.

Yuko and Michael were a heterosexual couple, both cisgender and in their late thirties with one child. Michael was born and raised on the west coast to a French-Canadian mother and father whose parents were Norwegian immigrants. Born in Japan, Yuko came to Canada to study English as an international student in her twenties. She and Michael met at university and fell in love immediately. They enjoyed a large social circle bringing together Yuko's cohort of international language students and Michael's cohort of North American University students. Their journey to be together after Yuko's student visa expired involved traveling long distances and immigration delays, but it only fueled their love.

Once Yuko moved to Canada permanently their life context changed considerably. Although their love continued to be strong, they were transitioning into the responsibilities of young adulthood. Out of college now, Michael was busy building his professional life as a financial advisor which also involved expanding his social network. Yuko's international friends had gone back to their home countries and she felt lonely. Distracted by his career, Michael did not tune into Yuko's isolation. He was also insensitive to the enormous pressure she was under to assimilate to a North American lifestyle. Fully expecting Michael to help her adjust to this massive move, Yuko was deeply disappointed by his lack of support. Michael's inability to be there for Yuko at a vulnerable time of need was experienced by her as a significant attachment injury.

Consistent with the norms of her cultural background, Yuko tried to set aside her feelings for the sake of the relationship or sometimes she would put her feelings out in subtle ways. For example, instead of telling Michael that she felt lonely, she would discourage him from spending evenings out. When Michael seemed oblivious and insensitive to her predicament, she held back as long as she could, but eventually would begin to complain, mildly at first, but then over time more bitterly. Her complaints were met with avoidance and coolness from Michael. Around and around the loop they went with Michael's avoidance evoking more desperation and anger from Yuko and her complaints evoking more emotional shut down and withdrawing from Michael.

After the birth of their baby, Michael and Yuko continued to drift apart. With a newborn and no family nearby, Yuko felt she needed Michael more than ever. Being deprived of sleep and support, Yuko continued to complain and criticize Michael for his unavailability. Michael felt very judged and strengthened his focus on work, spending long hours there, as a way of avoiding the negativity at home. This pattern continued throughout their daughter's early years. Once she entered school, however, Yuko found employment outside the home as a homestay recruiter. Yuko became quite involved in her own work and social life outside of their family and for a time there was a decline in the tension between them. Michael noticed Yuko's shift in priorities and was initially relieved as it appeared to make her happier and there was a decline in the endless complaining, defending and negativity between them. However, he began to worry when she stopped paying attention to him and no longer planned activities for them to do together. Indeed, Michael's worries intensified when he discovered she was spending time outside of work with her boss. Although Yuko denied that she was having an affair, she did acknowledge that her boss was a good listener and confidante.

The Negative Cycle

Initially, Yuko attempted to gain Michael's attention subtly and then complained when he did not respond. Michael experienced the climate of their relationship as quite negative. His response to Yuko's complaints was to placate her in the moment and try to convince her that "life was good." However, Michael did not truly respond to Yuko's need for his support, nor regain her trust after not being there during her immigration. Instead, Michael spent increasingly more time away from home to avoid *her* negativity. By the time they came to therapy, Yuko had given up trying to get Michael to respond to her and was slowly disengaging. She had developed her own life outside their relationship (with work and friends), had established an emotionally close and confiding relationship with her boss, and was indeed contemplating leaving Michael. Michael had not realized his bond with Yuko had eroded so much and it felt like his world was collapsing around him. That is when he made the panicky phone call to the couple therapy clinic.

YUKO

Originally the protesting partner, Yuko gave up and turned outside of the relationship to get her needs met

Behaviors

Initially Yuko hinted at her needs, then shifted to complaining and criticizing; Eventually she began to create a life outside of the relationship

Thoughts

"Michael would rather be out with his friends than with me. I should be able to handle this. I must be weak. If he loved me, he would know what I need"

Reactive emotions

Despair, bitterness, resentment toward Michael; Guilty for feeling disappointed

MICHAEL

Typically the withdrawing partner, he shifted dramatically to pursuing when he sensed he was losing Yuko

Behaviors

Michael placated and attempted to convince Yuko that their life was good; When that didn't work, he became defensive; Over time he became "remote" and avoided coming home

Thoughts

"Yuko is so negative and judgmental these days. I am inadequate as a husband"

Reactive emotions

Emotionally shut down; worried

YUKO

Core emotions

Sad about being so isolated and lonely; Hurt and abandoned by Michael after she had immigrated to North America for him

Unmet attachment needs

To feel supported and cared for by Michael

MICHAEL

Core emotions

Panicked that Yuko would leave him;
Sad about their lack of connection and not attending to Yuko adequately

Unmet attachment needs

To feel closeness and joy again

Figure 11.2 Yuko and Michael's relationship dance

Yuko and Michael's relationship illustrate what can happen when a partner grows weary of pursuing for connection, especially after an attachment injury in which trust has been broken and remains unrepaired. The person who has typically done the protesting can become exhausted and eventually gives up "knocking at the door." They can divest from couple life and move toward developing independent life goals. This kind of shift can sometimes evolve into a life of parallel existences for the couple or sometimes be a precursor to relationship break up. As in Michael and Yuko's case, it is not uncommon to see a cycle reversal with the partner who previously withdrew moving into a pursuing position in reaction to the threat or fear of losing the relationship.

Previous Attachment Experiences

Let's look at the cultural differences playing into how Michael and Yuko's disconnection evolved. Yuko, the middle of three daughters, was raised within a collectivist culture in a traditional Japanese home. Harmony within the family transcended individual needs and in general, emotions and relationship needs were intuited rather than expressed directly. It was difficult for Yuko to acknowledge the validity of her disappointments even to herself, as loyalty and commitment was valued in her family of origin. Therefore, it would have been uncomfortable for her to consider prioritizing and explicitly sharing her loneliness or need for Michael's attention and support. When Yuko complained it was only after frustrations had built up and she felt conflicted and guilty about it afterward. All Michael could hear was that she was unhappy with their life. He did not perceive her as expressing a need for his presence and comfort.

Michael, from his own parental modeling, defined their relationship in gender traditional ways. He also reinforced cultural expectations that Yuko would naturally assimilate to a North American way of life. He believed his role in marriage was to be a good provider and keep the peace. Michael had witnessed considerable conflict in his parents' relationship, with his mother being quite emotional when upset and his father responding by calmly rationalizing his position and eventually turning away until things cooled down. Not having a male role model for how to effectively respond to a person's feelings, Michael felt out of his depth when it came to emotional matters. Although he was concerned about Yuko's unhappiness, the only way he knew to handle it was to try to help her look at the bright side, which he did earnestly. However, when that strategy did not turn things around, Michael felt inadequate to help her, and so he eventually avoided her complaints in hopes they would pass.

Changing the Music, Changing the Dance

In therapy, Michael discovered that, in the beginning of their marriage, Yuko's complaints were an expression of her broken trust and need for his support and companionship, rather than unhappiness with her decision to be with him. This was a sensitive area for Michael as he had always wanted for them to have a happy life together in Canada, but he just did not know how to respond to Yuko's emotional needs. Michael shared that his efforts to convince her to be grateful were attempts to lift her spirits *precisely because he was concerned* when the transition did not go smoothly. Experiencing Michael's sadness in-session and hearing about his intentions to make her happy enabled Yuko to open the door to Michael, but only a crack at first. Reframing Michael and Yuko's unsuccessful attempts to reach each other as their "signals crossing" was a helpful non-blaming way to make sense of their predicament. Their relationship improved and they began spending more time engaging in activities and conversations together.

Embracing Attachment Needs

As therapy progressed, Michael was supported in exploring his relationship to his own emotions. Michael discovered that he tended to bottle up his feelings and distract himself, often by keeping himself busy when he was troubled by something. He realized that he viewed emotions as a "problem" to "get over" instead of being a normal part of being human. This was true of how he related to his own emotions and Yuko's. Also, by not paying attention to his feelings, Michael was missing out on the important messages they were giving him. When he tuned in to his emotional world, Michael began to understand that he had been unhappy for a long time too, feeling sad and inadequate when he heard Yuko's complaints, missing the joy and intimacy they once shared. He poignantly shared his regret that he had neglected her when she felt so vulnerable after her move, and his deep desire to attend to her and feel close again. Over time, as Michael experienced these feelings in their sessions and expressed them to Yuko as part of repairing their attachment injury, she indeed felt closer to him than she had in years.

With Michael now bringing more of himself to his relationship with Yuko and tuning into her needs as well, Yuko began to struggle with her fear of opening up to him. She acknowledged that a part of her was drawn to Michael and wanted to lean into the relationship as a source of security. However, another part of her was afraid to trust that she could let Michael in and he would be there for her. Michael was able to acknowledge Yuko's fears and say that he understood her reluctance to count on him and trust that they could do it differently. He also reassured her that he would be there for her if she turned to him and let him in.

For Yuko, part of re-engaging with Michael involved first acknowledging that she had become resentful and hardened toward him over the years. She felt she had become a bitter person and very much disliked this image of herself. She also acknowledged that similar to Michael, she felt equally out of her depth in the world of emotions. Yuko shared that she felt weak and vulnerable for not being able to handle her emotions better. However, with repeated invitations, support and reassurances from Michael, Yuko began to share the hurt and loneliness underlying her bitterness. She wept over all the years gone by when she needed Michael and could not reach him. Michael listened and held her as she cried, feeling compassion for her pain and sadness over their years of missing each other. Yuko had risked trusting Michael and he was able to be fully there for her. They were healing the injury and rebuilding their bond.

In the last stage of therapy, Michael and Yuko discussed how they were going to stay connected in their everyday lives. They used several of the strategies outlined in Chapter 12, including establishing regular times through the week to check in with one another. Michael and Yuko had drifted so much over the years, establishing almost completely separate lives. They needed to consciously interweave their lives and activities together again. They decided to establish a weekly "date night" that they protected fiercely even when presented with other invitations. Additionally, in order to mark the renewal of their relationship, Michael and Yuko decided to take up a new interest together—one that was a little out of both of their comfort zones. In their last session Michael and Yuko shared with shy excitement their decision to enroll in a dance class. Dancing represented their desire to move and become comfortable in their own skin and to celebrate their ability to create a new relationship dance together.

Rafael and Karan: We're So Different, Are We Compatible?

Rafael, age 43, and Karan, age 55, were together for 14 years before they came for therapy. Rafael identified as Latinx, genderqueer, and bisexual, whereas Karan identified as a gay, mixed race (South Asian and British), cisgender male. They presented in sharp contrast to one another with Rafael being more outgoing, talkative and animated; Karan being more introspective, introverted, and subdued. Being so different in personality from one another, they wondered if they were compatible and if they should stay together.

Rafael described himself as thriving on change and shaking things up just as they are getting settled, including changing jobs regularly and taking up new interests (such as antique car shows, traveling, skiing, rock climbing), regularly putting him on the move. Karan said that as a general rule he did not seek out change and felt uncomfortable with the pace of Rafael's lifestyle. Traveling regularly for work as a business auditor made Karan appreciate down time on the weekends. However, he reported that he feared being left behind if he did not go along with Rafael's plans.

Perhaps you know couples like Rafael and Karan or have even been in a relationship yourself where you seem to have profoundly different sensibilities from your partner, such that you wonder if there is enough in common to hold you together. Rafael and Karan asked: "Are we compatible?" Our experience tells us that couples can tolerate a lot in the way of being different from one another. It is *how* couples handle their differences in the relationship that can either expand their world or lead to isolation. Meeting personal differences with tolerance, curiosity and commitment to find a way to work creatively with the differences can have positive impacts on self-esteem, sense of control and satisfaction in the relationship. Negative behaviors around the differences can evolve into negative relationship cycles eroding a couple's connection over time.

The Negative Cycle

Rafael and Karan were threatened by their differences and responded by trying to eradicate them. Over the years Rafael tried to entice Karan into his plans by talking them up enthusiastically. When Karan would not respond in equal measure of enthusiasm, Rafael persisted, but experienced it as "pulling teeth." Given Karan's slower pace, Rafael also reported feeling held back and stifled in the relationship especially when he felt he was dragging Karan along. When Karan agreed to do activities, but seemed disgruntled or uninterested while participating, Rafael felt let down. Rafael personalized Karan's mood, feeling hurt and rejected when Karan appeared uninterested in activities. This hurt manifested in complaints to Karan and subtle threats, such as "You don't have to come along; I can always find other people who would be happy to hang out with me."

Karan felt neither able to satisfy Rafael by keeping up with him nor able to influence Rafael to slow down to a more comfortable pace. Karan agreed that he usually went along reluctantly because he was afraid to say "no" and risk losing Rafael. Although Karan attempted to be a good sport and go along, he wasn't always good humored about it. The dynamic between them left Karan feeling powerless and undervalued in the relationship because Rafael's desires seemed to overshadow Karan's. Both partners believed that they accommodated to the other without being appreciated for it.

RAFAEL

The protesting partner

Behaviors

Rafael persistently initiated activities to entice Karan and used subtle threats to “replace” Karan if he didn’t agree

Thoughts

“Karan’s always ‘in a mood’ - why does he have to be so grumpy? I am an inconvenience to Karan. I have to entertain people to keep them interested”

Reactive emotions

Irritated and stifled; Anxious

KARAN

The withdrawing partner

Behaviors

Karan debated a little but would eventually give in to Rafael begrudgingly; He held back his true feelings

Thoughts

“I’ll never be able to satisfy Rafael.
I am replaceable. I don’t have an impact on Rafael”

Reactive emotions

Quiet worry, unease

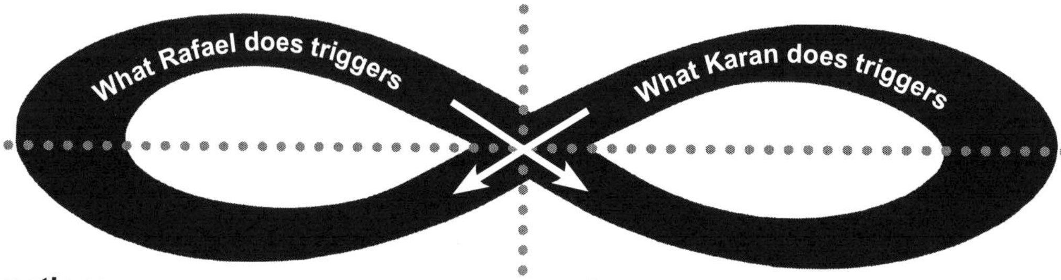

Core emotions (Rafael)

Hurt by Karan’s reluctance to participate with him; Rejected by his apparent lack of interest

Unmet attachment needs (Rafael)

To feel truly loved for himself

Core emotions (Karan)

Afraid of Rafael losing interest in him; Sad about disappointing Rafael; Angry because he felt undervalued and powerless

Unmet attachment needs (Karan)

To feel valued for who he is and safe to assert himself in the relationship

Figure 11.3 Rafael and Karan’s relationship dance

Previous Attachment Experiences

Karan, the younger of two boys, was raised primarily by his mother, who immigrated to North America from Britain. He had biweekly contact on the weekends with his father, who came from India originally. Karan described both of his parents as unassuming, conservative people. Their home was a quiet place, to the point that he and his brother were taken very much by surprise when their parents split up shortly after Karan's 10th birthday. He saw no prior indication of marital problems. Karan's mother became anxious and depressed after the breakup and remained so for years to come, whereas his father re-partnered and started a new family. Karan described his stepmother as quite opinionated, and he never felt truly at home at their place. On the other hand, he found the atmosphere at his mother's home to be heavy and depressing. Karan's parents guessed his sexual orientation, although he never came out to them explicitly. There was an unspoken understanding. Karan reported that he got along with family well enough but was not particularly close to them. Also, as a gay man of mixed race who always felt "different," Karan had never felt truly confident and secure in himself, which made it difficult for him to assert himself in his relationship with Rafael.

Rafael came from a family of Spanish heritage who were second generation American. As the eldest of five children, Rafael took a leadership role among his siblings. He saw that his siblings would bicker when they were bored at home and put their parents on edge. Uncomfortable with this chaos, Rafael carved out a role for himself in which he dreamed up adventurous ideas, rallied the troops, and took them out to play and explore the world. Rafael's tired parents appreciated the break and peace of mind that the younger ones were in capable hands. He became good at taking charge of situations and grew up feeling confident, capable and highly valued in that role. However, there was not much opportunity for Rafael to experiment and "find" himself until he left home to go to college.

Until leaving home for college, Rafael had never been exposed to any nonconforming identities. Deep inside he had inklings that he did not fit tidily into categories, yet he avoided delving into these questions. It was at college that Rafael began exploring his sexual orientation and questioning his gender identity which felt more fluid than binary. It was a relief to meet other young adults who were gay, bisexual or questioning their sexuality and/or gender. Rafael came out to his family in his third year one weekend when he was home from college. His parents were initially surprised by what they heard, but they were able to come around relatively quickly and say, "It doesn't matter to us what you are, we love you no matter what!" Although Rafael was very relieved by his parents' accepting response to his disclosure, he nevertheless continued to feel constrained by his "entertainer" role in the family, which carried over into new situations and relationships. Although this role afforded him success and lots of friends, it also constrained him. He held a deeply engrained belief that if he did not provide the entertainment, his friends would get bored and lose interest in him.

Changing the Music, Changing the Dance

Karan and Rafael began to shift their interactions when they stopped trying to convince the other of the merits of their own point of view and began listening. One day, out of a sense of futility, Rafael just decided to stop pushing. Although what happened next was quite unintended, it opened up new doors for this couple. When Karan was not fending Rafael off, it created room for Karan to experience the sadness of disappointing Rafael and fear that this was the beginning of the end. Fueled by witnessing Rafael's disappointment on a regular basis, Karan described his helplessness about how he could become a more dynamic individual who could hold Rafael's interest. He spoke poignantly about wishing he could keep up with Rafael, but time and time again, he felt the limits of his own energy. Sadly, he believed it was just a matter of time before his shortcomings would be the undoing of their relationship.

As Karan spoke, Rafael sat in silence, looking at him riveted. Rafael then remarked that he never knew how deeply Karan was affected by their arguments or that he even cared about pleasing him; it always looked to Rafael as if he was an inconvenience to Karan. Rafael agreed that, by nature, they moved through life at different paces. However, he went on to say that those differences had become magnified because his whole life he had lived with an internal pressure to be the organizer and entertainment provider. He acknowledged his own anxious insecurity that if he did not make life colorful, Karan would retreat (into a book) and he would lose Karan's attention. Karan drew closer and acknowledged that he did sometimes escape into more solitary activities. However, what he was escaping from was his own worry and feelings of inferiority, *not* Rafael, per se. They paused, absorbing these revelations before they were struck by a comical irony. The very act of letting each other "in" to their inner worlds both slowed and grounded Rafael and drew Karan out. They had stumbled upon a meeting place.

Embracing Attachment Needs

As Karan and Rafael became more "real" with one another, they were inspired by the curiosity and excitement it invoked in their relationship. It also allowed them to tune into themselves and further explore their identities, beliefs and feelings. Karan and Rafael discovered that although they were different "creatures," they were in no way incompatible. In fact, when they stopped fearing their differences and compensating for them in destructive ways, they could delight in them. Rafael loved Karan's reflectiveness, wry humor, and calm demeanor. Karan loved Rafael's warmth and generosity. They had resolved their initial question of "should we be together?" They realized that in their negative interactions they had been wrestling with the dilemma of how to be close without giving up the essence of who they are. With the relationship on more stable footing, it allowed Karan and Rafael to look more closely at their own insecurities, which lay at the heart of their common dilemma.

His whole life Karan had not felt solid inside himself. His parents' divorce had taken him by surprise and affected his sense of stability. Also, living between two cultures, being brown in a white world, and discovering his attraction to men, made Karan feel different from others on multiple levels. The fact that he had never shared his sexual orientation openly with either of his parents kept him in a world of self-doubt. Karan expressed his self-doubt by being reserved and unassertive in his relationship with Rafael because he feared stepping out and being rejected. However, Karan realized that his holding back made it difficult for Rafael to accept and respond to him, which was what Karan truly wanted. When Karan shared these revelations with Rafael, it gave Rafael a deeper appreciation for why Karan would agree to things and then seem disgruntled. On some level Karan was replaying a familiar scenario where his own wants and needs were not acceptable, and Rafael's pushiness had served to reinforce those beliefs. They both experienced sadness at this realization and there was a moment of closeness as Karan risked sharing and Rafael expressed regret about how his own reaction had played into Karan's insecurities.

Karan's courage to reveal his struggles paved the road for Rafael to look more closely at his own. Rafael explored the interpersonal role he had adopted over the years of providing the entertainment, as well as his persistence with Karan to go along with him. He experienced a mixture of feeling constrained by this role and also some emptiness without it. Who *was* Rafael, if not the entertainer? Rafael realized that most of his adult life he had been distracting himself from finding the answer to this question for fear that there was not much substance there. Karan reached over and reassured Rafael that he had many lovable qualities and that he did not have to "perform" for Karan's love or attention. In a solemn voice Rafael asked Karan for help in slowing him down and supporting him to discover himself. Karan and Rafael were establishing a bond that provided a secure base for self-exploration. They came to know themselves better and continued to confide openly with each another. Contrary to their expectations, sharing their differences now created intimacy, which had its own "energy" that was exciting and engaging.

On a final practical note, you might be wondering how Karan and Rafael resolved their differences in disposition and interests in daily life. With their increased security, both partners gravitated somewhat toward each other's energy level. As a result of the reflective work Rafael had done, his own internal pace slowed from its original frenetic quality. Karan on the other hand was more energetic when he felt able to be true to himself and open with Rafael. Both Karan and Rafael ensured that they scheduled quality time and activities together, including time for Rafael to pursue some outside interests while Karan engaged in quiet activities at home. Compromises were made openheartedly, based on their desire to accept and affirm one another. Karan and Rafael had found a way to embrace their differences and fold them into the fabric of their relationship.

Jamar and Holly: The Impact of Racial Trauma and Social Positioning

We introduced you to Jamar (age 32) and Holly (age 28) in Chapter 3, a couple who had been together for only two years when they reached out for therapy. Jamar was an African American cisgender man, and Holly a white, cisgender woman whose parents were third and fourth generation Polish and French, respectively. They poignantly illustrate how unacknowledged white privilege, racial trauma, gender expectations and class differences can strain a relationship, particularly if these influences are not discussed in an ongoing way. Jamar was raised in relative poverty on the "wrong side of the track." Both of his parents worked hard in their jobs; his mother worked long hours in the service industry and his father, who was a truck driver, was often away from home for long stretches due to his work. Jamar's grandmother lived in the family home along with his three siblings. Jamar had overheard many arguments about money among the adults throughout his childhood, which unsettled him. As a teenager, Jamar made a vow to himself that when he grew up, he would be a good earner so he would never have to worry about money.

In contrast, Holly, an only child, was raised in an affluent home in which she had much freedom, but not much involvement from her parents. Her father was a senior partner at a large law firm and her mother a surgeon who specialized in organ transplants. Holly had felt lonely as a child and always dreamed of having a warm, close-knit family with lots of children. She worked on and off as a caterer and met Jamar at a party that she had catered, thrown by mutual friends. Holly and Jamar felt an instant strong attraction. Their relationship developed quickly with them being almost inseparable for the first three months. Within six months of meeting, they had moved in together. That's when things began to change. With Jamar's focus on getting ahead and proving himself by excelling in his position as a web designer, he began to take on extra jobs and work overtime to impress his employer. Holly once again felt on her own much of the time, which was especially difficult after the intense romance at the beginning of their relationship.

The Negative Cycle

Holly began to experience Jamar as emotionally absent. She missed being the center of his world and longed for the passionate love they shared at the beginning of their relationship. At first, Holly tried hard to get Jamar's attention by making elaborate gourmet meals, candle-lit dinners and planning bike trips and picnics on the weekends. Disappointment shifted to repeated phone calls at the end of the workday to pin Jamar down and demand that he come home by a certain hour. When Jamar did arrive home, always later than expected, Holly's upset would spill over into tearful episodes and sharp criticism for working too much and ignoring her.

For Jamar, Holly's criticisms felt like attacks that cut to the core of his identity as a "good" man and dependable partner. He felt judged by Holly and it angered him that she didn't seem to appreciate his hard work and aspirations to get ahead. Jamar initially responded by defending himself, explaining that for him work was symbolic of escaping poverty and doing his family proud. However, when Holly discounted these arguments and escalated to stormy tears, he clammed up and shut down in stony silence. Jamar admitted that when they argued he would feel very distressed and turn to work to manage his anxiety. At other times Jamar would roll his eyes in contempt and question how she could be so needy when she had everything she could possibly want. When Jamar turned away from her, Holly flipped into panicky thoughts that she was about to lose him, and she would beg for his forgiveness. This reconnected them and would be followed by a brief period of closeness and passionate lovemaking until the negative cycle reared its head again.

Previous Attachment Experiences

As mentioned before, Holly's parents were both very career oriented and high achieving. They compensated for their busyness with expensive gifts and summer holidays, many of which only one parent could attend due to their high-level work responsibilities. Holly had several nannies throughout her childhood, one of whom she became quite attached to, but her parents let this person go without any warning or adequate explanation. By the age of 13, Holly was a "latchkey kid," coming home to an empty house and beginning to prepare family meals as a distraction from her loneliness. She had picked up a variety of cooking tips from helping the nannies (from the Philippines, Brazil and Germany) in the kitchen over the years and her parents praised Holly for her culinary creations. At the age of 16, Holly fell head-over-heels in love with an 18-year-old boy who coerced her into becoming sexually active. They had an "on again off again" relationship for several months in which the young man gave her attention for short periods and then turned cold, never bringing her around to meet his family or friends. Holly rode an emotional roller coaster for the better part of the school year until he lost interest completely. This first relationship experience sadly reinforced insecurities that already sat deep within Holly about how attractive and lovable she was.

Unbeknownst to Holly, her sharp words triggered a deep sense of inferiority that Jamar had internalized as a young boy of little means who was bullied by the white kids at his school. Simply walking home was frightening, especially if he wasn't with a group. He was sometimes even teased by other black kids for being "too black" and for wearing second-hand clothes. Jamar had lived with the stress of racism on a daily basis ever since he could remember. It did not help that even the well-meaning white teachers and fellow students didn't expect him to excel in school. He was instead encouraged to pursue sports. He was always told by his parents that he would have to work twice as hard and be twice as successful than white folk to get anywhere in life. They also urged him to be compliant and polite around authority figures in order to escape harm. As a young adult Jamar had many times been followed around businesses and harassed by store clerks and stopped by the police for no reason. On one occasion on a particularly frigid day someone had called security on Jamar at his university campus and made a report about someone "loitering" in the foyer of an administrative building. In these situations, Jamar always heeded his parents' advice to be quiet and cooperative in order to avoid being perceived as in any way intimidating or dangerous. Jamar never discussed these painful experiences with Holly, believing that as a white person growing up with privilege, she would never be able to truly understand.

HOLLY

The protesting partner

Behaviors

Initially Holly worked hard to please Jamar; Later she became demanding and begged for reassurance

Thoughts

"I am invisible. I'll never be really important to anyone"

Reactive emotions

Anxious, angry and then desperate when Jamar became cold

JAMAR

The withdrawing partner

Behaviors

Jamar defended himself briefly and then clammed up; He turned to work

Thoughts

"Holly doesn't appreciate me. I am being judged"

Reactive emotions

Anxiety that he was not being a good partner; Contempt in response to Holly's neediness

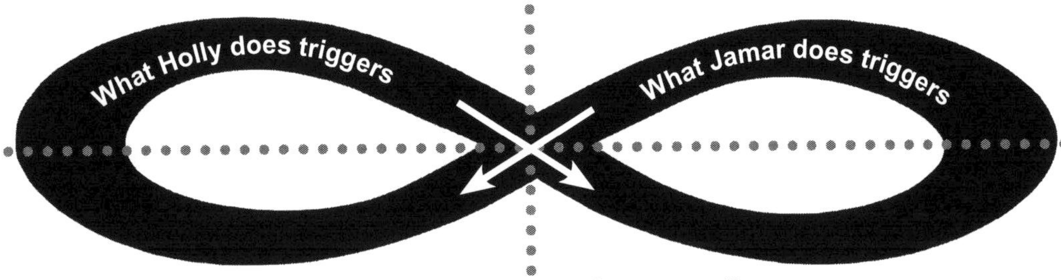

Core emotions

Sad and lonely; Panicked that Jamar would lose interest in her

Unmet attachment needs

To feel the security of belonging with Jamar and being loved by him

Core emotions

Afraid of Holly's disapproval; Hurt and angry at being put down

Unmet attachment needs

To feel true partnership, safe with Holly and reassured she "has his back"

Figure 11.4 Holly and Jamar's relationship dance

Changing the Music, Changing the Dance

Early in therapy Holly and Jamar's clinician recognized how racial trauma, chronic discrimination and differences in social position intersected to amplify their negative cycle. Jamar's experience of being bullied and racially profiled throughout his life kept him in a one-down position which he mostly handled by holding in his anger and keeping quiet, although it would occasionally leak out to Holly through contemptuous actions or remarks. Holly's privileged position conditioned her to express her distress loudly and stridently. The systemic pattern was replayed and reinforced in their relationship through the dynamic of Holly criticizing and demanding when she felt lonely and Jamar distancing when he felt judged. It took some time but Jamar eventually opened up about how diminished he felt inside by their arguments and perception that she was looking down on him. In his mind, work was a way Jamar could restore some dignity in himself and do something useful for their relationship, especially since Holly was only working sporadically. Jamar also explained that contempt was a shield that gave him self-respect and elevated him from the one-down position where he lived.

Living in a world with systemic racism shaped Jamar's identity and worldview in a way that made it difficult for him to trust Holly's ability to understand and respond to him. However, when he did open up to Holly, she was able to take Jamar's focus on work less personally and make room for his feelings and aspirations. It helped to quell the nagging sense that Holly had lived with all her life that she could be easily ignored or cast aside. When Holly was able to express her hurts less reactively, Jamar felt less attacked and took in the message that she missed his company and wanted more balance in their lives. Being able to express their core emotions helped this couple understand where each was coming from and softened their responses to each other. Although they still had friction occasionally, their relationship began to improve, with Jamar being more attentive in the relationship and Holly more respectful. She also showed more interest in developing her own career. Both partners found relief in their cycle calming down as they were able to have L-O-V-E conversations outside of therapy.

Embracing Attachment Needs

Creating some stability was a great start for Holly and Jamar in improving their relationship. However, talking about their cycle and the deeper feelings it stirred up revealed that they were still miles apart. Holly began to ask more about what led to Jamar feeling so diminished, which led them into conversations about the impact of experiencing racism on a daily basis. To the present-day, Jamar acknowledged that he never felt like he belonged in the social circles they frequented and even in Holly's family who were slow to accept him at the beginning. Somehow, he always got the feeling they were expecting him to fail. It wasn't easy for Jamar to open up about the profound influence of these experiences with Holly and with a white therapist. It made him feel very vulnerable and exposed and so, after some discussion, their therapist helped him to connect with a black clinician for some individual work.

When they returned to couples therapy several months later, slowly and in a measured way Jamar began to speak to Holly of the traumas in his childhood that led him to be a person who moved through life afraid in the world. He enumerated the many ways he relived these devastating events in microaggressions at work, walking down the street, on the transit system, at the bank, in the differing treatment he received when they were out together . . . and so on. Jamar shared that when Holly didn't seem to notice these differences it reopened old wounds and made him feel terribly alone in all that he was up against to survive, never mind succeed. Finally, Jamar said he recognized how hard it would be for a white person to understand, but he needed her to see him fully, accept that the wounds within him were valid and reassure him that she had his back with her parents, among their friends and in their community.

Holly admitted thoughtfully that it was hard for her to enter Jamar's world and understand what it was like to live as a person of color. However, she reassured Jamar that he meant the world her and she would do everything in her power to stand by him, including calling it out when she saw injustices occurring around them. Holly began reading books to better understand the trauma and history of racism, as well as to examine her own racial biases. Through her reading, Holly became more aware of the privileges of her own upbringing and the individualistic culture she was raised in that left her feeling lonely much of the time. She realized her parents assumed that she was "just fine" even as she struggled as a young teenager to feel a sense of belonging. In her sessions with Jamar, Holly revealed with sadness that she always felt like an accessory in her parents' busy lives and unsure she was wanted in her early love relationships. She hungered to feel truly loved and irreplaceable to someone—like she felt for the first time in the early days with Jamar but feared she had sabotaged with her outbursts. In a soft, timid voice Holly expressed her longing for reassurance and then held her breath. Jamar drew her into his arms, telling her how precious she was to him, as she sank in and sobbed with relief.

Holly and Jamar finally felt like their relationship was on solid ground. Holly continued her social justice work by enrolling in seminars aimed at combating racism and she and Jamar deepened their involvement in activism. It was an uphill battle, but their relationship stayed strong despite having to endure the many stresses of discrimination. They continued to stay closely connected and leaned heavily on their partnership as a source of strength and support. In one of their last sessions Jamar warmly shared a story illustrating just how far they had come together. Holly had surprised him at the office earlier in the week with a packed dinner and they ate side by side, working together on the website design for her new soon-to-be launched catering business!

In closing, we hope you have been touched, as we have by these stories of change. Our couples have truly been our greatest teachers. Their stories are the stories of individuals who had the courage to look inward, meet each other in their true feelings and chosen to travel together. To us they reveal so much about the resilience of the human spirit to move toward positive transformation when given the conditions for growth, namely the healing love of another.

CHAPTER 12

MAINTAINING INTIMACY AND REVITALIZING OUR SEX LIFE

As the stories in the previous chapter reflect, most couples who progress through the steps outlined in this book and who have engaged in intimate and reparative conversations have put a lot of energy into rebuilding their relationship bond. Couples talk about the quality of their attachment bond in terms of closeness, tuning in to each other's needs, reaching and responding, sharing experiences and confiding fears and insecurities. At the heart, it is about *feeling secure enough to be who you are and knowing that your partner will be there for you.* All that is left is to develop strategies for maintaining the connection you have worked so hard to establish. In this chapter we will look at how to keep each other close and how to address any remaining unresolved issues, including the important area of sexuality.

Staying in Tune

Many of the exercises in this book have helped you tune more deeply into yourself as an emotional being. If you are like many people, this may have introduced you to a whole new part of yourself. Most find it satisfying to gain self-knowledge and find that it increases their confidence in making solid decisions in love, work and leisure. However, as with any important ability (such as sports, yoga, meditation, music, languages, and so on), you need to keep an active practice of tuning into yourself in order to maintain your ease with it. We recommend establishing a regular time to check in with yourself. Some people will choose to do this daily, others several times a week, but we recommend doing it at least weekly. Table 12.1 provides some suggestions for staying in tune with yourself.

Table 12.1 Staying in tune: How to "check-in" with yourself

Finding a regular check-in time	Establish a time in your schedules when you will do check-ins, and create a quiet, reflective space. You can sit together and take turns asking each other the questions that follow or work through them on your own and share later.
Monitor your general wellbeing	Use your emotions as a barometer to monitor your general wellbeing by simply asking yourself: What's my general emotional state these days? Notice peaks and dips in your mood; notice how stable and/or labile your emotions are. Do you feel a sense of balance, security and wellbeing?
Debrief important events or stressors	Tune into yourself about how important events in your life are affecting you: How am I feeling about this recent/upcoming event? What was I struck by during the event? How did I feel about it? Do this more than once about a significant event and notice how your emotions shift and evolve over time.

DOI: 10.4324/9781003009481-12

Pay attention to warning signs of emotional distress	How is your quality of sleep, appetite and exercise? Have there been changes in your mood? If you notice you are edgy, impatient, quiet or preoccupied, create some space for yourself (even if it is not your usual check-in time) to examine what's troubling you. Imagine performing a "scan" of your inner emotional world. You might start out with a broad emotion like upset or frustrated, but linger and stay with it, follow it, starting with saying "I am upset." Allow yourself to feel and embody the upset emotion until it becomes clearer and more specific (e.g., sad, worried, hurt, angry). Now ask yourself: What is this hurt, anxious or angry feeling about?
Listen to your body	You can also perform a body scan and notice any bodily sensations such as a knot or butterflies in the stomach, heavy or sinking chest, flushed or sweaty, heart pounding, clenched jaws or hands. Focus your attention on those sensations and ask yourself: What am I feeling weighed down by? Is there something worrying me? Am I keeping some important feelings bottled up inside? Might this part of me need to express or do something to bring resolution?

Staying in touch with your emotions is an important self-care activity. However, when you and your partner come together and share emotions, it's a way of staying close and connected to each other. You and your partner have likely done a lot of deep sharing about your relationship throughout the pages of this book. However, sharing your feelings about daily happenings, outside of your family life as well can become part of the "glue" that keeps your relationship feeling close. One couple we worked with established Sunday evenings as a special time for connecting before their hectic work-week began. They completed the chores of the weekend and tucked kids into bed on time so they could relax together with a cup of tea and a leisurely chat. They spent time sharing what was on their minds, revealing worries and concerns, and also looking ahead to the coming week. They would let each other know of important dates and events coming up and how they could support each other through the week. They described that adding this time into their schedule was a very minor adjustment that yielded amazing results in their ability to stay in contact with one another, feel anchored and be in control of their busy family and work lives. They did say, however, that they had to protect this time stridently and say "no" to other invitations for their time, but the feeling of togetherness was worth it!

Your Relationship as a Top Priority

You are not alone if you feel that there are numerous competing demands for your time and attention. You may be wondering how you are supposed to add something more into your schedule when work responsibilities, caring for children or supporting elderly parents in declining health already feel overwhelming. However, when a relationship is neglected and the closeness diminishes, this in itself can become a substantial stressor. Decades of research also shows that close relationships can be a very important source of support and resilience against the impact of stress. You can cope with almost any stress, strain or trauma if you are not handling it alone. It is possible to keep your relationship close through high stress and demands by staying in tune on a regular basis as described. What follows are some other ideas to integrate into the "culture" of your relationship.

Establish Relationship Rituals

Close couples establish rituals such as date nights, a shared bedtime routine, or simply marking anniversaries and special occasions, such as birthdays, graduations and promotions, in ways that are uniquely theirs. Research studies have found a positive association between couple "play," such as shared jokes, terms of endearment or private nicknames and relationship satisfaction.[1,2] We also recommend paying attention to partings and reunions, as suggested by Dr Sue Johnson and her colleagues.[3,4] How do you say goodbye and how do you acknowledge each other when you come back together? Watch and notice; does your family pet give your partner a better greeting than you do? Although these ideas sound obvious, it may be surprising to hear that many couples miss out on creating joyful moments simply by overlooking everyday opportunities and important milestones. *We invite you to take some time to talk as a couple and come up with* three *new relationship rituals, at least one or two of which would happen daily.* They could be as simple as checking in with each other at lunch time or a ritual around bedtime.

Make Time to "Play" Together

Balance emotional intensity with joy and play. Discover some shared interests and make time to pursue them together (e.g., forest walks, gardening, cooking, listening to music, exercise). If you are not enthralled by some of your partner's interests, can you stretch yourself to participate in some way, even as a spectator or supporter? When you plan with the intention to increase shared quality time with your partner, you can make small adjustments that make qualitative differences in your life together. *Find a shared interest to engage in together.*

Make Decisions Together

Our experience and research show that couples who share personal goals and decisions, inviting each other's input, achieve more satisfying outcomes.[5] First, the act of discussing your wishes, goals, and decisions invites your partner into your world. Second, when your partner has the opportunity to share input or concerns, and a creative solution can be negotiated, they will likely be supportive in helping you achieve your goal. So, for example, when your partner says, "One of my personal goals is to become more fit, so how would you feel if I joined a gym and started exercising three times a week?" it acts as an *acknowledgment* that my actions have an impact on you and an *invitation* to discuss how to pursue my goal in a way that works for you and our family. This type of conversation is important in a variety of contexts, including changes at work, starting new projects around the house or leisure time activities, to name a few. It's not about asking permission; it is about pursuing goals and decisions in a way that is inclusive, and collaborative with the important people in your life. Conversations that open in this way lead to outcomes that are more positive for all concerned because care has been taken to integrate everyone's wants and needs.

Future Planning

Expanding from the topic of personal goals, consider your future goals as a couple or family. While the "joie de vivre" that comes from being spontaneous can breathe new life into your close relationship, planning ahead can ensure that life does not pass you by without meeting important long-term goals. *Ask each other, "What is your vision for our lives two, five, and ten years down the road?"* Future planning conversations can keep you aligned in your goals or at least let you know if you are not so that you can address your differences and minimize disappointment. Don't despair if you bump into differences, with a secure bond and some good will, as you will see, usually partners are able to solve problems creatively.

Resolving Longstanding Differences

When partners feel a sense of security within themselves and within their relationship, they can be more open and flexible. This is a good time to address specific content areas in your relationship that remain unresolved, such as redistributing household tasks, deciding where to live, or resolving religious differences in raising children, to name a few. The first step is to approach a conversation about your differences as an opportunity to bridge the gap between the two of you rather than as a threat. We want to reassure you that when couples can maintain this overarching goal, we have found them to be incredibly creative problem solvers.

Sandra and Brian used to go around and around in circles arguing about Brian's smoking habit. Due to significant addiction in her family, Sandra disliked everything about smoking and let him know it. She also adamantly demanded that Brian stop smoking and announced that his refusal to do so was evidence of his lack of love for her. When Brian felt pressured and disparaged, it squelched his own motivation to quit. He would defend himself weakly by making excuses for his inaction. Once they resolved Sandra's doubts about his love through therapy and Brian found some ways to turn to Sandra to cope with stress, they were ready to return to this significant area of disagreement. However, when they returned to this problem, it was with a completely new approach. Sandra asked Brian if he was open to having a new conversation about smoking and he agreed. Sandra started by stating that his smoking was still an issue for her, both because of concern for her own exposure and for fear of losing Brian prematurely. She continued by recognizing that he alone had the power to decide about his own health, so she would stop pushing and prodding him, but she still needed to eliminate her own exposure to smoke. Brian responded by letting her know that he understood and had wanted to quit smoking for a long time, but he knew he had to do it when he was ready to make the commitment from his own volition. He offered to smoke outside away from the house until he gathered his willpower to quit altogether. Sandra accepted his compromise and he stuck to their agreement. Within six months of their arrangement Brian began a program to actively quit smoking.

Sandra and Brian demonstrate how a very contentious issue can be resolved when partners are no longer in the grips of their negative dance. When your energy is not focused on coping with attachment distress, it frees up all kinds of resources and goodwill to tackle problems effectively. Sandra and Brian used L-O-V-E conversations, Listening with an Open heart and mind, Validating the legitimacy of each other's perspective, and Expressing their own needs openly and caringly. Sandra listened to Brian's need to be in control of his life. Brian listened to Sandra's concern for her own health and fear of losing him prematurely. They took turns expressing the significant meanings, feelings and needs embedded in their respective positions, without dismissing each other's perspective.

An important ingredient of Sandra and Brian's success in coming up with a mutually agreeable solution was their ability to honor each other's needs. Many people feel threatened when faced with a different point of view on a topic that is important to them. The tendency is to alleviate disagreement by trying to convince the other of the merits of your own point of view, becoming insistent until your partner gives in, or sometimes going behind your partner's back to avoid dealing with the issue head on. Disagreements can turn into arguments and resentments because partners feel unseen or unheard. It simply does not work to attempt to eliminate your conflicting viewpoints in these ways. Rather, partners need to acknowledge and respect their differing perspectives and then find a solution that takes both of their needs into account.

Remember: A good solution integrates and satisfies the needs of both of you.

Reflection 12.1 Resolving differences

What, if any, left over issues, decisions or differences do we still need to resolve?

What fears do I have about this conversation?

What are my most important needs about this issue?

Now generate a list together of all possible solutions. Be creative and think outside the box. Do not critique or eliminate any idea no matter how unrealistic it seems:

Circle the solutions that meet both of your needs. Take some time to "try on" the different ideas or scenarios. Trust your gut feelings. Ask yourselves, does this solution honor your relationship as well as meet your personal needs? Although not always possible, optimal solutions feel good personally and take care of your relationship as well (or at least are not detrimental to it). Once you decide on the best scenario or solution write down your plan for putting it into place, including the steps involved and estimated timelines.

Table 12.2 Tips for resolving specific issues

1.	Choose an agreed-upon time to discuss the issue when you are well rested and the atmosphere between you is amicable.
2.	Remember to use L-O-V-E conversations: Listen with an Open heart and mind. Validate and acknowledge each other. Express your thoughts and feelings softly, simply and slowly.
3.	Brainstorm a variety of alternative solutions without critiquing them right away.
4.	Allow some time before making a decision so that you can "try on" various scenarios and settle on the one that fits for your own unique set of circumstances and needs.

We hope that these ideas help you to stay aligned and feeling close. The remainder of this chapter we focus on enhancing physical affection and sexual intimacy in your relationship. For many couples, life stress and relationship distress can erode their sexual connection. We would be remiss if we drew this book to a close without addressing this important component of close relationships.

Maintaining Sexual Intimacy

Sex in Couple Relationships

Creating and maintaining a happy and mutually satisfying sexual connection is usually, but not always, an important part of most love relationships. Not only can physical touch excite and arouse, affectionate touch between partners comforts and soothes, contributing to the creation of strong emotional bonds. As we have noted throughout this book, secure attachment promotes exploration, creativity, risk taking in all areas of an individual's and couple's life, and this includes in the bedroom.[6] Professor Sue Johnson writes,

> Emotional connection creates great sex, and great sex creates deeper emotional connection. When partners are emotionally accessible, responsive and engaged, sex becomes intimate play, a safe adventure. Secure partners feel free and confident to surrender to sensation in each other's arms, explore and fulfill their sexual needs, and share their deepest joys, longings and vulnerabilities.[7]

While "making love" is satisfying, joyous and deeply bonding for many couples, for others, it can be the source of great disappointment, frustration and emotional distress. Sex also appears to influence the way that couples appraise their relationship. Sex therapists and educators, Professor Barry and Emily McCarthy[8] report that when the sexual relationship is going well, sex is regarded as adding only 15–20 percent to the couple's perception of their relationship vitality and satisfaction. However, when there are sexual dysfunctions present or sex is non-existent, sex assumes a much greater role (between 50 and 70 percent) in determining perceptions of relationship vitality and satisfaction.

Further, the typically private nature of a couple's sexual relationship can deter people from seeking help from health professionals or family and friends, leaving partners feeling very alone with their difficulties. While it is common for couples to talk over child-rearing issues or financial concerns with their relatives or friends, thereby gaining information, reassurance and perspective, it is highly unlikely that individuals will open up at a barbeque or party about their sexual pain or ineffective erections. As a result, many individuals erroneously believe, "We are the only couple in our neighborhood who can't . . . or don't . . ."

Individuals across the world, in all segments of society, can have difficulties at different stages of their lives with sexual pain, low desire, discrepancy of desire between partners, lack of orgasm, premature ejaculation or erectile dysfunction. *If you or your partner is experiencing these or other sexual difficulties, we encourage you to seek medical advice and/or help from a relationship therapist who has specialized training in sex therapy.* Many difficulties can be overcome, or at least managed to reduce the negative impacts that can otherwise result.

Also, if you are tempted to compare your sexual relationship with that of others, especially couples in the movies, you may be interested to read the following comment from Dr. Michael Plaut, and his colleagues,

> There is a vast gulf between the popular image of beautiful couples having magnificent sex virtually without limit and the reality of the ordinary couple battling to succeed at an emotionally and

technically demanding sport without coaching . . . Couples are often reassured to know that the only thing that matters is their satisfaction; there are no standards, either in what is done or how often.[9]

As this quote aptly reminds us, in securely connected, committed relationships sex is most often about the giving and receiving of pleasure. Simply put, "pleasure is the measure" is what sex educator and researcher Emily Nagoski espouses in her popular book, *Come as You Are*.[10] How easily though, we can get focused on *frequency* of sex and become too outcome and *performance* oriented. This could be narrowly defining sex as intercourse and orgasm or striving for the "ultimate" simultaneous orgasms. We forget at times that we have many erogenous zones on our bodies that can respond to sensuous touch, excite and delight us. The more items we can put on our "sexual menu" to select from, the more it allows us to express our sexuality fully and our preferences in a clear, specific and lighthearted way.[11]

Sexual satisfaction is much more about erotic attunement than sexual gymnastics—tuning into each other's sensual energy, being present in the moment, communicating desires, exploring each other's bodies, taking risks, being playful, having fun and moving in rhythm together.

These were some of the most significant components described by individuals who identified themselves as having experienced "great sex" in a study that included diversity in age, sexual orientation, gender and number of years in relationship.

Sex researcher Professor Peggy Kleinplatz found that relational factors such as feeling connected, vulnerability, authenticity and deep empathy were more salient in optimal sexuality than intense physical sensation, "chemistry," attraction and desire.[12]

The lovers who experience "great sex" in this study beautifully illustrate a model of sexuality first proposed by Professor Rosemary Basson[13] which acknowledges that "female" sexual functioning proceeds in a more complex and circuitous manner than "male" sexuality. Professor Basson reports that female sexuality is significantly influenced by relationship factors such as emotional connection, trust and level of conflict, and also personal factors such as how confident, attractive and relaxed a person is feeling. A person's *sexual scripts*, or view of what sex *should* be like, based on previous sexual experiences or cultural, religious or familial messages, can also either make a person feel more open or closed off to sex.

We are also learning that men's sexual desire is more nuanced than the stereotypes of super high libidos, always ready for sex, would lead us to believe. It is time to take some of the pressure off men to meet this impossible standard. After interviewing hundreds of men for her book, *Not Always in the Mood*, Sarah Hunter Murray[14] concluded that sex was not at the forefront of their minds when they were sick, tired, stressed or feeling emotionally disconnected from their partners. What stood out most clearly in increasing sexual desire for men was the potent message that they were wanted and desired by their partners.

Thus, whereas some people's sexual desire is *spontaneously* sparked as soon as they think about making love, for others desire is more *responsive*, which means it can be cultivated often with romance, foreplay, flirtation and playfulness. Responsive desire can be just as powerful and passionate as spontaneous desire once it gets turned on. The key question for couples then is: *What opens the window of willingness to be sexual?*[15] Emily Nagoski describes how sexuality is influenced by accelerators (turn ons/ reasons to be sexual) and brakes (turn offs or reasons not to be sexual). In trying to rekindle sexual desire couples can do well to focus on pressing the accelerators and taking their foot off the brakes.[16] Accelerators could include romantic ambiance, a seductive look, a flirty joke, specific nonsexual touches, being thoughtful, sharing feelings and so on. Examples of brakes might be when the house is a mess, worrying your child could walk in on you, not feeling good about your body, not feeling emotionally close or safe, fatigue, stress, pain and so on.

Lending some support, researchers have found that heterosexual couples where men do more housework report greater sexual satisfaction;[17] women who report greater happiness with their couple relationships typically experience more sexual arousal, desire and enjoyment of sex; and conflict and emotional distance interferes with sexual desire and satisfaction.[18] Not surprisingly, couples presenting for sex or relationship therapy are typically less playful and spontaneous than couples who report high relationship satisfaction.[19] However, there are no "right" or "wrong" responses or ways to get turned on, barring sexual coercion or hurting someone against their will. Sexual accelerators and brakes are as unique and personal as each individual is and they are a great place to get started in exploring your sexuality as a unique individual and couple.

Talking About Sexual Issues or Problems

How you and your partner talk and respond to any sexual issues or problems will be the critical ingredient that determines what happens next for you. Awkward silences, unresolved arguments and unspoken hurts and fears will keep you feeling distant from each other as you struggle to avoid the sensitive issue at hand. Perhaps you already feel like many couples who seek help for sexual difficulties: "There are now two problems, the sexual difficulty, and what happens between us as a result of the sexual problem." It is also possible that the distress and negative interactions that affected your emotional connection have drifted into your erotic connection. Or that difficult interactions surrounding the original sexual problem may now be fueling further anxiety and stress, which typically makes all sexual problems worse.

Talking about sexual issues and problems can be hard. Maybe that is the reason that you have picked up this book and started reading. Difficulties and differences around sexual needs and expression can trigger a host of negative feelings, such as sadness, anger, fear, hurt, disappointment or shame; if you cannot talk comfortably about these feelings or if you get caught in expressing these feelings in destructive ways, it is likely that you and your partner may be experiencing deep levels of distress, even anguish.

Perhaps you are saying little, because you want to protect your partner or yourself from embarrassment; maybe your partner misunderstands your silence as not caring or that the topic doesn't matter to you. Maybe in the past you have said too much to your partner about this sensitive topic, leading to conflict, more hurt and lots of misunderstanding. It is quite likely, however, that *because your partner and your relationship matter to you so much*, you are *both* experiencing strong feelings associated with the sexual issue. Strong feelings that overwhelm, as we have discussed before, can lead to difficulties in talking things over. Strong feelings of distress can also sometimes confuse us into reaching inaccurate conclusions, like "You obviously don't love me anymore" or "If my partner really cared, they wouldn't do that."

Maybe you feel shy to talk about your sexual needs and preferences; perhaps the family or culture you grew up in held rigid views or made negative comments about your body, sexual expression and intimacy. Maybe previous partners have ridiculed you about your sexual needs and left you feeling inferior, anxious or "odd." Perhaps you feel resentful toward your partner for pressing for more frequent sexual contact than you would ideally like. Maybe you have kept silent about that for years and now can't tolerate it any more. Whatever your previous experiences, you and your partner can overcome your difficulties by working together, asking each other for help, and being willing to open up little by little. Let's look now at a few stories of couples who showed us that solutions can be found, even for sensitive issues like erectile problems, pain with intercourse and post-traumatic sexual difficulties.

Lorraine and Keith

The quality of a couple's relationship will typically influence how they handle sexual issues or difficulties. Keith and Lorraine, for example, were a cisgender heterosexual couple in their mid-fifties who had experienced many years of relationship conflict. Lorraine often felt dissatisfied with Keith's lack of emotional support for her; she expressed her dissatisfaction in a blaming and angry manner that typically left Keith feeling hurt, inadequate and angry. Their sexual relationship had been an important part of keeping their marriage alive, and it was definitely an effective way for them to "make up" after big fights. However, with the onset of middle age, Keith encountered problems with erections; he felt very embarrassed about even thinking about discussing the problem with a doctor, and his reluctance to seek medical help led Lorraine to the mistaken belief that he didn't care about her or their relationship. She became increasingly tense and angry with him, leading to more conflict and heartache. The more Lorraine nagged him to go to the doctor, the more ashamed Keith felt and the more he withdrew into his shell. The more he withdrew, the more desperate Lorraine felt and the more she nagged. Their negative cycle was very much alive and their sexual problems didn't go away.

Inside, both partners were feeling alone and afraid, and very distant from each other. For Lorraine and Keith, it took painstaking effort and a lot of support for them to be able to break the negative cycle (nag-withdraw) that had kept them distressed. Overtime, however, they learned to try something new. Instead of blaming and attacking, Lorraine expressed her concern softly to Keith that she was worried he might have diabetes or high blood pressure which can cause problems with erections; she also risked being vulnerable and told him how afraid she felt that if they couldn't make love, they may not manage to stay together.

Gradually this couple increased their levels of understanding and trust and Keith finally sought a medical assessment. Both were relieved to find that Keith had no medical problems, but that his erectile problems were likely to be associated with aging, stress and relationship anxiety. His doctor encouraged him to get more physical exercise, try to reduce his long work hours and keep working with their relationship therapist. The couple learned to handle his erectile problems with a lighter, more philosophical attitude ("Sometimes this happens; don't worry about it; wait a few minutes and things may get better again; let's enjoy cuddling for now"). Through breaking the negative cycle of interactions Lorraine and Keith grew to feel more secure with each other, and more confident about their ability to work together with their sexual problem rather than ignoring it or fighting about it.

Steve and Karen

Steve and Karen, on the other hand, were a younger cisgender, heterosexual couple with a strong history of love and companionship, who presented for help for Karen's pain during intercourse. She had grimly endured the pain for some time before fully disclosing to Steve the extent of her suffering. As a consequence of suffering in silence, Karen had become increasingly anxious, even repulsed by the very thought of sexual intercourse. "Even the thought of him touching me now makes my skin crawl," she sadly admitted. It was heartening to meet Steve on her first visit and hear him say: "I'm glad you agreed I could attend as well. As I see it, I am 50 percent of this partnership and I want to help Karen. I don't always cope well with her rejection and avoidance of me, so I think I need some help too." Steve wanted Karen to know that her problem was really *their* problem and that together they would solve it.

This couple had the critical ingredients for success evident right from the start of treatment. They were committed to finding a solution, both partners were willing to open up and work with the vulnerable feelings that were associated with the treatment process, and both partners were able to help each other be patient and resilient in the face of setbacks and disappointments. Barry and Emily McCarthy[20] say that couples with a sexual problem need to become "an intimate team," working together with a shared problem, rather than against each other like enemies. Karen and Steve were definitely an intimate team, and it was pleasing to see the progress they made.

They were patient and supportive with each other as they worked on exercises to help reduce Karen's anxiety and the association of intercourse with pain; Steve felt supported and included and learned to manage his feelings of rejection when Karen said "no" to sex. At the end of the treatment, it was poignant to hear them admit that they were almost glad they had encountered their sexual problem, because working together on solving it had drawn them closer together and helped them achieve a safety in their relationship that they could never have imagined was possible. This disclosure, along with a photo of their beautiful baby who was born about a year later, reminded us that couples can, and do, overcome big problems.

Suzie and Tai

In the aftermath of sexual trauma, it can be complicated to create a healthy, mutually satisfying sexual connection with your partner. Suzie, a survivor of childhood sexual abuse, and her female partner Tai, illustrated how a couple can rekindle their connection in spite of deep historical wounds. At the beginning of therapy, Suzie pursued Tai emotionally, but was less interested in physical contact. Early in their relationship Tai was less emotionally open, but she pursued Suzie in the sexual arena. They were committed companions, however, with years of rejection and "empty" sex Tai withdrew sexually as well. With hard work, Suzie and Tai were able to rebuild their emotional bond and become close. Suzie and Tai looked like a happy couple now, but felt their sexual connection was still complicated and left their relationship vulnerable. Their level of security and safety shored them up to tackle the sensitive area of physical intimacy.

In one session Suzie revisited an experience common to her during lovemaking in which she flipped suddenly from pleasure to reliving traumatic memories fraught with terror and panic. In the past, she would shut down so completely at these moments that she was hardly there, contributing to Tai's experience of emptiness. Suzie said, "What I really need in my moments of terror is to interrupt our sexual encounter and just be held by Tai." Highly motivated to rekindle their sexual connection, Tai agreed to try. For several months Suzie and Tai experimented with this simple strategy of shifting gears from sex to comforting when it became necessary for Suzie. Sometimes their lovemaking was not visited by terror, but when it was, they always switched gears.

As Suzie and Tai experimented, their intimacy grew and their sexual menu expanded. In recognition of Tai's fear of rejection, Suzie stretched herself to initiate sex more often when she felt open. Tai began to feel desired again. Suzie felt less fearful of sex knowing that she could be in control of the process if she felt at all triggered. When she did need to exit from being sexual to being comforted, Tai met her with protective arms every time. Suzie spoke of feeling soothed in the comfort of Tai's embrace. Tai, in turn, felt good about being both a source of comfort and desirable to Suzie. Incredible trust, this couple was able to build, which led to more regular, pleasurable and intimate lovemaking. As their sexual connection grew, their relationship became infused with new energy and vitality.

These couples illustrate that if you encounter sexual problems or personal limits, whether caused by previous trauma, health issues, other life stressors or relationship difficulties, the best way beyond it is through it—together holding hands! Bring the problem into your relationship and work on it together. Restoring a secure relationship bond is important for creating an environment conducive to experimenting and being flexible. Commitment to work as a team, mutual desire to find a solution, willingness to be vulnerable and open, patience and persistence; these ingredients make good outcomes much more likely.

Reflection 12.2 Let's talk about sex

What positive memories and feelings come up for me about our sexual relationship? What positive messages would I like to give to you/my partner?

____

____

____

What is my own sense of myself as a sexual being or sexual partner? How might this impact the way I approach sex?

____

____

____

What are my "sexual scripts"? What cultural or religious messages did I receive about sex from my family?

____

____

____

What are some of my sexual "accelerators" and "brakes"? Can you identify three of each?

____

____

____

Are there any problem areas in our sexual relationship that I would like to discuss? Have we tried before to talk about this topic and got into a fight? How did a negative cycle get triggered and stay active?

____

____

____

What would I like to say to my partner today about my needs for intimacy or physical touch? Could I share a couple of my "accelerators" and "brakes"? How could I approach this conversation in a different way from previously so that negative interactions between us are not triggered? (Tips 4–7 as listed might be helpful here.)

____
____
____

How do I feel about sharing these reflections with my partner?

____
____
____

What are my hopes for our future sexual relationship?

____
____
____

Table 12.3 Tips for keeping your sexual connection alive

1. *If you like the way your partner touches/hugs/kisses you*, express your appreciation from time to time. If you would like that touch to happen more frequently, let your partner know, but in a positive way. "I like . . . and would really love you to do that more often please." *If your partner is sick, sad or troubled in some way*, offering affectionate touch without sexual demands may be a very effective way to convey that you care.
2. *If you are feeling disappointed or dissatisfied with aspects of your sexual relationship, ask yourself how you both communicate about what you want and need?* Reflect on your interactions with your partner and ask yourself if you get triggered into negative cycles (e.g., demand-withdraw; mutual avoidance) over the sexual problem. It is likely to help if you address the negative interactions first. ("It seems like whenever we try to talk about our problems with . . . we get stuck in me pressuring you and you turning away. I don't like nagging but I do want to talk to you. Can we figure out a better way?"). You may need to go back to some to the earlier chapters on relationship cycles and emotions to work through some of the exercises again.
3. *If you are attempting to talk to your partner about your sexual concerns or disappointments*, work at disclosing your feelings rather than blaming your partner. "I feel awkward when . . ." rather than "You never . . ." Work at identifying the vulnerable feelings underneath your frustration or disappointment and tell your partner about them. "I feel hurt/lonely/scared/undesirable when . . ." Your partner will find it easier to listen if they do not feel "in the firing line."
4. *If you and your partner have differing levels of sexual desire*, use L-O-V-E conversations to talk about it. Help each other to understand: What is it like to be the partner who wants more? What is it like to be the partner who wants less? What is it like to be on the receiving end of "no"? Talk about your own experience without criticizing or blaming your partner. Tune into your sexual "accelerators" and "brakes" and take care in beginning to share them. See if you can engender a spirit of playfulness and curiosity together. Don't worry about how often or what sort of sex other people are having, focus on making your sexual relationship a happy, fulfilling and loving experience, just for the two of you.

(*Continued*)

Table 12.3 (Continued)

5. *If you are experiencing sexual problems such as difficulty achieving or maintaining erections, premature ejaculation, pain during intercourse,* consult a medical practitioner who specializes in sexual health. Erectile problems in particular may be associated with health problems (e.g., smoking, weight gain, blood pressure, hormonal issues) or certain medications. Similarly, there are many causes for painful intercourse including vaginal infections, inflammation, changes resulting from menopause, and so on. A consultation with a pelvic floor physiotherapist could also be life altering!
6. *If your sexual difficulties are caused by relationship problems or are causing relationship problems,* seek help. Relationship therapists are accustomed to working with intimate issues and will treat your disclosures respectfully. Working through relationship struggles, performance anxiety, issues with body image or psychological distress concerning sex can help you become closer and available for affectionate touch and renewed energy in the bedroom.
7. *If you are wondering how to safeguard your sexual relationship into the future,* a good place to start will be to look after your physical health and fitness, look after the trust and closeness in your relationship and help your partner to feel loved, appreciated and special every day.

Additional resources . . .

Hold Me Tight®—Hold me just right is a Relationship Education and Enhancement Program for couples of all identities and orientations who would like to cultivate a sensual and sexual connection. It was developed by Michael Moran and Nancy Knudsen.

Workshop Listings can be found on *fulfilledcouples.com/couple-workshops.html, coupleandfamilyinstitute.com/for-the-public/ or ICEEFT.com*

A website for helping both men and women to better understand women's pleasure:
omgyes.com

A reference book:
Male sexuality by Michael Bader, Lanham, MD: Rowman & Littlefield Publishers, 2008

References

1. Vanderbleek, L., Robinson, E. H., Casado-Kehoe, M., & Young, M. E. (2011). The relationship between play and couple satisfaction and stability. *The Family Journal, 19,* 132–139.

2. Betcher, R. W. (1981). Intimate play and marital adaptation. *Psychiatry, 44,* 13–33.

3,7. Johnson, S. M. (2008). *Hold me tight* (p. 186). New York, NY, Boston and London: Little, Brown and Company.

4. Furrow, J., Johnson, S., Bradley, B., Brubacher, L., Campbell, L., Kallos- Lilly, V., Palmer, G., Rheem, K., Woolley, S. (in press). *Becoming an emotionally focused therapist: The workbook* (2nd ed.). London: Routledge.

5,17. Gottman, J. (1999). *The marriage clinic.* New York, NY and London: W.W. Norton and Company.

6. Johnson, S. M., Simakhodskaya, Z., & Moran, M. (2018). Addressing issues of sexuality in couples' therapy: Emotionally focused couples therapy meets sex therapy. *Current Sexual Health Reports, 10*(13), 65–71.

8,20. McCarthy, B., & McCarthy, E. (2019). *Enhancing couple sexuality: Creating an intimate and erotic bond.* New York, NY and London: Routledge.

9. Plaut, S. M., Graziottin, A., & Heaton, J. (2004). *Sexual dysfunction.* Oxford: Health Press.

10,16. Nagoski, E. (2015). *Come as you are: The surprising new science that will transform your sex life.* New York, NY and London: Simon and Schuster.

11. Iasenza, S. (2010). What is queer about sex?: Expanding sexual frames in theory and practice. *Family Process, 49,* 291–308.

12. Kleinplatz, P. J., Menard, A. D., Paquet, M., Paradis, N., Campbell, M., Zuccarino, D., & Mehak, L. (2009). The components of optimal sexuality: A portrait of "great sex". *The Canadian Journal of Human Sexuality, 18*(1–2), 1–13.
13. Basson, R. (2000). The female sexual response: A different model. *Journal of Sex and Marital Therapy, 26*(1), 51–65.
14. Murray, S. H. (2019). *Not Always in the mood: The new science of men, sex, and relationships*. Lanham, MD: Rowman and Littlefield Publishers.
15. Loulan, J. (1984). *Lesbian sex*. San Francisco: Spinsters, Aunt Lute.
18. Sprecher, S., & Cate, R. M. (2004). Sexual satisfaction and sexual expression as predictors of relationship satisfaction and stability. In J. H. Harvey, A. Wenzel, & S. Sprecher (Eds.), *Handbook of sexuality in close relationships* (pp. 235–256). Mahwah, NJ: Lawrence Erlbaum.
19. Moore, D., & Heiman, J. (2006). Women's sexuality in context: Relationship factors and female sexual function. In I. Goldstein, C. Meston, S. Davis, & A. Traish (Eds.), *Women's sexual function and dysfunction*. New York, NY and London: Taylor and Francis.

CHAPTER 13

LOOKING AHEAD

Anticipating Life Transitions

Before bringing this book to a close we would like to revisit the steps you have taken to improve your relationship. We also want to invite you to take a look ahead to help navigate future transitions proactively. Recapping and retracing the steps you took in this book to get where you are today is an important part of creating your own story of change. Creating a shared story about your journey through the pages of this book celebrates the distance you traveled and can become a reference for you in the future. As you read the paragraphs that follow, be sure to take time and acknowledge the important steps along your journey, moments of discovery and closeness.

Retracing Our Steps

In Chapter 1 you were introduced to L-O-V-E conversations, a general framework for approaching personal conversations. We hope that using the L-O-V-E conversation guide has been useful in helping you to open up to each other through listening and expressing yourselves in ways that draw you close rather than driving you apart. Chapter 2 helped you to try on the lens of attachment theory, which views your relationship as an emotional bond where you strive to attain your universal needs for safety, security and closeness. Chapter 3 invited you and your partner to look at various influences that shape your own attachment experiences. Do they help you better understand how you relate to each other when your sense of security or connection is threatened? In Chapter 4, you saw how couples can get stuck in negative patterns of interaction; the exercises in this chapter gave you a chance to notice your own ways of getting caught in negative cycles. These first chapters were intended to help you discover how you and your partner can get pulled into negative patterns that drive you apart. We hope you could see how you *both* contribute when your interactions spiral out of control and, similarly, are *both* affected by them. As Sue Johnson says, the negative cycle is your enemy, the source of your hurt and disappointment, not each other.

Embedded in the distressing relationship dance is a complex mixture of emotions, which we addressed in Chapters 5 through 8. Chapter 5 described the function of emotions and distinguished between the reactive emotions that fuel negative relationship cycles and the core, vulnerable emotions that help people switch tracks and engage meaningfully with each other. Chapter 6 described the main, core emotions people typically can experience in close relationships. In Chapter 7 we focused on drawing out the positive intentions that are hidden by the reactive or defensive behaviors you might be expressing when ensnared in negative interactions. Being able to recognize and share these intentions with the core emotions that go along with them is often a profound turning point for couples. When you see the sadness on your partner's face because they want to, but cannot reach you or witness your partner's fear of not being able to please you, it helps you realize that you are both hurting. You are in this together and need to work together to get your relationship back on track. Chapter 8 returned to

DOI: 10.4324/9781003009481-13

your world of emotions to help you make sense of how hurt, jealousy, guilt and shame can be useful in tending and mending relationship ruptures.

As couples get to know their own and their partner's behaviors, emotions and positive intentions, they begin to find ways to diffuse tension and conflict in their relationship. We hope you have found good ways to exit from your negative dance and gained a sense that, working together, you *can* change your interactions. This is an important milestone providing the foundation necessary to build a stronger relationship bond. Chapter 9 walked you through conversations that helped you delve deeper into feeling your core emotions and attachment needs. By expressing them and being emotionally responsive to each other, you strengthen the security and intimacy of your relationship. These are the cornerstone conversations that rebuild your emotional bond. However, sometimes wounds left over from profound relationship hurts, for example infidelity or not supporting your partner during a particularly difficult time (such as a health crisis), can prevent a couple from fully re-bonding. Therefore, Chapter 10 was included to describe the process of repairing and forgiving significant hurts.

As you took the steps outlined in this book to create your own story of change, we included Chapter 11 to help you realize you are not alone. Chapter 11 let you in to the lives and intimate journeys of four different couples who used EFT to address their goals and transform their relationship. Their stories were intended to both encourage you to see that change is possible and to show the path, highlighting important steps along the way. Finally, Chapter 12 addressed how to revive your sexual connection and resolve lingering problems in other areas. You might have noticed how much easier it is to solve problems together, when there is a felt sense of security in your relationship. Security fosters goodwill, openness, curiosity and creativity, all of which are important ingredients for good problem-solving. Finally, as you have likely experienced, relationships require continued attention and energy. Chapter 12 also offered some suggestions for maintaining all the hard work you have put into reconnecting with one another.

What If We Slip Back to Our Old Ways?

It is our heartfelt hope that in the process of building a secure relationship bond, you have met your own unique goals for picking up this book. Fortified with a strong emotional bond, useful ways to exit negative interactions, and effective ways to reconnect, we believe you will have invaluable tools for navigating the ups and downs of life together. However, we want to let you know that even with putting your best efforts forward, you will likely still experience some times of tension, friction and occasionally even revert to an "old style" argument. We see it as very normal to experience slips at times, particularly when fatigued or stressed, and we tell our own clients to *expect* they will occur. We all know that old habits die hard. Slip-ups are evidence of your humanness, not necessarily an indication that things are unraveling, and all your work was for naught.

If you can . . .

- *Slow down*
- Be patient and give yourselves some grace
- Remind yourself you have the tools you need
- Recognize you got caught in the old dance again
- Calmly go back to L-O-V-E communicating,

. . . then you can find your way back to each other.

Common reasons for sliding back into negative interactions are related to stress and letting your relationship slip down the list of priorities. High stress, fatigue, or sleep deprivation make it difficult to respond well in any context, including close relationships.

Remember that whatever is happening in your world, sharing it authentically in a non-blaming way with your partner is an important stress reliever and emotional buffer.

Keeping your struggles inside not only leaves you alone in shouldering your problems, but also can create a barrier between you and your partner. Similarly, over time not attending to your relationship on a regular basis with the rituals you developed in Chapter 12 may result in your drifting apart, which makes room for doubts and insecurities to creep in. Couples create their own unique ways for nurturing their relationship, but all relationships need attention to thrive. You may take some comfort in remembering that even if you find yourselves slipping back into the old negative dance, you now have the tools to recognize it and specific ways of sharing your concerns that can help you find your way back to one another.

Additional resources . . .

Hold Me Tight® is a Relationship Education and Enhancement Program for couples developed by Susan Johnson

Look for workshop listings in your area on *iceeft.com/hold-me-tight-workshops*

The *Hold Me Tight®* program can also be conducted independently online at *holdmetightonline.com*

We now turn to the topic of transitioning to new life circumstances, as change is an inevitable part of life and is a key time of redefining family roles and relationships.

Navigating Future Transitions Together

Whether you have been together for few years or many, you know that life brings about many changes and adapting to new circumstances together is an essential part of being in a couple. You have likely already encountered some transitions as a couple, for example relocation, changes in employment, starting or expanding your family. You may also have seen changes in each other's health, physical appearance, or mood. Some people thrive on change, looking forward to the new challenges it brings, whereas others prefer stability and take longer to adapt to new circumstances. As we hope you have experienced throughout this book, there are not "right" or "wrong" ways of feeling about change, only your own unique responses to share and weave creatively into the fabric of your relationship.

In the paragraphs that follow we look at some of the common life transitions that couples face during the course of their relationship, particularly around the family developmental cycle and coping with adversities such as health issues or losses. Although it is beyond the scope of this book to delve deeply into these topics, we draw your attention to them because transitions can be stressful and may awaken old fears, insecurities and patterns of interacting, throwing you back to the old cycle. Wherever possible, we will refer you to helpful resources on these topics.

We would also like to acknowledge that peoples' life courses vary to a greater or lesser degree according to many variables, including culture, social position, gender and sexual identities, experiences of oppression, health factors and life circumstances, including divorce, re-partnering and blending families.[1] These diverse experiences create unique realities. We hope this book helps prepare you to tune into your and your partner's specific life journey and resulting emotional realities, voice them to each other and respond sensitively. Our goal here is to highlight *just a few* important defining times in a couple's life that create opportunities to take pause, touch base and come together. In this chapter we will focus on phases throughout the family life cycle and some circumstances that force couples to redefine their current situation, transform their relationships and adapt to new ways of living. However, the underlying message is always the same.

Lean into each other when faced with new realities or concerns. Your best chance of coping with what life brings your way is TOGETHER.

Transitions occurring throughout a family's life cycle stir up strong emotions precisely because they often involve major adjustment in our closest relationship bonds.[2] You might be interested to discover that changes in family constellation, that is, births and especially exits (e.g., a child starting school, leaving home or death of a family member) have the most impact on couples.[3] Transition can bring up fears and insecurities, making them sensitive times when partners have greater needs for closeness and reassurance. Next we offer some thoughts to help you not only navigate the transitions that apply to you as smoothly as possible, but even experience them as opportunities to "lean in" and deepen your relationship.

Developmental Milestones in the Family Life Cycle: Young Couples

Young couples embark on an exciting time once they decide to share their lives together. Coupling involves bringing together two lives and forming an "us" that honors you as individuals and shapes your relationship bond. Along with settling into work (whether paid or unpaid), setting up a home and establishing a joint friendship network, another big transition for many couples involves having children. Of course, having children is not a given for all couples and considering how life altering it is, the decision itself can create considerable angst. Parental indecision is a growing area of counseling and we offer a couple of websites with helpful resources: *thebabydecision.com* and *motherhoodisitforme.com*

Bringing children into your world: Couples who decide to become parents look to the arrival of their first child with much excitement and anticipation. For some couples the process of becoming pregnant and the pregnancy itself goes smoothly. Some couples begin parenthood unplanned, while other couples encounter issues with infertility and struggle for years before becoming pregnant or alternatively opt for adoption or surrogacy. Couples who wish to become parents but cannot conceive typically have many painful emotions to deal with. Adjusting to the grief of infertility can place strain on the best of relationships. If this applies to you, we encourage you to be gentle and patient with yourselves as you adjust to the loss of a special dream.

The arrival of children whether planned or a surprise is typically an intense, emotional and sensitive time for parents. The bond between you as romantic partners needs to expand and make room now to include children. As Mary Dankoski[4] puts it, the challenge is how to become "partners in parenthood," without losing sight of your intimate relationship. Many women who have given birth to children struggle with their physical transformation and fatigue, wondering if they are still attractive to their partners. Many men and partners, on the other hand, report feeling left out since the focus of medical appointments and procedures is on the expectant mother. This feeling may even escalate after the baby is born and becomes the center of attention. The road can be bumpy at first as new parents get to know their infants and work through challenges with feeding, fussiness and sleepless nights.

Two important studies conducted in Brisbane, Australia and Minnesota, USA, were both guided by attachment theory and investigated the transition to parenthood, following heterosexual couples from late pregnancy to when their babies were several months old.[5, 6] The Australian study is described in a book for parents and practitioners, *Becoming parents: Exploring the bonds between mothers, fathers and their infants*.[7] These researchers draw attention to the diversity of experience for parents, both in terms of joys and difficulties, and to the value of addressing relationship insecurities before the baby is born.

Couples with high levels of relationship anxiety (Does my partner love me? Will they be committed for the long term?) were found to be more likely to have difficulties adjusting, needing more understanding and support arising from the pregnancy and arrival of the baby. Further, many couples reported that having different expectations about sharing household tasks after the birth was a stressful factor in their adjustment to parenthood. In both studies, relationship anxiety and perceptions of partner support were important factors in the experience of post-natal depression.

Investigation of the difficulties that new parents can experience has also identified that couples are more likely to have success in dealing with their anxieties and stress if the new mother or main caregiver (if family roles are defined as such) is able to state clearly where or how they need help rather than just getting frustrated and angry that "No one seems to know or care!" Asking for help directly and being specific, such as "Could you please get the groceries on the way home from work tonight? Would that be possible?" opens the way for clear discussion about what is needed and what is doable. Especially since investigations have also noted that sometimes new fathers or co-parents think they are being helpful, but actually are not always attending to tasks that have high priority in the other's mind. Working as a team where tasks are discussed and prioritized can help both partners feel more confident in their capacity to cope with all the new responsibilities that parenting brings.[8] Offering reminders of love and support even on days when things are going quite smoothly is another suggestion that the researchers offer.[9] The good news is that relationship education programs for couples making the transition to parenthood have demonstrated some success in preventing deterioration in relationship satisfaction across the transition.[10,11]

Table 13.1 Recommendations for maintaining relationship wellbeing across the transition to parenthood

- Make time to stay emotionally connected, sharing your worries, feelings and needs using L-O-V-E conversation. During pregnancy or while waiting for your new addition, being extra attentive and reassuring is a good way to allay insecurities about how important you are to each other.
- New parents who are primary caregivers usually have extra needs to know that their partners are close by and engaged. Co-parents, you are profoundly needed! Plug in wherever you can. From pitching in with changing and feeding the baby, taking on more of the workload around the house, to holding and comforting your partner and young children, you can be an invaluable source of practical help and emotional support.
- Similarly, co-parents have additional needs once children come on the scene, often struggling to find their place with their young. They typically want to be engaged in family life and decisions about parenting, but may feel peripheral or unequipped, so it is vital to encourage and value their involvement.
- Simple efforts such as checking in with each other, asking how you are each coping and feeling since your lives turned upside down, asking what you each need to feel supported will all go a long way.
- The hormones that support lactation tend to suppress libido, so it is not uncommon for lactating mothers to not feel as interested in lovemaking as they did before the pregnancy or birth. This is typically a temporary change that can be handled with L-O-V-E conversations to express reassurance and understanding to one another.

Additional resources . . .

Diary of a baby: What your child sees, feels, and experiences by Daniel Stern, NY: Basic Books, 2008

Becoming parents: Exploring the bonds between mothers, fathers, and their families by Judith Feeney, J., Hohaus, L., Noller, P and Alexander, R., Cambridge: Cambridge University Press, 2001

Young children: After the initial transition to parenthood there is ongoing juggling of the demands of work, running a household and child rearing. As children grow into the preschool and elementary school years parents also need to develop a shared vision and philosophies around parenting. Use L-O-V-E conversation as you explore parenting values that are important to each of you, knowing that you may have some in common and some different. Be prepared to exercise flexibility as you weave your perspectives together and develop parenting practices that reflect your *joint* vision.

Partners who have children with chronic health or mental health concerns face unique and additional parenting demands that can tax their relationship. A recent study of families with children on the autism spectrum found couples reported several common themes that characterized their relationships.[12] After diagnosis, couples had to mourn the loss of their expectations and adapt to a "new normal." Couples reported that the fatigue from emotional demands and additional caregiving responsibilities affected how close they felt to each other. They also felt socially isolated in their experience of parenting and lacked desperately needed social supports. Finally, these couples expressed a healthy need to give attention to the impact that having an autistic child had on their relationship. Based on our clinical experience we would venture to extrapolate that some of these themes may be relevant to parenting with other childhood concerns of a significant nature (e.g., diabetes, asthma, learning differences, major anxiety and depression, etc.). Even to begin naming how the relationship is impacted can help partners feel a little closer, which is an important goal since relationship quality is the factor that has been linked to co-parenting quality more reliably than any other factor studied.[13]

Here are some helpful resources on attachment-based parenting of young children. As you link arms to tackle the ups and downs of parenthood, turning to each other when you feel uncertain, imagine the foundation of security you are laying for your children.

Additional resources . . .

Parenting from the inside out, 10th anniversary edition: How a deeper self-understanding can help you raise children who thrive by Daniel Siegel and Mary Hartzell, NY: Tarcher/Penguin, 2013

Attachment-focused parenting: Effective strategies to care for children by Daniel Hughes, NY: Norton, 2011

Hold on to Your Kids: Why Parents Need to Matter More Than Peers by Gordon Neufeld & Gabor Maté, NY: Ballantine Books, 2019

The Dolphin Parent by Shimi Kang, Penguin Canada Books, 2015

How to talk so kids will listen & listen so kids will talk by Adele Faber & Elaine Mazlish, NY: Avon Books, 2012

The Invisible String by Patrice Karst, Geoff Stevenson (Illustrator), CA: DeVorss & Co., 2020. For ages 4 and up.

Midlife

If you are in midlife and life is feeling full, if not overwhelming at times, there is a good reason. Midlife is marked by reworking roles with children who are entering adolescence, launching young adults, and increased caregiving to the older generation. It involves the most entrances and exits in family life,[14] all of which are quite emotionally involving.

Parenting adolescents: The years pass quickly and can feel like a blur between school, extra-curricular activities and extended family. We hope that you pull together, enjoy the busy years and create many happy memories as a family. Before you know it, your children will have graduated from elementary school and moved into adolescence. Developmental changes naturally bring about new challenges and shifting dynamics in family life. Adolescence typically prompts some revision of parenting practices, loosening the reins of control and offering increasing amounts of responsibility and independence to your teenager.[15] Experts agree that parenting adolescents involves a balance between providing enough structure to support them in navigating their natural strivings for autonomy, while maintaining the family ties that are so important for their development and adjustment.[16,17] This can be more challenging than it sounds as teenagers begin to put more distance between themselves and their parents in ways that can be hurtful at times. Differences in parenting styles concerning boundaries and permissiveness may become accentuated at this time, exposing areas of disagreement. However, research suggests that when parents work together as a team in making decisions and jointly participate in activities with their youth, teens are less likely to engage in risky behaviors or experience symptoms of depression.[18] This finding reminds us of the importance of staying engaged and united to support your teenagers' development, preventing potentially unhealthy splits and alliances within the family. A common example occurs when the more permissive parent becomes favored and the less permissive parent is shut out. When parents are not on the same page and thus handle issues inconsistently, a variety of unhelpful dynamics can emerge, resulting in one or both of you feeling unvalued, undermined or overburdened in the parenting role. Your teens will pick up mixed messages making it more difficult for them to navigate their way. Teenagers are betwixt-and-between childhood and fully-grown adulthood; they need their home to be a loving, secure place to lean into when they need support and a solid base from which they can launch into exploring the world.[19] Table 13.2 offers some tips for parenting adolescents.

Table 13.2 Tips for parenting adolescents

- Open up conversation between yourselves as parents, sharing your own fears and concerns. Maintain a strong partnership in parenting and work together to keep your bond with your teen flexible yet connected.
- Even though seeking more autonomy, your teenager still needs you! They are looking for you to provide a *safe haven within arm's reach and a secure base with space.*
- Expect to revise your parenting practices, to *integrate* your perspectives as parents and also respond to your teen's changing needs. Be prepared to stretch, be flexible and collaborative in negotiating the rules.
- *Listen* to your teen's perspective and feelings first without trying to drive your point home. Finding a balance between limit setting and listening will strengthen your relationship with them and help you make better decisions.
- Of course, some boundaries need to be firmly, yet lovingly maintained. Joining and connecting with your teen first will make it easier for them to accept your limits when you need to be firm about them. Don't forget to validate their *feelings* about your limits.
- Remember, our kids don't need us to be perfect. Hurt feelings, anger, repair, apology, forgiveness is the stuff of family life. Our acceptance is what teenagers need the most so they can focus their energies on discovering and defining themselves in the world.

Additional resources . . .
Hold Me Tight®—Let me go is a Relationship Education and Enhancement Program for families with teens developed by Paul and Nancy Aikin
Workshop Listings are on *aikinassociates.com/workshops/* or *ICEEFT.com*
Hold on to your kids by Gordon Neufeld and Gabor Maté (Also attachment based), NY: Ballantine Books, 2019

Brainstorm: The power and purpose of the teenage brain by Daniel Siegal, NY: Tarcher/Penguin, 2015
Siblings without rivalry—How to help your children live together so you can live too by Adele Faber & Elaine Mazlish, NY: W.W. Norton & Co., 2012
How to talk so kids will listen and listen so kids will talk by Adele Faber & Elaine Mazlish, NY: Scribner, 2012
Positive discipline for teenagers by Jane Nelsen & Lynn Lott, NY: Three Rivers Press, 2012
Information for parents of LGBTQ+ Teens:
healthychildren.org/English/ages-stages/teen/dating-sex/Pages/Four-Stages-of-Coming-Out.aspx

The "empty nest" myth of middle age: Nowadays difficult economic times and uncertain prospects are making it difficult for young adults to launch careers, move out, and start their own families. In the US approximately 68 percent of parents provide financial support to adult children (who are no longer students).[20] Not surprisingly, couples who are aligned in providing their adult children with support report higher relationship satisfaction.[21] With increased mobility and a difficult job market, the process of launching kids out into the world tends to happen more gradually than in previous generations. It is quite typical for young adults to leave home and then return for periods, drawing out the launching era. This trend of back-and-forth movement has been captured in the Western literature as the "boomerang age."[22]

At the same time, with advancements in medicine and health care, aging parents are living longer than ever[23] and needing assistance from caregivers, a role often fulfilled by family members. Research in the US and Canada[24,25] on issues of aging and longevity reported that approximately 25–28 percent of adults provide personal care or financial support to a parent or relative. As you can imagine, helping adult children establish themselves, while also caring for aging parents, places heavy demands on middle-aged couples. They also report feeling unprepared for relationship changes with parents that come with declines in cognitive and physical health (e.g., renegotiation of roles, assuming decision-making power, coping with parental dependency).[26]

So how does the middle generation feel? Middle-generation couples report feelings of angst, uncertainty and exhaustion.[27] Middle-aged adults summed up their daily lives as "time starved" and "on hold" because they put off making future plans due to uncertain health of an aging parent, increased financial commitments and caregiving responsibilities being in a state of flux. A Canadian study that took into account immigration and parenting stress during this period found differences among ethno-cultural groups with Chinese and Iranian families experiencing greater parenting stress than British families, likely due to added stressors such as immigration challenges, discrimination and socio-economic disparity. The most important variable related to parenting stress across all the cultures studied, however, was intergenerational conflict.[28] Of note was that intergenerational conflict was more pronounced in the cultural groups that embrace collectivist values, likely caused by tensions in raising their children within an individualistic culture that may conflict with their own cultural values. These studies highlight how our familial bonds remain the most significant factor related to our wellbeing throughout the life cycle. However, culture, immigration experiences and other variables can certainly shape our experience of the family life course. Given the many possible stressors and potential for burnout at this time of life, it is especially important to stay connected, as you experience both the strain as well as the rewards of caring for your loved ones at this time in your lives.

As little as 20 minutes of L-O-V-E conversation can ground you, give you strength and recharge your battery. Spend 20 minutes together in daily talk time, discussing the events and feelings of the day.

Eventually, however, the kids do leave home, and the sad day will come when parents die. For many couples, the reality of their young adults leaving home permanently and the relinquishing of caregiving responsibilities for aging parents are met with mixed emotion. The end of an era can bring up feelings of loss and regret. It can also open up new possibilities, which in time can be experienced as exciting. For example, an 18-year study found marital satisfaction to improve for women aged 40s to 60s once children leave home.[29] These results likely reflect relief from angst about an uncertain future for their children and relief from multiple demands on their time and energy.

The loss of parents: The death of anyone close is experienced as a loss and it is natural to feel sadness, protest and longing for the deceased person.[30] However, the loss of a parent can be particularly profound, whether or not your relationship with your parents was close. Whether you have had a close relationship with the deceased parent or a complicated one, it can unsettle your own sense of security in the world, bring up losses or regrets about the relationship and/or put you in touch with your own mortality. If you have had a complicated relationship with your parent, this may make the resolution of your grief longer and more effortful.[31] Similarly, recovery from loss can be more difficult if there are other crises and life stressors occurring at the same time.[32] However, if your parent has been struggling with ill health for a long time, and you have been the main caregiver, you may also experience a sense of relief that their suffering is over and look forward to shifting the focus in your life.

The main way that partners can lose their way at this time is by not recognizing their unique role in providing each other with comfort and support. It is also a time to reach out to extended family and friends for help. Although the decline and death of a parent is an expected part of life, it can feel overwhelming with the ongoing demands of everyday life. It is natural to need to feel close and taken care of by your partner during this difficult time. Most people need to turn to and lean on their partner to get through the practical tasks, weighty decisions, and intense emotions of losing a parent.

Do not assume that if your partner loves you, they will be able to anticipate your needs. Turn to each other to ask *and* offer:

- Practical help with running the household, caring for the dying parent, making funeral arrangements, and winding up affairs of the deceased;
- Help with reaching out to extended family, friends and neighbors;
- Support with medical decisions and other matters;
- To listen, hold and comfort, soothe difficult feelings.

Remember, people can handle all kinds of trying, painful experiences if they do not feel alone. You may feel small and overwhelmed by the enormity of your partner's emotions. Even if you feel helpless and not sure how best to support your partner, don't turn away. Stay available and express your willingness to "be there."

As you heal from your loss and begin to feel restored with fewer caregiving responsibilities, your relationship can once again become a central focus of your lives, along with the pursuit of career and/or personal interests. Give yourselves the opportunity to go through this transition together. Discuss your vision of what your lives look like now that you have more freedom. By expressing your fears, hopes, and expectations, you can stay on the same page and shape your future together.

Additional resources . . .

Hold Me Tight®—Let me be me is a Relationship Education and Enhancement Program for families with adult children developed by Paul and Nancy Aikin

Workshop Listings are on: *aikinassociates.com/workshops/ or https://iceeft.com/hold-me-tight-workshops/*

Empty nesting: Reinventing your marriage when the kids leave home by David Arp, Claudia Arp, Scott Stanley, Howard Markman, & Susan Blumberg, San Francisco, CA: Jossey-Bass, 2001

I can't stop crying: Grief and recovery, A compassionate guide by John D. Martin & Frank D. Ferris, Toronto, ON: McClelland & Stewart, 2013

sharongreenthal.com/category/empty-nest/
caregiverstress.com
stagesofseniorcare.com/resources/
refugeingrief.com
These are helpful websites on caregiver stress, empty-nesting and grief.

The Senior Years

In terms of the family life cycle, retirement and taking care of yourself and each other as you age involve the final transitions in roles, responsibilities, and relationships. Older couples face unique challenges in retirement and their own health challenges.[33] Next are some thoughts on keeping your relationship strong in the later years.

Retirement: Winding up work and professional life represents a major transition involving changes in your identity, lifestyle, roles and priorities. As we found when researching the empty nest phenomenon, nowadays retirement seems to occur in phases as opposed to being a discrete event. Many people retire from their primary careers, to pursue secondary careers, work or volunteer activities, often part time, that reflect long-term hobbies or interests.[34] For some, retirement is anticipated as the "golden years" of freedom from the grind and opportunity to pursue special interests, including focusing on grandchildren and other family members. Others, who retire out of necessity for health reasons or because of organizational restructuring, may suffer feelings of loss without the structure and identity that work affords, particularly if one partner is retiring before the other.

With fewer roles and responsibilities, older couples tend to spend more time together, making it important to talk about the changing nature of their lives and relationship. Researchers studying retirement in heterosexual couples find that both newly retired men and women report decreases in the quality of their relationship shortly following retirement while they are still transitioning (especially if their partner is still working).[35,36] However, within two years relationship quality improves again, giving us hope that although the road can be bumpy, most couples navigate the transition to retirement happily. Another interesting finding is that among dual earning couples, those retiring at the same time report the highest relationship satisfaction.[37] Perhaps transitioning to retirement at the same time makes it easier for couples to synchronize their lives. As you can imagine, the quality of your relationship and the way you relate before retirement are also important in your happiness together as you navigate the changes ahead.

So, how might you be feeling? The years of retirement can be a joyful time of reconnection for couples who have been busy with careers and possibly raising a family. However, it is also natural to experience some apprehension about spending lots of time together and getting to know each other more intimately again. Avoid the urge to distract yourself from your worries by making yourself super busy independent of your partner. Or at the other extreme, resist stepping into an area of the household that has been the domain of your partner without exploring how it will impact them (e.g., "Now that I'm retired, I want to take over the cooking!"). Potential disappointment occurs when partners differ in their expectations and vision of retirement, says Ohio gerontologist Christine Price:[38] for instance, if one of you looks to retirement as a time for togetherness and shared activities and the other one focuses on pursuing independent interests that demand time away, such as a business venture. Indeed, the three main areas that couples struggle with most at this time focus on leisure activities, intimacy and finances.[39] Discussing your fears, hopes and goals well ahead of time can help you work together to develop a shared vision of your future years; one that brings your lives together *and* also allows space for you as individuals. Consider covering the topics listed here using L-O-V-E conversation as a way to help you get in sync. Prepare to extend yourselves for each other and make room for your differences instead of trying to convince each other to agree.

Table 13.3 A retirement conversation checklist

- How will we time and sequence our retirement(s)?
- How do we feel about the (anticipated) loss of identity and fulfillment of work roles and activities?
- What are our *shared goals* (e.g., spending time with grandchildren, traveling, exercising, engaging volunteer work)?
- What goals do we have for *our relationship* (e.g., to develop shared interests, feel closer, improve our physical intimacy)?
- What are our *personal goals* and passions (e.g., health and wellness, a specific hobby, taking up an area of study, pursuing a long-term interest)?
- How will we pursue our personal and mutual goals in a way that takes care of our relationship bond? What specific activities will we undertake?
- How will we spend leisure time activities, balancing our time together and apart?
- How will we divide household chores in retirement (i.e., Will we assume the same roles as before? Will distribution of tasks be equitable?)? Structure and decide how the specific tasks of your household will be divided.
- What are our financial goals and considerations? How will we meet them?
- How will we cultivate a circle of friends or keep our social network alive?
- How will we protect our time together (i.e., create boundaries with family and/or friends to protect our relationship, mutual goals, and activities)?

Adjustment to aging: In addition to retirement, the senior years bring about physical changes in health and mobility. Although aging is an inevitable part of life, it is understandably saddening to encounter your own physical limits and loss of independence. It is natural to experience these declines in health and physical functioning as very real losses. Caregiving can have a significant impact on the interactions of older adult couples. Whereas for some couples caring for a frail or disabled partner can be rewarding, for other couples strain can occur for both caregiver and care recipient alike, prompting a group of researchers to recommend relationship enhancement programs for caregivers and their spouses who were cardiac patients.[40] Research with older couples has identified two potential problem issues: overly protective care (e.g., able-bodied partners doing things for the other that they are fully capable of doing unaided, thus creating unnecessary dependency) and patronizing communication or care (e.g., able-bodied partners acting on their own accord as if they "know better" what the other partner needs). Some caregiving, however well meaning, can be intrusive and make the care recipient feel unnecessarily dependent. Lack of sensitive listening and communicating can also erode self-respect.[41] On a more positive note, studies of older adults aging well indicate that engaging in meaningful and valued activities is an important part of maintaining high quality of life in the senior years.[42]

The love, acceptance and devotion that close relationships offer enable older adults to face painful realities and adjust to changes in health and functioning. Your relationship can be a huge source of strength if you turn to each other for support. Share your struggles and accept help and compassion from each other, extended family and friends. With a strong support network, you will have the best chance of accepting the inevitable changes that are on the horizon, finding new ways to navigate your world and planning for future living arrangements. A willingness to be flexible and adapt to new circumstances, as well as keeping each other close are key to enjoying a rich quality of life in the senior years.

Table 13.4 Giving and receiving care

- Listen with an open mind to what your partner needs (rather than what you think is needed), particularly if it involves assistance with personal care like showering and toileting.
- Balance being available and helpful with letting your partner undertake whatever self-care that can be managed unaided.
- Share your need for help clearly and express gratitude for support provided.
- Engage in activities that provide joy and meaning to daily life.
- Enjoy time together with extended family and friends.
- Stay connected and active in your local community as a form of self-care (e.g., seniors center, volunteering and special interest groups such as book clubs, bridge, gardening, etc.).

Additional resources . . .
The perfect home for a long life: Choosing the right retirement lifestyle for you by Lyndsay Green, Toronto, ON: Thomas Allan Publishers, 2013
gransnet.com/relationships/how-retirement-affects-marriage
caregiverstress.com and
stagesofseniorcare.com/resources/
These are websites with helpful resources on family caregiving.
Healing Hearts Together is a relationship education and enhancement program for partners facing cardiac disease developed by Heather Tulloch, Paul Greenman, Natasha Demidenko & Sue Johnson. Check out iceeft.com for more information or google Healing Hearts Together to find workshop locations.
In closing, we hope that looking ahead proactively will help you anticipate some of the changes and challenges inherent in different life cycle transitions. Although lifespan transitions can evoke both anticipation and worry, we see them as an opportunity to revisit your personal and relationship needs. They are really an invitation to reflect and connect, to become closer.

References

1,14. Carter, B., & McGoldrick, M. (Eds.). (2015). *The expanded family life cycle: Individual, family, and social perspectives* (5th ed.). Boston, MA: Pearson Higher Education.

2,4. Dankoski, M. E. (2001). Pulling on the heartstrings: An emotionally focused approach to family life cycle transitions. *Journal of Marital and Family Therapy, 27*, 177–187.

3. Menaghan, E. (1983). Marital stress and family transitions: A panel analysis. *Journal of Marriage and the Family, 45*, 371–386.

5. Feeney, J., Alexander, R., Noller, P., & Hohaus, L. (2003). Attachment insecurity, depression and the transition to parenthood. *Personal Relationships, 10*, 475–493.

6. Simpson, J., Rholes, W. S., Campbell, L., Tran, S., & Wilson, C. L. (2003). Adult attachment, the transition to parenthood and depressive symptoms. *Journal of Personality and Social Psychology, 84*, 1172–1187.

7. Feeney, J., Hohaus, L., Noller, P., & Alexander, R. (2001). *Becoming parents: Exploring the bonds between mothers, fathers, and their families*. Cambridge: Cambridge University Press.

8. Simpson, J. A., Winterheld, H. A., Rholes, W. S., & Orina, M. M. (2007). Working models of attachment and reactions to different forms of caregiving from romantic partners. *Journal of Personal and Social Psychology, 93*(3), 466–477.

9. Feeney, J. A., Alexander, R., Noller, P., & Hohaus, L. (2003). Attachment insecurity, depression and the transition to parenthood. *Personal Relationships, 10*(4), 475–493. https://doi.org/10.1046/j.1475-6811.2003.0006.1x

10. Halford, W. K., Petch, J., & Creedy, D. K. (2010). Promoting a positive transition to parenthood: A randomized clinical trial of couple relationship education. *Prevention Science, 11*, 89–100.

11. Petch, J., Halford, W. K., Creedy, D. K., & Gamble, J. (2012). A randomised controlled trial of a couple relationship and co-parenting program (couple CARE for parents) for high- and low-risk new parents. *Journal of Consulting and Clinical Psychology, 80*(4), 662–673. https://doi.org/10.1037/a0028781

12. Lee, N. A., Furrow, J. L., & Bradley, B. A. (2017). Emotionally focused couple therapy for parents raising a child with an autism spectrum disorder: A pilot study. *Journal of Marriage and Family Therapy, 43*(4), 662–673.

13. Sanders, M. R., & Keown, L. J. (2017). Parenting in couple relationships. In J. Fitzgerald (Ed.), *Foundations for couples' therapy: Research for the real world* (pp. 302–309). New York, NY: Routledge.

15. Riina, E., & McHale, S. M. (2013). Bidirectional influences between dimensions co-parenting and adolescent adjustment. *Journal of Youth and Adolescence, 43*, Online First Articles.

16,18. Collins, W. A., Gleason, T., & Sesma, A. (1997). Internalization, autonomy, and relationships: Development during adolescence. In J. E. Gyrusec & L. Kuczynski (Eds.), *Parenting and children's internalization of values: A handbook of contemporary theory* (pp. 78–99). New York, NY: Wiley-Blackwell.

17. Masten, A. S., Hubbard, J. J., Gest, S. D., Tellegen, A., Garmezy, N., & Ramirez, M. (1999). Competence in the context of adversity: Pathways to resilience and maladaptation from childhood to late adolescence. *Development and Psychopathology, 11*, 143–169.

19. Furrow, J. L., Palmer, G., Johnson, S. M., Faller, G., & Palmer-Olsen, L. (2019). *Emotionally focused family therapy: Restoring connection and promoting resilience*. New York, NY: Routledge.

20. Harris Insights & Analytics® (2017). *Parents supporting adult children 2017 survey*. National Endowment for Financial Education. Retrieved May 30, 2021, from www.nefe.org/research/polls/parents-supporting-adult-children-survey.aspx

21. Polenick, C. A., Birditt, K. S., & Zarit, S. H. (2018). Parental support of adult children and middle-aged couples' marital satisfaction. *The Gerontologist, 58*(4), 663–673.

22. Mitchell, B. (2007). *The boomerang age: Transitions to adulthood in families*. New Brunswick: Aldine-Transaction.

23. Warraich, H. (2017). How medicine has changed the end of life for patients with cardiovascular disease. *Journal of the American College of Cardiology, 70*, 1276–1289.

24. MetLife Mature Market Institute. (2011). *The MetLife study of caregiving costs to working caregivers: Double jeopardy for baby boomers care for their parents*. Westport, CT: MetLife.

25. Turcotte, M. (2013). *Family caregiving: What are the consequences? Insights on Canadian society*. Ottawa: Statistics Canada.

26,29. Gorchoff, S. M., John, O. P., & Helson, R. (2008). Contextualizing change in marital satisfaction during middle age: An 18-year longitudinal study. *Psychological Science, 19*, 1194–1200.

27. Igarashi, H., Hooker, K., Coehlo, D. P., & Manoogian (2013). "My nest is full": Intergenerational relationships at midlife. *Journal of Aging Studies, 27*, 102–112.

28. Mitchell, B. A., & Wister, A. V. (2019). Are the parents all right? Parental stress, ethnic culture and intergenerational relations in aging families. *Journal of Comparative Family Studies, 50*(1), 51–74.

30. Fraley, C., & Shaver, P. (2016). Attachment, loss and grief: Bowlby's views, new developments, and current controversies. In J. Cassidy & P. Shaver (Eds.), *Handbook of attachment* (pp. 40–62). New York, NY and London: The Guilford Press.

31. Bowlby, J. (1979). *The making and breaking of affectional bonds*. London: Tavistock Routledge.

32. Raphael, B. (1994). *The anatomy of bereavement*. Northvale, NJ: Jason Aronson.

33,39. Henry, R. G., Miller, R. B., & Giarrusso, R. (2005). Difficulties, disagreements, and disappointments in late-life marriages. *International Journal of Aging and Human Development, 61*, 243–264.

34,35. Moen, P., Kim, J., & Hofmeister, H. (2001). Couples' work/retirement transitions, gender, and marital quality. *Social Psychology Quarterly, 64*, 55–71.

36,37,38. Price, C., & Nesteruk, O. (2015). What to expect when you retire: By women for women. *Marriage and Family Review, 51*(5), 418–440.

40. Bouchard, K., Greenman, P. S., Pipe, A., Johnson, S. M., & Tulloch, H. (2019). Reducing caregiver distress and cardiovascular risk: A focus on caregiver-patient relationship quality. *Canadian Journal of Cardiology, 35*(10), 1409–1411.

41. Edwards, H., & Noller, P. (2002). Care giving and its influence on marital interactions between older spouses. In P. Noller & J. Feeney (Eds.), *Understanding marriage* (pp. 437–464). Cambridge: Cambridge University Press.

42. Williamson, G., & Christie, J. (2009). Aging well in the 21st century: Challenges and opportunities. In C. Snyder & S. Lopez (Eds.), *Oxford handbook of positive psychology* (pp. 165–170). Oxford: Oxford University Press.

FINAL WORDS

As we wind up this workbook, we want to acknowledge the commitment you have shown to your relationship by picking up and working through this book, with or without the help of a therapist. The exercises throughout the pages of *The Two of Us* have required emotional strength and courage. We hope they have helped you deepen the intimacy, trust and security in your relationship.

The most obvious rewards of a good relationship are joy, love and companionship throughout life. While we acknowledge that our health is influenced by many factors, recent research is reporting that happy couples in long-term, committed relationships are at lower risk for heart disease, have stronger immune systems and have fewer visits to their doctors than unhappily partnered couples. People in long-term, stable relationships also report mental health advantages, including less anxiety, depression, drug use and heavy drinking.[1,2] Loving physical touch and expressions of affection also lower the body's response to stress and experience of pain.[3,4] All of this research seems to be saying that cultivating a solid love relationship is not only one of life's greatest pleasures; it is also good for your health!

We hope that you are indeed enjoying the many physical and emotional benefits of love. However, if in the future you find yourselves getting stuck again in unfulfilling relationship patterns, you now have the ability to see and acknowledge them to one another. You will probably be able to recognize when you are missing your partner, or something is feeling awry in your relationship. You can use the reflections and notes you made throughout this workbook as a reference to help you share your feelings and needs, so you can put them out to each other in ways that help you become close again. We hope you will be able to see your needs as evidence of your attachment to one another rather than as flaws in either of you. Finally, you now have the L-O-V-E conversation framework as a way of expressing yourselves and responding to each other. In other words, you now have practical tools to talk to each other about your emotions, needs, hopes and longings in a way that strengthens your relationship bond. The energy you invest in becoming closer will be rewarded in spades with happiness, harmony and intimacy. Our wish for you in the days and years ahead is to experience the warmth love has to offer, for as our attachment mentor, John Bowlby, expresses, it is the heartbeat of life!

> Intimate attachments to other human beings are the hub around which a person's life revolves, not only as an infant or a toddler or a school child but throughout adolescence, and the years of maturity as well, and on into old age. From these intimate attachments a person draws their strength and enjoyment of life and, through what they contribute, they give strength and enjoyment to others.[5]

References

1. Kiecolt-Glaxer, J. K., & Newton, T. (2001). Marriage and health: His and hers. *Psychological Bulletin, 127*, 472–503.
2. Reis, H. T., & Sprecher, S. K. (2009). *Encyclopedia of human relationships*. Los Angeles: Sage Publications.

DOI: 10.4324/9781003009481-14

3. Coan, J. A., Schaefer, H. S., & Davidson, R. J. (2006). Lending a hand: Social regulation of the neural response to threat. *Psychological Science, 17*, 1032–1039.
4. Johnson, S. M., Moser, M. B., Beckes, L., Smith, A., Dalgleish, T., Halchuk, R., . . . Coan, J. A. (2013). Soothing the threatened brain: Leveraging contact comfort with emotionally focused therapy. *PLoS One, 8*(11), e79314. Retrieved November 21, 2013, from www.plosone.org/article/info:doi/10.1371/journal.pone.0079314
5. Bowlby, J. (1980). *Attachment and loss: Vol. 3. Loss, sadness and depression*. New York, NY: Basic Books.

APPENDIX A

REFLECTIONS

Chapter 1 Introduction: Who is This Book For?

Reflection 1.1 Ready to have a L-O-V-E conversation?

Let's begin your first L-O-V-E conversation on a positive note. Identify the last time you had a good moment or interaction with your partner, felt close, relaxed, enjoyed an activity together or noticed something you appreciate about your partner. Describe the situation or quality you appreciate and the good feelings it evokes. Take turns sharing your good moments.

Description of Good Moment: ____

____

____

____

Good Feelings Evoked: ____

____

Debrief Together: How do you feel inside about sharing your good moments and feelings with each other? In this moment how do you feel toward each other (e.g., closer, warmer, embarrassed, cautious, happy, calm, relaxed)? ____

____

Chapter 2 Attachment Bonds: The Best Chance of Survival

Reflection 2.1 Look at your relationship through the "lens" of attachment security

Safe haven

Partners give each other support and comfort in a number of ways. Some examples might include:

- Listening when the other is worried
- Being attentive when the other is sick
- Helping practically when the other is tired
- Inquiring about your partner's feelings
- Staying engaged patiently when your partner is confused
- Discussing and debriefing events of the day together
- Expressing concern and/or providing physical comfort when your partner is sad or hurt.

How does my partner give me support, comfort and encouragement? *(Take your time. Try to find at least* one *positive answer to this question.)*

____

____

____

If you can't find a positive answer to this question, acknowledge that you feel blocked on it instead of shifting the focus to your partner's flaws. Sometimes past hurts and current anger can make it difficult for us to see the positive ways in which our partners are attempting to respond to us.

How could I offer my partner a safe haven in hard times? Think of specific things you do/could do (no matter how small).

____

____

____

Secure base

Partners encourage each other to grow and develop, for example, by:

- Supporting each other's work and activities
- Asking questions that reflect curiosity in each other's opinions
- Listening to each other's hopes and dreams
- Taking an interest in each other's studies, community activities, hobbies
- Acknowledging each other's capabilities and possibilities for growth
- Bolstering each other's confidence with encouragement ("You can do this").

How has my partner encouraged me to grow and develop? *(Try to find at least* one *positive answer to this question.)*

____

____

____

How could I support my partner's dreams and aspirations to grow and develop?

____

____

____

Reflection 2.2 How is our emotional presence?

Describe a recent example of when you were accessible to your partner.

In the scenario outlined, how did you respond to your partner?

How would you describe your level of engagement?

What would a casual onlooker say about the quality of your engagement as a couple?

Now, describe a recent example of when your partner was accessible to you.

In the scenario outlined, how did your partner respond to you?

How would you describe your partner's level of engagement?

What would a casual onlooker say about the quality of your engagement as a couple?

Reflection 2.3 Insecurity creates fear and distress

Perhaps you or your partner has said some of the statements listed. As you read the statements again out loud, *SLOWLY*, notice which ones strike a chord with you. Notice (and note down) the impact of saying and feeling those words. Do you sense the distress in these statements? How would you describe it in your own words (feelings or sensations in your body)?

____

____

____

Share with your partner how you are impacted. Remember to: Listen with an Open heart and mind, Validate and Express yourself softly, simply, slowly.

Chapter 3 My Partner and Me: What Influenced Who We Are and How We Are in Close Relationships?

Reflection 3.1 Attachment beliefs and expectations

The following questions look at how confident you feel that others will be there for you and how comfortable you feel about getting close to others and letting others get close to you. MARK AN ESTIMATE ON THE LINE FROM 1 (NOT AT ALL) TO 10 (VERY MUCH).

To what extent do I feel confident that my partner or close others will accept me?

1 (not at all) 10 (very much)

How confident do I feel that my partner or important others will be there for me if I need them?

1 (not at all) 10 (very much)

To what extent do I see myself as a person who is worthy of care and support if I need it?

1 (not at all) 10 (very much)

To what extent do I feel comfortable letting my partner or important others close to me?

1 (not at all) 10 (very much)

How confident do I feel about asking others for help or closeness?

1 (not at all) 10 (very much)

To what extent do I feel comfortable giving support to my partner or important others?

1 (not at all) 10 (very much)

Reflection 3.2 My own attachment history

Take some time now to reflect on your own history of attachment relationships.[4]

Childhood

When you were upset by something as a child, did you have a "lap"[5] to climb up onto to be held and comforted? Who, if anyone, did you go to for comfort when you were young? How did this person or people generally respond to you?

How consistently did you get these responses?

What did you learn about asking for comfort and security from these experiences?

If your first answer was "no," how did you comfort yourself?

How did you learn *not* to turn to others for comfort?

Observations of your parents' or caregivers' relationship

Choose three adjectives to describe your caregivers' relationship:

What did you learn about relationship bonds from observing your own parents' or caregivers' relationship, or being reared by a single parent or being reared by multiple caregivers?

Adulthood

Have there been times when you have been able to confide and find comfort with your partner? Describe a time when this went well.

____

How do you typically approach your partner for attention and contact?

____

Have you ever turned to alcohol, drugs, sex or material things for comfort?
Please describe what was going on and what you did to cope.

____

Have there been any particularly traumatic incidences in your previous romantic relationships that make it difficult to approach your current partner?

____

Reflection 3.3 How my past influences me

How have your own child and adulthood attachment relationships shaped your beliefs about being able to expect others to be attentive to your needs?

____

____

____

How have societal influences or norms shaped your expectations of others being attentive to your needs (for example, concerning your culture, race, birthplace, religion, social class, abilities, etc.)?

____

____

____

Complete the sentence(s) that apply to you:
When my antenna is turned up, I notice myself engaging in these behaviors:

____

____

____

When my antenna is turned down, I notice myself engaging in the following behaviors:

____

____

____

Reflection 3.4 Reflection on our cultural influences

How have culture, race, ethnicity, religion, gender roles, social position/power or other contextual influences shaped my identity? What positive or negative messages have I internalized about myself? Who has helped me in exploring my identities in these various areas?

____

____

____

____

How might the pain of racial, cultural, social class or religious oppression play a role in my life? How do I cope?

____

____

____

Upon reflection, what assumptions do I bring to our relationship based on my background that affect us?

____

____

____

What disagreements do we have that can be better understood if we look at them through the lens of racial, cultural, social position/power or religious impacts or stressors?

____

____

____

How have we handled these differences? What have been some positive or negative aspects of the way we have dealt with our different backgrounds?

____

____

____

What are still sensitive issues from our backgrounds that can trap us into negative interactions?

____

____

____

These conversations can be sensitive, and misunderstandings based on differences in background can contribute to hurts and distress. Meeting in L-O-V-E will help you care for each other and perhaps also discover something new.

Reflection 3.5 Reflections on the pathways to developing LGBTTQIAP+ identities

What do I remember as important experiences in my pathway to developing my gender identity, identities or sexual orientation?

____

____

____

Who helped me on that journey? Who didn't help me, and instead made it hard and painful? What messages have I internalized about myself, positive or negative, as a result of these interactions?

____

____

____

Did I have peers who provided a sense of safety and belonging? Who else has helped me develop my identity?

____

____

____

Do we have differences in how open and "out" we are with family, friends or co-workers? How do we navigate these differences as a couple?

____

____

____

How is our relationship impacted by the ongoing stress of marginalization and discrimination? Do I tend to turn my "antennae" up or down? How do I cope?

____

____

____

How could we help or better support each other as a couple?

____

____

____

Reflection 4.1 What's our relationship pattern?

Identify for yourself and/or discuss with your partner which relationship pattern fits most of your difficult interactions. *It will help to remember a recent problematic interaction or conversation.* You are looking for *patterns*, not every interaction needs to fit the pattern. Read through the behaviors on the protesting and withdrawing lists. Take turns circling any behaviors that seem familiar to you in your part of the relationship dance. Recall how your partner has described your behavior in difficult or conflictual interactions. Resist the temptation to discount their description, get triggered or defend yourself. You can also try recounting and writing down a recent disagreement to track the steps in the dance you each made.

Complete the sentence: I feel threatened when ______________________________

____

and then I do ____ to manage.

As long as you are not currently in conflict, share your observations with your partner.

Reflection 4.2 How our cycle feeds on itself

Complete the following sentences together. They are similar to and fit with exercises from Conversation 1 from *HMT*.[8] Example: The more I go after you by *criticizing and complaining* (What I do; How I cope), the more you avoid me by *retreating and going quiet* (What you do; How you cope).

Name: ____________________

The more I go after you by ___________________________________, the more you avoid me by ____.

Name: ____________________

The more I avoid you by ___________________________________, the more you go after me by ____.

When I (Name) __________________________ don't feel on solid footing (secure, connected) with you, I react by ____, and then you ____ in response.

When I (Name) ____________________ don't feel on solid footing (secure, connected) with you, I react by ____, and then you respond by ____.

Reflection 5.1 Emotion tracking exercise

If my partner . . .	Immediately in my body I sense . . . (Is this safe or is it threatening for me?)	Other feelings in my body may emerge . . .	Typically I feel . . .	Typically I think . . .	Typically I do . . .
Example: Arrives home early from work looking serious	Uh-oh	My eyes widen and my mouth might open. My attention focuses on the unexpected arrival	I feel surprised and curious to find out more	What is going on? Something must have happened!	Stop what I am doing and walk toward my partner, to find out more
Example: Frowns sternly at me	Uh-oh	My stomach clenches	I feel afraid or "on edge"	What have I done to upset you?	I find an excuse to distract myself
Arrives home from work announcing they have good news					
Calls my name in a panicky voice					
Cries in response to something insensitive I said					
Calls my name in an angry voice					
Calls my name in a playful voice					
Criticizes someone I love					
Walks away when I raise something important to me					

Reflection 5.2 My emotions

What messages did I get about experiencing and expressing emotions from my culture or social context? Were there conflicting messages (e.g., between my family of origin and the culture where I lived, or between my parents and grandparents living in the home)?

____

____

____

Were some emotions OK but others not acceptable?

____

____

____

How did my family respond to my emotions?

____

____

____

What messages did I get about my emotions in previous romantic relationships?

____

____

____

How did previous significant relationship partners respond to my emotions?

____

____

____

Reflection 5.3 Unhelpful intensity of negative emotion

Do I sometimes experience extremes of emotion such that I find it hard to manage the intensity of negative emotion I am feeling OR experience lack of emotion, such that I find it hard to know what I feel? If so, this is what typically happens for me:

____

____

____

How do I try to manage it?

____

____

____

Have there been times when I have experienced emotional responses about which I am now not proud (for example, jealousy about my partner's success; pleased to see someone hurt or humiliated)? If I sit and reflect on that memory, am I able to identify an insecurity in myself that explains my reaction?

____

____

____

Reflection 5.4 What do I feel and express in our negative dance?

Before we take a closer look at some of the common core emotions in your cycle, reflect for a few minutes on the predominant reactive emotions you express if you and your partner get caught in negative interactions. Could they be a reaction to a deeper core emotion? For example, do you sometimes feel frustrated anger in response to not feeling understood; anxious withdrawal in response to fear of disappointing your partner; numbing out to avoid expressing your legitimate anger?

What reactive emotions do you notice yourself typically expressing in the negative cycle?

____

____

What is happening in your interaction with your partner when you express this reactive emotion? What is your trigger? It may be a particular phrase, action, look or tone of voice. *Remember that the reason for identifying triggers is to provide each other with important information on how you experience your interactions; it is not about blaming each other.*

Here are some common examples. You can indicate ones that fit for you or write your own.

___ When I hear you become louder and more persistent, I react with defensive anger.

___ When I sense that we are headed for conflict, I shut down/go numb.

___ When I don't know how to respond to you, I feel helpless and overwhelmed.

___ When your wall goes up and I can't reach you, I get frustrated.

___ When I see you close off or walk out of the room, I express reactive anger.

____

____

____

What do you think or say to yourself when you see or experience your partner's reactive emotions (e.g., "You don't care about me," "It's pointless to talk, I'll never get heard!").

____

____

____

What impact does your expression of reactive emotions (or non-expression of emotion) have on your partner?

____

____

____

How might this contribute to a negative cycle of interaction between you and your partner?

____

____

____

Complete this sentence together:

When I express my reactive emotion of __________________, you come back with a reactive emotion of __________________________.

When I express my reactive emotion of __________________, you come back with a reactive emotion of __________________________.

Chapter 6 More About Emotions: What Are We Both Feeling?

Reflection 6.1 How do we view love?

So how do you relate to these comments about love and happiness in couple relationships? What do you consider important aspects of a loving relationship?

How have your views on love been shaped by your religion, ethnic or family culture?

What do you and your partner do to nurture and nourish your love for each other?

Reflection 6.2 Happiness, joy and love

What are some memories of happy or joyous times with my partner?

____

____

____

Describe your idea of a happy time with your partner.

____

____

____

How do I express love to you/my partner? How does my partner express love to me?

____

____

____

Reflection 6.3 Sadness and loss

What experiences of loss or grief have I had in my life?

How do I feel sadness in my body (e.g., sinking feeling, heavy heart, tears)?

What sadness do I experience in my current relationship?

What do I typically do when I feel sad?

How do I express sadness to my partner?

What happens for my partner when I am sad? How does my partner typically react to me when I express sadness?

What sadness have I caused my partner? How do they typically react to feeling sad?

What do I feel now, recalling these experiences of sadness for either my partner or myself?

What helps me to cope with sadness, to heal from disappointment or loss? What comforts me?

What did I learn from this experience about my partner or myself?

Reflection 6.4 Anger

How do I experience anger in my body (e.g., clenched fists; feel hot/cold; feel agitated and restless; feel pressured to speak)?

____

____

____

What typically triggers my anger?

____

____

What typically triggers my partner's anger?

____

____

What happens between us when either of us is angry?

____

____

Do I "bottle up" anger so much that I don't speak to my partner for days? If so, what is it like for me to be angry in this detached way? What does it feel like for my partner to experience my cool withdrawal?

____

____

____

Do I sometimes lose control of my anger, becoming explosive or out of control? If so, what does it feel like to be exploding? What is it like for my partner to receive this fiery treatment?

____

____

____

Do either of us try to minimize anger through intellectualizing, making jokes, blaming or crying instead? If so, what makes it difficult to express anger directly?

____

____

How else do my partner and I manage anger?

____

____

What helps us to calm down?

____

____

How would I *like* to manage my anger?

____

____

Reflection 6.5 Fear and anxiety

In what kinds of situations do I feel afraid? What/who typically triggers my fear?

Do I sometimes feel generally anxious or uptight without any *apparent* reason to be afraid? If I tune into myself deeply, is there an attachment threat fueling my fear?

What fears are typically triggered in my relationship?

When I feel fear or anxiety, what do I experience in my body (e.g., clenched stomach, shaky inside, whole body freeze, scattered thoughts)?

What do I tend to do inside myself and in our relationship?

What helps me to calm my fears/anxieties?

What happens for my partner when I feel afraid?

What do I notice when my partner is afraid?

What helps my partner to cope when feeling afraid? How can I help?

Do I ever feel fearful that I am not lovable and important to my partner? What do I do with that fear? How do I express it?

Reflection 6.6 Contempt

Have I ever felt anger at a violation and established a protective boundary by expressing contempt? How did I handle it?

____

____

____

How else could I have handled that experience so that I showed respect for myself and also the other person?

____

____

In my current romantic relationship, have I experienced contempt (e.g., rolled eyes, sarcastic putdowns, being mocked or a milder version such as feeling overly teased)? If so, what was that like for me? How did I feel? How did I then behave toward my partner?

____

____

____

Have I expressed contempt to my partner? If I look deeply inside, how did these feelings of contempt evolve for me in our relationship?

____

____

If I express contempt, my partner typically responds by

____

____

How do I feel now reflecting on these experiences?

____

____

Reflection 6.7 Discovering our core emotions

Find a time and place where you can be quiet and reflective. Think of a recent time you and your partner got stuck in your usual negative cycle. It may help to write down some of the details.

Name: ____________________

Ask yourself: When I look deeper into what is going on for me in our negative cycle, what am I feeling at the core?

____

____

____

Name: ____________________

Ask yourself: When I look deeper into what is going on for me in our negative cycle, what am I feeling at the core?

____

____

Reflection 6.8 How we impact each other

Think about the impact your emotions and behaviors have on your partner. How do your partner's emotions and behaviors impact you? It may help to do the sentence completion exercise together. There is a sentence completion set for each partner.

Name: ____________________

In my *core*, when I am _________________________ (e.g., afraid, sad, hurt, angry), but don't feel able to share openly, I *react* by expressing ____________________________ (e.g., frustration, reactive or defensive anger, irritability, detachment). I typically *cope* by ______________ ___________________________________ (e.g., complaining, lecturing, going silent).

You then typically *react* by expressing _________________________ and *coping* by _____________________________. I wonder what you are feeling in your *core*? _____________ ____

How do your vulnerable core emotions impact me?

____

____

Name: ____________________

In my *core*, when I am _________________________ (e.g., afraid, sad, hurt, angry), but don't feel able to share openly, I *react* by expressing ____________________________ (e.g., frustration, reactive or defensive anger, irritability, detachment). I typically *cope* by ______________ ___________________________________ (e.g., complaining, lecturing, going silent).

You then typically *react* by expressing _________________________ and *coping* by _____________________________. I wonder what you are feeling in your *core*?

____

How do your vulnerable core emotions impact me? _____________________________________

____

Name: ____________________

When I feel positive *core* emotions _________________________ (e.g., happiness, joy), I typically express/act with ____________________________ (e.g., love, affection, openness, attentiveness, empathy). You then typically *respond* with _____________________________ ______________ (e.g., joy, playfulness, relief, listening, disclosing your own feelings.

The more I interact by voicing my _________________________ (e.g., openness, encouragement, love, core feelings), the more you respond with ____________________________ (e.g., smiles, relaxing, listening to me, sharing your own feelings with me).

How do your positive core emotions impact me? _____________________________________

____

Name: ____________________

When I feel positive *core* emotions ______________________ (e.g., happiness, joy), I typically express/act with ____________________________ (e.g., love, affection, openness, attentiveness, empathy). You then typically *respond* with ________________________________ ________ (e.g., joy, playfulness, relief, listening, disclosing your own feelings.

The more I interact by voicing my ____________________________ (e.g., openness, encouragement, love, core feelings), the more you respond with ______________________ (e.g., smiles, relaxing, listening to me, sharing core feelings with me).

How do your positive core emotions impact me? ____________________________________
____

Reflection 7.1 Our attachment intentions

To look for the attachment intentions behind your behavior in the negative dance, begin by reflecting on the following:

1. I get most triggered and distressed when I feel ______________________________

   ______________________________ in our relationship.

2. What is missing for me most in our relationship is ______________________________

   ____

3. When I do my part of the dance, I am trying to ______________________________

   ____

4. My desire and/or intention is to ______________________________

   ____

Reflection 8.1 Hurt

In my current relationship with my partner, when have/do I experience hurt? What happens? What do I feel? How do I then act toward my partner?

____

____

____

How have I/do I hurt my partner's feelings? How does my partner react? What effect has this event/these events had on our relationship?

____

____

____

What attempts, if any, do we make to repair the damage? How successful have those attempts been?

____

____

____

Please note that when you and your partner share your reflections, it is quite likely you may have differing "versions" of the same hurtful events. Partners tend to tell the story of a hurtful event from their own perspective. This is to be expected. Try hard to listen to your partner without jumping in with "corrections," justifications or to tell your own version of the story. Try to learn something new about your partner from listening to their feelings and experience. *The goal of this exercise is not for the two of you to agree on the events, but to hear and understand your differing experiences.*

Suggestions for dealing with hurt feelings will be offered in Chapter 10, Relationship Injury: How Can We Repair the Damage?

Reflection 8.2 Guilt and shame

In my current relationship with my partner, when have I experienced guilt? What happened? What else did I feel? How did I then behave? What helped?

Have I felt chronic or unproductive shame in my life? Who triggered for me the feelings of being worthless, small or of little value? *This may be a painful reflection for you; take it slowly and be gentle with yourself.*

What did I want to do (e.g., hide away or retaliate with anger)? What happened then? What happens for me now as I recall those feelings?

Do I ever feel shame in my couple relationship? What evokes the feelings of shame?

What does my partner say or do that triggers feelings of shame in me? How do I typically behave? What impact does that have on my partner? Is it helpful?

Do I provoke feelings of shame in my partner? What is that like for them? Is it helpful? What am I really trying to achieve when I act in a way that makes my partner feel shamed?

Chapter 10 will further the reflection on relationship repair

Reflection 8.3 Jealousy

In my current relationship with my partner, have I felt jealous? What evoked my jealousy?

What else did I feel? How did I then cope and behave? What impact did that have on my partner?

What helped me feel better or made me feel worse?

Does my partner experience jealousy related to my interactions with other people? How does my partner typically behave when feeling jealous? What has my partner told me about those feelings?

What have I done that has triggered jealous feelings for my partner?

If I look closely at my motives, was I trying to send my partner a message through my triggering behavior? If so, what emotions inside of me were being expressed through my behavior?

What have we found helpful as a way of dealing with jealousy in our relationship?

See Chapter 9 for the story of Brad and Janine, a couple who struggle with the issue of jealousy and find a way to create security together.

Chapter 9 Rebuilding Our Bond

Reflection 9.1 Relationship stability checklist

Check off the following indicators of relationship stability as they apply to you and your partner.

1. __I believe we each have our own part to play in the sequence of steps in our negative interactions.
2. __ The nickname for our negative cycle is ______________________________
3. __ I can describe my part in the negative dance as ______________________________
4. __ I can describe my partner's part in the negative dance as ______________________________
5. __ I know these things I do or don't do (behaviors) that trigger my partner

   ____
6. __ I know that these behaviors from my partner trigger me

   ____
7. __ I know that these reactive emotions of mine fuel our negative dance

   ____
8. __ I know that these reactive emotions of my partner's fuel our negative dance

   ____
9. __ I know these core emotions are stirred up for me in our negative dance

   ____
10. __ I know that these core emotions are stirred up for my partner in our negative dance

    ____
11. __ We have strategies for interrupting or diffusing the negative dance, such as

    ____
12. __ It seems like we can be more flexible during disagreements.
13. __ We are now more able to share our feelings.
14. __ I believe our problems are caused by the negative dance we *both* contribute to and suffer from.
15. __ We are no longer blaming each other as much in conversations.
16. __ I understand that my benevolent intention in the negative dance is

    ____
17. __ I understand that my partner's benevolent intention in the negative dance is

    ____
18. __ We are arguing less than we were in the past.
19. __ We feel more relaxed in each other's presence.
20. __ Our relationship feels more stable than before.
21. __ When we do get caught in the negative cycle, we are able to recover more quickly than before.

Reflection 9.2 Guided reflection for partners in the withdrawing position

____
(name)

1. How has the negative dance hurt or taken a toll on you? Be specific.
Take time with this question and allow yourself to check in and notice what you feel inside. (Possible examples include physically carrying tension in specific parts of your body, losing touch with yourself, how your mood might be affected or your self-confidence being eroded.)

2. If you have dealt with challenges at work, with family or in your relationship on your own, how has that been for you?
What have been the benefits of handling things on your own?

3. What have been the downsides of handling things on your own?
For example, have you ever felt overwhelmed, anxious, depressed or alone?

4. What kinds of experiences and feelings in your relationship have been difficult to share with your partner? What has been hard about sharing with your partner—what did you fear might happen?

5. What negative messages or beliefs have you internalized *about yourself* that have created insecurity and made it hard to show yourself fully?
(For example, I feel like I am not good enough for you. I am a complete failure no one would ever want me. Or any vulnerability is a sign of weakness and will turn you off or open me up to hurt.)

6. What fears have you internalized *about your partner or relationship*?
(For example, I am afraid you will eventually get fed up with me and leave. You will be burdened by my issues. Or you don't really want me or at least not all of me.)

7. What support or reassurance do you need right now from your partner to help you be able to bring more of your true self into this relationship? What do you long for?
   a) What do I need right now in our relationship to help me feel more secure within myself?

   ____

   ____

   b) What do I need right now to help me feel more secure with you, emotionally safer or closer to you?

   ____

   ____

Can you look at your partner now, meet their eyes and share your reflections and longings? It's okay if you are nervous about this conversation. Perhaps you could start by expressing that first, sharing what are your fears about this conversation and what could help you get started.

____

Reflection 9.3 Guided reflection for partners in the protesting position

__________ (name)

1. How has the negative dance created pain or insecurity in you? Be specific.
   How/where have you felt this in your body? Take time with this question and allow yourself to check in and notice what you feel inside. (Possible examples include physically feeling anxiety in specific parts of your body, feeling unable to settle yourself, how you feel energetically or how you view yourself.)

   ____

   ____

2. If you have dealt with challenges at work, with family or in your relationship on your own, how has that been for you?
   What have been the benefits of handling things on your own?

   ____

   ____

3. What have been the downsides of handling things on your own?
   For example, have you ever felt overwhelmed, anxious, desperate or lonely?

   ____

   ____

4. What doubts or fears have you internalized *about your relationship or your partner* being there for you?
   (For example, I'm afraid you will be turned off by my feelings. I'm afraid you don't really want me to need you because no one has ever taken care of me. Or people always abandon me, I'm sure you will too eventually. Relationships don't last.)

   ____

   ____

5. What doubts or fears have you internalized *about yourself*, your own lovability or your own needs for security?
   (For example, it hurts so much to imagine, but I must be hard to love—I'm too much, too angry or too needy; not attractive or intelligent enough. I'm afraid with the person that I am, no one could truly love or cherish me.)

   ____

   ____

6. What kinds of experiences and feelings in your relationship have been difficult to share with your partner in a vulnerable way? What has been hard about letting your partner see your vulnerabilities or insecurities—what did you fear might happen?

   ____

   ____

7. What support or reassurance do you need right now from your partner to help you be able to share your true insecurities and vulnerabilities with them? What do you long for?
   a) What do I need right now to help me feel more secure with you, emotionally safer or closer to you?

   ____

   ____

   b) What do I need right now in our relationship to help me feel more secure/better about myself?

   ____

   ____

Can you look at your partner now, meet their eyes and share your reflections and longings? It's okay if you are nervous about this conversation. Perhaps you could start by expressing that first, sharing what are your fears about this conversation and what could help you get started.

____

Chapter 10 Relationship Injury: How Can We Repair the Damage?

Reflection 10.1 Exploring our hurts

What does this chapter mean for our relationship?

What injuries (small or large) in our relationship call for repair? There may be many incidents that come to mind. The one I choose to work on today is

____

When I felt hurt . . .

What exactly caused me hurt? (State clearly what the event meant for you.)

____

____

____

Are there any aspects of that hurtful event that still cause me to feel hurt? What other emotions are involved for me (e.g., anger, sadness, fear)?

____

____

____

What can I forgive? What can't I forgive? What do I need from my partner at this point? What would help me to let go of the hurt?

____

____

____

Has my partner apologized or acknowledged their part in my hurt? (Does my partner even know I was hurt?) What might be potential barriers or obstacles to my partner's apology/acknowledgement in relation to the listed incident/s? Might my reactions be keeping alive the conflict and distress between us?

____

____

____

What do I see as potential barriers or obstacles to my letting go of hurt and forgiving in relation to the outlined event/s? What might help me overcome these obstacles?

____

____

____

Reflection 10.2 Attachment injuries

If Reflection 10.1 opened up awareness for you of more serious injury, take some time to go deeper by reflecting on the following questions.

What was lost in the hurtful event?

What were the negative, helpless or hopeless feelings for me that followed?

How have I tried to protect myself since that event occurred?

What assumptions about safety in our relationship were shattered that day?

How have our negative interactions developed since that event?

How have we attempted to mend the damage caused?

What hopes and longings for closeness have I suppressed?

Before talking to your partner about these reflections, we suggest that you reflect on whether it is safe to share your reflections. You might like to revisit the checklist in Chapter 9 (Reflection 9.1) to review your readiness to talk about a topic that is possibly loaded with "raw spots."

Reflection 10.3 Talking it over

What is it like for me to contemplate talking to you, my partner, about events from our past that still cause me hurt? What would I like to say?

____

____

____

How can I express those thoughts and feelings in a way that will be clear but not hurtful and destructive to our relationship?

____

____

How can I start the conversation in a way that is not harsh?

____

____

What do I need to do to express my hurt clearly without getting caught up in outrage and venting?

____

____

Do I have concerns about such a conversation?

____

____

If so, it will help to look back over earlier chapters on the negative cycle and reactive versus core emotions. Think about what you have learned about your emotions, how you express them, your part in any negative cycles of interaction. Think some more about using the simple guidelines for L-O-V-E conversations: Listen to each other with an open heart and mind; validate and acknowledge each other; express thoughts and feelings simply, softly and slowly.

It may help to begin such a conversation by expressing your concerns about the process, rather than going straight into the content of what you want to say. For example, "I'd like to talk to you about something that is important to me, but I feel uneasy, a bit scared that I'll lose my cool. This is hard for me, but I also don't want it to be bad for you. I've made notes from the reflections in The Two of Us workbook to help me stay on track. Is this an OK time for us to talk or would you rather I wait until . . .?"

Reflection 10.4 If I have hurt my partner

What exactly caused my partner hurt? What other emotions are involved for my partner (e.g., anger, sadness, fear)? What specifically did I do/not do that was hurtful?

____

____

What does my partner need from me now? What would help tend to the hurt?

____

____

____

Are there any barriers or obstacles to my offering a sincere apology to my partner in relation to the listed incident/s? What is it like for me to anticipate apologizing to my partner?

____

____

____

What do I see as potential barriers or obstacles to my partner forgiving me in relation to the listed event/s?

____

____

What would I like to do for my partner or say to my partner now?

____

____

____

If offering an apology, stay focused on what you REGRET, take RESPONSIBILITY for your role in the injury and talk about how you hope to REMEDY[36] the hurt caused. Avoid defending yourself or making excuses. It may help for you to write out what you want to say and then read the letter to your partner or give it to your partner to read.

Important as it is to offer apology and seek forgiveness, remember that forgiveness cannot be engineered or forced. While waiting for forgiveness, work on reducing negative behaviors (such as criticizing, excessive drinking, gambling or flirting) and work on increasing positive behaviors such as kindness, listening and supporting with family responsibilities. In particular following affairs, it is usually very helpful to be open and honest about your whereabouts and activities while away from your spouse. This will help rebuild their trust in you.

Reflection 10.5 Debriefing about the reflections and conversations with my partner

What has it been like for me to engage in the reflections of this chapter?

____

____

What was helpful?

____

____

What still feels unfinished?

____

____

What was it like to talk to my partner?

____

____

What was it like listening to my partner express their vulnerable feelings?

____

____

How did I feel expressing my vulnerable feelings?

____

____

Was there anything that felt too hard to talk about to my partner?

____

____

If any of these reflections open up issues for you individually or as a couple that feel too hard to handle on your own, we encourage you to seek some professional help. Find a counselor, therapist, pastor or doctor in your local area who is willing to work with you to find a way through these difficulties.

Chapter 12 Maintaining Intimacy and Revitalizing Our Sex Life

Reflection 12.1 Resolving differences

What, if any, leftover issues, decisions or differences do we still need to resolve?

What fears do I have about this conversation?

What are my most important needs about this issue?

Now generate a list together of all possible solutions. Be creative and think outside the box. Do not critique or eliminate any idea no matter how unrealistic it seems:

Circle the solutions that meet both of your needs. Take some time to "try on" the different ideas or scenarios. Trust your gut feelings. Ask yourselves, does this solution honor your relationship as well as meet your personal needs? Although not always possible, optimal solutions feel good personally and take care of your relationship as well (or at least are not detrimental to it). Once you decide on the best scenario or solution, write down your plan for putting it into place, including the steps involved and estimated timelines.

Reflection 12.2 Let's talk about sex

What positive memories and feelings come up for me about our sexual relationship? What positive messages would I like to give to you/my partner?

____

____

____

What is my own sense of myself as a sexual being or sexual partner? How might this impact the way I approach sex?

____

____

____

What are my "sexual scripts"? What cultural or religious messages did I receive about sex from my family?

____

____

____

What are some of my sexual "accelerators" and "brakes"? Can you identify three of each?

____

____

____

Are there any problem areas in our sexual relationship that I would like to discuss? Have we tried before to talk about this topic and got into a fight? How did a negative cycle get triggered and stay active?

____

____

____

What would I like to say to my partner today about my needs for intimacy or physical touch? Could I share a couple of my "accelerators" and "brakes"? How could I approach this conversation in a different way from previously so that negative interactions between us are not triggered? (Tips 4–7 as listed might be helpful here.)

____

____

____

How do I feel about sharing these reflections with my partner?

____

____

____

What are my hopes for our future sexual relationship?

____

____

____

APPENDIX B

OUR RELATIONSHIP DANCE

Name:______________________

What I do

____

____

What I think to myself

About me: ____________________

____

About you: ____________________

____

I react emotionally with

____

____

Name:______________________

What I do

____

____

What I think to myself

About me:____________________

____

About you: ____________________

____

I react emotionally with

____

____

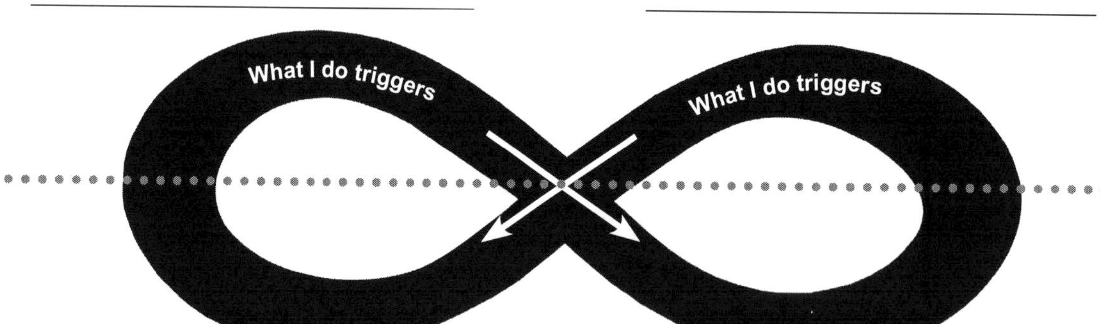

How I feel inside

____

____

____

What I need, what my intentions are

____

____

____

How I feel inside

____

____

____

What I need, what my intentions are

____

____

____

Figure B.1 Our relationship dance with behaviors, thoughts, reactive emotions, core emotions and attachment intentions

INDEX

Page numbers in *italics* indicate figures and page numbers in **bold** indicate tables.

9780367444037